T0380749

The Outdoor Perils of Cats

Kathy S. Thompson, M.A.,
Education and Counseling

authorHOUSE®

AuthorHouse™
1663 Liberty Drive
Bloomington, IN 47403
www.authorhouse.com
Phone: 833-262-8899

Published by AuthorHouse 10/26/2021

ISBN: 978-1-7283-5923-6 (sc)
ISBN: 978-1-7283-5924-3 (e)

Library of Congress Control Number: 2020906632

Print information available on the last page.

Any people depicted in stock imagery provided by Getty Images are models, and such images are being used for illustrative purposes only.
Certain stock imagery © Getty Images.

This book is printed on acid-free paper.

Edubooks by Kathy S. Thompson

Poems and Short Works Books (57 in each)

Young Readers Books

Charlie and Mom Cat (early readers)

The Cygnet (young readers, and all ages)

Madame Spider (tweens, teens, and all ages)

Philpot and the Forest Animals (young readers, and all ages)

Disclaimer

The author makes no claim to the accuracy of all details in this book. The author has attempted to remove any noted errors and has checked out what could be checked out, as well as possible. Efforts towards accuracy have been made but the author makes no claim to there being full and complete accuracy of all the book's contents. Any errors brought to the attention of the author will be corrected in the future. Any medical-related content in this book is not intended to encourage any type of medical orientation or treatment. When there is a medical issue centering on kittens or cats, always seek the advice of a veterinarian.

Apology

I know this book is not perfectly written. Though I majored in English as an undergraduate, I've forgotten some grammar, plus some grammar and even spelling rules have changed over the years and I have not kept up with those new ways, although, many of them are optional. Still, grammar can get to be a little muddled in the mind. So, apologies for any and all imperfections. Just getting the book out was the priority. Therefore, you may find some irregularity, in that the book was not professionally edited. I hope there's no typing errors (but my eyes are not so good). So, apologies go out for any and all oversights or undersights. There may be some repetition, too. Some is purposely there, to drive in a point. Some is accidentally there but is put in a different context. Because I was working on more than one book at a time, I would sometimes forget what I had already written so I occasionally put the same information in twice—almost always in a different context. Also, this book was a bit of a rush job. Because the book was somewhat rushed, all sentence construction may not be immaculate but most of the content generally makes sense in so far as I know. Though not likely, there could be typing or grammar errors in this book.

Furthermore, you may think some text information does not directly relate to the included covered subjects. There is, perhaps, some borderline material in there. With what may seem extraneous, if you give it more thought, you would likely make the connection that the material does relate to the overall subject and certainly to what is generally being covered in the text. There are one or two covered areas that may be more remotely related to the principal subject but I wanted to add in those subjects and felt that they were connected. All points made tie in with the overall subject, and they generally or specifically relate. Some points that were made do, more than others. I tried to be thorough; I am a detail-oriented writer. Putting so many details in so the book would be more comprehensive was not always so easy to do and so the organization of the book is not quite all that I would have wanted it to be, but I'm not unhappy with it. Mainly, I got everything in that I wanted in and that was my priority. Again, this book was a little rushed.

Foreword

There is a negative, and I believe fallacious idea out there that cats should be outside and that they have a primal desire to be outside. Even a few shelter workers believe this way, and they sometimes have more personal reasons for believing that. Cats do not have a primal need or desire to be outside. I've been around cats and had cats for close to thirty years now and have seen and experienced much, which is all in my long compendium, titled *I Care for My Cats (and other animals)*.

The debate goes on but truly, cats are happy and safe, inside, and there is no valid reason why they should be outside because they are unprotected, outside. In other words, all kitties that are outside must be rescued and brought inside and there should be considerably more effort to do so. It should become a national goal to do this. Several new laws need to be passed. More effort to retrieve strays and ferals to bring them inside permanently should be made, which will require laws, and organization.

No, cats need to be inside of a loving home because there, it is safe. I've fostered many, many cats and kittens and they've all much preferred being inside where they are fed, given water, and are sheltered. Once they are altered (neutered or spayed), they settle in and do not need to or want to go outside. Cats have very little desire to go or be outside because cats have been domesticated—considerably domesticated. At first, until a kitty gets used to their new life inside, they may want to go outside, if they were outside before but that desire subsides and then goes away. Old habits get forgotten.

Cats are <u>so</u> domesticated now that they are way more defenseless outside than is commonly thought. Domestication tames animals, and it changes them. Again, anything primal is not really all that present in today's kitties. Domestication has changed that. Therefore, all kitties should be brought inside—every last one of them should be. Way more no-kill shelters should be established and evert stray and feral should be taken there and rehabilitated. More field workers are needed to go get them and bring them in. Then, more transition workers will be needed. All kitties can be transitioned from the outdoors to the indoors and I emphasize this in my noted longer book.

Even feral cats can be rehabilitated. Some say "no they can't", but they truly can. I've experienced this myself, many times. It is a process (this rehabilitation) and the process is all clarified and expanded on in the previously-noted cat book. All outdoor kitties should be rescued and brought inside. Anyone with enough patience can rescue and rehabilitate feral cats, and certainly general strays. People can actually be trained to have this patience.

No cat should have to live outside, principally because of all the perils. This is the whole point. There's so many perils, and I relay that to people every chance I get. They are all highlighted throughout this book. The first chapter has, perhaps, the longest sentence in the world. Despite possible grammar errors, the extremely long sentence lists the majority of outdoor perils of cats, but there are many more and they can be in and around any country and sometimes all countries.

Vet care information in the book was checked over by a local veterinarian, who checked over the medical information in my longer compendium, noted above, but there is very little in this particular book about specific vet care. It is more about specific perils, which increase the need for vet care. There are, however, several CAT-egories in my noted compendium that center on a number of vet care issues and matters. Kitties forced to be outside will need extra and additional vet care because outdoor kitties will fall victim to some of perils they will continually encounter. Because outdoor kitties do not get the vet care they need, they die young, or very young.

If many more people would rescue and help outdoor kitties, and see that they got into a home, these wonderful companion animals would live longer and be so much happier. Some people could do a lot. Some people could do a little. More need to jump in and take animal rescuing much more seriously. Ideas behind Operation Rescue need to be spread far and wide. Animal rescue is a subject that should be continually brought up in a conversation. Outdoor kitties cannot help themselves and so much more needs to be done for them. People need to be aware of these perils, and to date, not enough people are. They know about a few but there are many more than just a few and they all add up.

Contents

Contents

The Long Sentence List of Outdoor Perils

I will be using the word, kitty (versus cat) somewhat regularly in this book because it is a catch-all word that includes for both kittens and cats. It is also a more affectionate word to use and is more informal (as opposed to the word, cat).

Most people do not realize all the outdoor perils that are dangers to kitties. Most people are aware of some and can list off a few, but they are not aware of the long list of outdoor problems that are out there for kitties. There are real and actual dangers that are associated with the existing outdoor perils. I know that if I need things to be spelled out for me, which I often do, that other people need things to be spelled out for them. Writing on this subject spelled things out for me, about the subject of outdoor perils and dangers for kitties. It's a sad, pathetic life that outdoor kitties have to live. No outdoor cat has nine lives—that is a myth because kitties don't live very long, outside. Unfortunately, at the present time, many cats are forced to be and are destined to be outside and I hope this unfortunate trend changes and sooner would be better than later.

Because of all the outdoor perils, cats should never be outside, not even for short periods of time. People will put a predominantly indoor kitty outside from time to time and they assume the kitty will always stay around but the kitty can wander away. Most kitties do. Even one that tends to stay around a home can one day wander off. Something can frighten the kitty, for one thing. Curiosity could get the better of a kitty and the kitty may leave the area, to explore. The kitty may see something, hear a noise, or smell something strange, and then off it will go. Then anything can happen. Sometimes, they can get lost. Contrary to common belief, kitties can get disoriented and lose their way. Wind and rain can weaken and eliminate any recognizable smells and scents and a kitty can get lost forever.

Outdoor perils create and cause <u>cat</u>astrophes. Some people try to cocoon themselves into living in a dream world and will try to escape the reality that there are outdoor perils that kitties cannot escape, but reality is reality. Do not be 'like an ostrich, and bury your head in the sand'. Face the truth, if you haven't already, and join the rank and file of people everywhere who are doing all they can to keep kitties protected by keeping them indoors, and by strongly encouraging others to do the same.

Because there are more perils and dangers out there than most people realize, this brings me to one of the most important points of the book—that all <u>kittens and cats should be kept indoors all the time and only be given over to people who honestly and sincerely intend to follow that principle and practice.</u> After you have read this book, I think you will agree with these ideas or will agree with them more strongly.

The outdoors is dangerous for any kitty, but one of the most thoughtless acts that anyone can commit, and a very cruel one, is to put a kitty that has been indoors for some time, outside. That kitty has been used to comforts—a nice home, attention, and continual access to food, and water. Indoor temperature was pleasant for them and the home was cozy, and safe. To put a kitty outside, when the kitty is not aware of the dangers, is so cruel. The kitty has not been prepared to live outside (and to be so alone, either). The kitty cannot understand why he or she can't come back inside to live. The kitty can't talk, and tell the person who put them outside how uncomfortable and unhappy they are outside and how lonely it is for them. Kitties cannot express the stress they are undergoing. The outdoor life is a difficult life for any kitty. It's not good to put any kitty outside, or to not bring in outdoor kitties, either. Life is riddled with perils for kitties when they are outside, and, life is unpleasant for them, too. It isn't a good life for them. All kitties deserve a comfortable and safe life.

Frankly, when kitties are put outside, for whatever the reason—and some of the reasons are very flimsy I have to add—the kitty can't really be called a pet in the truest sense of the word. A pet should be around—even underfoot—24/7. If a pet is out of sight, they are out of mind. You cannot enjoy your kitty if it is not around your home. You cannot form and keep strong bonds with the kitty. If you convince yourself that you can, sorry, but you will be being illogical and will be under an umbrella of delusion. For too long a period of time, purebred cats, and certain others, have been overbred, which means that cats put outside and born outside have had less chance, or no chance of being rescued. Therefore, way fewer purebred cats should be bred—as of yesterday and as of today.

<u>Every kitty owner everywhere should do everything in their power to keep their kitty indoors and to make it a point to regularly spread this message around because outdoor perils can kill kitties.</u> I'm covering many of the outdoor perils here but I know I have left some out. There are many more

but I believe I covered the main ones. Soon to come, here, is a very long sentence about these perils but it is really a sentence <u>list</u>. Many of these listed perils are noted in the rest of the book, too, and they are all covered in my longer compendium, *I Care for My Cats (and Other Animals)*. The compendium covers considerably more content, which is why it is referred to as a compendium.

<u>Now starts the long sentence.</u> Some of these outdoor perils are stepping on thistles and thorns (in some areas of the country) and on broken glass and sharp metal pieces, running into barbed or razor wire, getting infections from puncture wounds on the skin, getting ear-mites and other kinds of mites that are found in some areas, getting fleas and bird fleas (that don't hop, they stick to a kitty, especially around the head and the ears and eyes (and are, therefore, unlike the regular fleas that hop around and spring), getting bit by chiggers and mosquitoes, getting other tiny insects or parasites in their fur, getting ringworm, being in cat fights and experiencing resulting mutilations (ear splits, scratches, slashes, cuts, and damaged eyes, particularly from claw wounds), getting minor or even severe fractures or broken bones, getting blood, lead, walnut, or frog or toad poisoning, encountering fast moving and heavy vehicles, accidentally eating and drinking poisonous substances, accidentally eating bad, spoiled and decaying food that is often bug and parasite-laden (as from garbage cans) accidentally eating poisonous plants, accidentally eating parasite-infested birds, reptiles, rodents, and various other animals (and insects), including snails and slugs and thereby becoming internally infested with various types of worms and parasites, accidentally eating similar animals infected with bacteria, viruses, and some kind of disease

and thereby becoming infected, encountering and even eating fungus, which includes toadstools and mushrooms, some of which are poisonous, getting larvae cysts in their skin (like from the botfly), getting screwworms (from the larvae of the blowfly), getting maggots (that burrow into and lay eggs in the skin), being stung or bitten by ground ants, encountering and being stung by Killer Bees (in some warmer, more southern areas), running into stinging honeybees, yellow jackets, wasps, hornets and now, Giant Hornets), and spiders, being bit by mosquitoes, encountering snakes, alligators, vicious dogs, coyotes, wolves, foxes, and encountering dangerous or hostile animals, in general, being prey to eagles or hawks and other birds (with talons) that can sweep down on a frightened kitten or cat and carry a kitty away for a meal for itself or perhaps for its young, being kicked or stepped on by a hoofed animal, being harmed by an antlered or horned animal, being harmed by a tusked wild pig, a porcupine, or even a raccoon, being sprayed by a skunk, running into and walking over animal droppings, getting an electric shock, being caught in a steel-jawed trap, being shot because they're mistaken by a hunter for another animal, being shot intentionally because some individuals choose to be cruel to domestic animals, encountering and being abducted by demented-thinking people who mean to do harm to kittens and cats (and puppies and dogs), including certain cruel-minded adolescents and children (who can do harm to a kitty inside of a home, too), experiencing sudden-change occurrences relating to the general theft of a kitty by people who want a free pet or experiencing sudden-change occurrences relating to an accidental loss of a kitty to people who think the animal is a stray and so they, therefore, take the kitty in to a shelter (this situation may end out being a positive, however), experiencing extremes of weather which can include hard rains and lightning storms and also thunder (very scary for kitties) and in some areas, experiencing cold and freezing snow and ice (yes, it is good to take in strays and to bring all kitties in before the winter season hits), experiencing heat extremes and heat exhaustion, being in harsh wind storms, including hurricanes (wind swirls), being in dust storms, including tornadoes, experiencing lack of fresh, and consistently available drinking water and having to drink dirty outdoor water, experiencing lack of proper and consistently available food and nutrition (kitty will not be filled-out and will become bony), getting paw splinters or slivers, getting foreign bodies in the eyes, experiencing pavement burns (asphalt and cement) on the paw pads, running into abusive and thoughtless children and young people (who throw rocks, shoot a kitty with bullets, shot, or bee-bees, kick a kitty, pick a kitty up by the tail or by the neck, bending a kitty's tail, etc.), coming into contact with various transmitted animal diseases and viruses such as Feline Leukemia (FeLV) and Feline Immunodeficiency (FIV) (and many others, too, including SARS because of the coronavirus), not being able to get immediate access to veterinary care in the event of an accident, or some kind of harm, or getting very sick, acquiring bad behaviors from untamed, feral kittens and cats, being exposed to rabid animals (including other felines) that might attack kitty and spread the diseases, like Rabies, getting over-exposed to the sun (especially white or white-based kitties) and getting sunburn and necrosis of the tip of the ear flaps, falling into and drowning in swimming pools, getting closed into or locked into empty or unoccupied places and dying a slow death, eating outdoor vegetation that could have parasites or parasite eggs on the leaves, stems, or blades (kitties love to eat grass and leaves, which is not good for them, in that respect), being exposed to carcinogenic and immune-affecting

6

elements from certain lawn and garden sprays and covers, including lawn and garden fertilizers or agricultural field and product sprays and cover, including field fertilizers, getting muddy, dusty, and filthy dirty and trying to groom themselves afterwards and having to licking all that dirt into their mouth, experiencing multiple pregnancies (for a female kitty, not spayed) and then the kittens having to suffer because of all the many specific related problems or dangers, such as inadequate food and water, especially if the mother dies or is separated from her babies), acquiring eye problems (for the kittens), (particularly bacterial and because of secondary infections if the mother cat is not there and able to clean the kitten's eyes), and the existence of various traumas kitties of all ages can experience when in the wild and even in general neighborhood communities.

Again, these are some of the outdoor perils but there's many more that could be added. I will be covering most of what is on this rather extensive sentence list, in subsequent pages. This just-noted sentence could be the longest sentence in the world (but it probably isn't). My cat book, *I Care for My Cats (and Other Animals)* is rather long, too. It may have broken a record for long books? I have no idea how that even happened. I never even thought about length as I was writing the book. I only thought about getting all the content in. There was so much to put in. Again, this *Outdoor Perils* book came from the longer book (*ICFMC*) because I thought the content was so important. I felt it needed to be a completely separate book.

2

Cold and Heat

When it rains, and some areas get rain more than other areas do, outdoor dry food for kitties becomes soggy, then it starts to decay. Meanwhile, outdoor kitties try very hard to find a dry area to be sheltered in, when it is raining, and if it rains for a long time, as it often does, outdoor kitties can't get out from their shelter (if they have found shelter) to get to any food, since they need to keep as dry as possible. They may be away from food for a long time, because it is raining. If they do go out in the rain to get food, obviously, they will get drenched.

Another problem with raining is that someone's outdoor kitty may run away. If you put your kitty outside, realize that rain and thunder and lightning can cause a kitty to run to another place because of fear and stress. They could even run far away. They can get lost and not be able to return to the area it came from. Then, their problems really start because no one is around to take any kind of care of them, not even a little care. Rain removes familiar scents so a kitty can't smell their way back home—not very well. They get disoriented and can wander even further away.

No kitties should ever have to be outside when it is raining. Once they get wet, and it's cold and damp, they have no way to get dry unless they can get inside of a home or warm building. Their fur gets wet, and it is very thick so it will take a while to dry even if the temperature is warm. And, kitties' paws always get wet when it rains and after it has rained. They can't avoid puddles, when puddles are all over the place.

Kitties don't do real well out in the wind, either. When there is both wind and rain, poor kitty must find some kind of shelter, quickly. It is sometimes hard for humans to fight the wind. Think of how hard it must be for small, light-weight kitties to fight the wind. They don't have much strength. Also, when the wind is strong enough and it is dry, kitties get debris in their eyes, just like humans do, and this is very problematic for kitties. Winds can mean chilly weather, too, and windy weather can chill a kitty, just like it can chill a human. A kitty can't exactly put on a windbreaker. True, fur keeps kitties warm, but only to a point. The cold gets through to the skin. Cold, past a certain point, will kill kitties. The smaller ones will be the first to die.

El Niño brings about terrible storms and can cause mudslides to occur. It can cause droughts and even plagues. It can cause animals to do unpredictable things. It can bring about warmer and hotter weather. (Air pollution is but one factor surrounding climate change.) El Niño winds can be powerful and cause a great deal of damage. Warm air from the ocean can flow upward and then cool too fast. This is one factor relating to El Niño. El Niño was around before Global Warming started to be noticed.

All animals on the planet are being affected by Global Warming. Some animals on the planet are being affected by El Niño. However, the two affect each other, causing unwanted, unexpected weather conditions. With warming comes less ice up north and less water on land (but for the rains). Warming affects breeding patterns and will ultimately force animals to go to new areas,

9

where they may or may not survive. El Niño causes unpredictable and radical storm systems, which end out being dangerous for animals. Everyone should be more than concerned. La Niña relates to El Niño. It seems to be a response to El Niño and the two are related to each other, as a sister is to a brother. All weather conditions are currently being recorded and studied more than they were before. Outdoor kitties are affected by weather, which is why they should live indoors and be companion animals.

When it snows, kitties can get frostbite just like humans can. They can lose ears and limbs to frostbite, and possibly tails. Freezing causes necrosis of a kitty's skin. Kitties can freeze to death fairly easily. Snow blizzards occur in the winter in a number of places around the world. Kitties should never be out in snow and ice. Certain kinds of cats are more vulnerable to cold then others are, but if it gets really cold, no domestic cat can survive. If there is snow and ice, whether the air is dry or moist, kitties are vulnerable. When they're moving around, it may or may not be all right, but when they sleep, they'll get chilled to the bone. And, they eventually have to sleep. Even during the day, it can be too cold for a kitty.

Just because a kitty may have a dense underfur that holds body heat close in to the kitty's skin, this does not mean that the kitty doesn't get cold. Most breeds or mixes have this dense undercoat, and they can be long or short-furred. Some undercoats are thicker/denser than others are. Some, you may not even be able to detect. A mixed-breed kitty will have an undercoat and one way to know exactly where an undercoat is, is that when you bathe the kitty, the undercoat won't soak in the water very fast, like the topcoat soaks it in. An undercoat will resist the water at first, but then it can eventually get saturated. The undercoat helps, but it's not the 'be all end all'. All kitties will get real cold when it is real cold. They don't have an extra layer of fat on them, like penguins have.

If you are ever outside when it's real cold and you are wearing a warm coat, don't _you_ still get cold? What if you had to be outside hour after hour? The undercoat is really just like wearing an extra sweater in the cold. The kitty can still get cold. Quite a few areas on a kitty's body do not have that undercoat, and those areas are more vulnerable to the cold. The Norwegian Forest Cat has this wool-ish undercoat, but the cat still shouldn't be out in real cold weather. (Quite a few kitties have little, or no undercoat. It's cruel to make kitties stay out in the cold. Some get sick. Some get frostbite. Some freeze to death. They are most uncomfortable and miserable when they are forced to be out in the cold. Who wants that for a poor defenseless kitty? Many think kitties are OK in cold weather just because they have fur but that kind of thinking is a fallacy. Our domesticated kitties have been bred down to be small so always keep in mind how small domestic cats are, even the larger ones. Large cats in the wild cope better when it is cold, but domesticated kitties suffer, and often die.

Also, it takes more energy for kitties to keep warm during the cold months. Whenever more energy is expended, animals need more food and calories. For this reason, outdoor kitties and strays will lose more weight during the colder months, unless there is plenty of food around for them, which there usually isn't. Only if there are people around who regularly put food out for a colony of cats, will there be enough food.

Realize, too, that kitties are unable to even get non-commercial cat food if they are in snowy areas. They can't get insects, birds, or small animals, since many of these will hibernate or hide. Some of these animals stay up in trees. Birds go elsewhere. It's hard for kitties to follow scents when snow is on the ground. If the cold doesn't get the kitties, and it usually does, starvation will. Slowly starving to death is a very cruel way for any animal to have to die. So many kitties die that way. When kitties are outside, they often have to go great distances to get a meal, and all this walking around burns up calories and cause them to be even hungrier. They might not find any food at all, especially when there is a blanket of snow. Chasing prey, or, running from predators, causes them to burn calories. The time can come when they have absolutely no fat left, to live off. That time will come sooner, not later, no matter what the season, whenever food is hard to come by. Food is hard to come by most any time for kitties that are outside. That is a fact.

If the temperature dips to be cold and you know night temperatures will be too cold, bring all the kitties in that you can. Especially when it's snowing, bring them all in. And if it's real damp outside <u>and</u> there is snow and ice, it's just too cold out there for all kitties. <u>They suffer, hour by hour, as they feel the cold.</u> But where can they go? Who can they complain to, and hope will listen? No one, is the answer to that. All they can do is come around, hoping there will be food and hoping someone might relieve their suffering, some way.

Certain kinds of kitties, absolutely, should never be out in even mild, cold weather (nor mild, hot weather) and these kinds of kitties are the Sphinx, the Devon Rex, the Selkirk Rex, and the Rex. They have no coat, to speak of, that will protect them from the outdoor elements. Even in winter, the sun can shine and cause them to get sunburn. These breeds should never be outside in any season.

One story I heard, reference kittens and the cold, occurred in Iowa. A friend of mine was walking her dog when it was icy cold outside. Snow was all around. Her dog, for some reason, headed over towards the bushes and started to act real curious about something. The woman went over to the bushes and, low and behold, there were two tiny kittens there, around four weeks old. The woman quickly picked up the kittens. She lived a block away. She took care of them until she could place them in homes. Come to find out, a resident in the area had seen a car stop right before the woman had come by with her dog. It appeared that the car had just dumped the kittens by the bushes, right before my friend had walked by. Had my friend not come by when she did, the kittens would have died of hyperthermia. Iowa, and many of Iowa's neighboring states, get so very cold. So does Canada, just up north.

The whole time when I lived in Canada, I never once saw any cat out in the snow and ice, but I know some end out in the cold. When I was up there, fewer people had kitties. More had dogs that were larger, and dogs do better in the cold, as a general rule, but even dogs should not be forced to be out in really cold weather (and it gets much colder, through the night). It is insensitive to force them to be, and can be considered to be negligent and in some cases, cruel. More people up north have cats these days so cats are more in jeopardy because of the cold. The trend to get a smaller dog to be a pet came about later (in the 1980s and 1990s), but for many years, people had mid-sized to large dogs.

It is true that many kitties get too cold and die from hyperthermia, but on occasion, kitties do get rescued from such a plight, as is noted in the two books written about an Iowa kitty named Dewey (The Library Cat). There is a children's version and an adult version of the book. Dewey almost freezes to death in the book-drop area at the library, and he gets some frostbite but he gradually makes it through. Dewey wins everyone's heart.

A major problem with cold weather occurs when kittens are born. Females that are not spayed can still get pregnant late in the summer so if they have their kittens in the fall, when it is cold (especially at night), the mother cannot do enough to keep the kittens warm and so the kittens can die. Even in desert areas, temperatures can get too cold during fall and winter months, particularly at night, so kittens will even die if they are born in warmer areas.

Before you have your female kitty spayed and if the kitty is outdoors for all or much of the time, the kitty can get pregnant and be forced to have her kittens outside, where the perils are many. (Never allow an unsprayed female to go outside.) If the weather is extremely hot, it will be quite uncomfortable for mom cat and the kittens. Plus, there will likely be fleas around. Again, if it is real cold, one or more of the kittens could die. If they don't die, they'll be miserable because of the cold, especially after the sun goes down and all through the night. Again, fur isn't always enough to keep them warm.

Too many people think that older kitties can be out in the cold. Well, they can be, but they're miserable, and they can freeze to death the same way as the younger, smaller kitties can. Cold is cold. They can get frostbite and partly freeze. Whether a kitty is long-fur or short-fur, they still get cold in the cold. Like humans, they <u>feel</u> the cold but kitties can't dress in warmies, or put a blanket over their bodies. They can't put gloves or boots on. Or turn on a heater, or turn it up. And so it goes.

Kittens should never be out in the cold, because of their size. But kittens that are born outside are often forced to be outside on a regular basis. Some people get a kitten and just dump the kitten outside. They think it is all right to do that. They put food and water out on the porch. Such people should read this book about outdoor perils and become aware of all the problems connected with putting any kitty outside. (Outdoor perils is noted in my larger book that has sixty CATegories or chapters in it.)

In November of 2005, in a northern American state, a woman put at least thirty-five kitties out in the cold. They were different ages and sexes. She just dumped them out in the snow and ice. A judge sentenced her to one night out in the cold, but she only stayed out four hours, as it turned out. He also gave her two weeks of jail time. Some of the kitties ended out with severe Upper Respiratory problems and were just too sick and those ones (nine of them) ended out being euthanized, but the other ones made it through after receiving medical care and they ended out being adopted. The kitties were fortunately retrieved before it was too late for some of them. Why the woman didn't take the kitties to an animal shelter or even the pound is what people were wondering. How could the woman not have known that what she was letting happen was very cruel? So many kitties are just dumped outside, too, and that is what is key. There were two issues—kitties being dumped, and kittens forced to be out in the cold. The judge felt that she needed to experience what the kitties had experienced and, for a while, she somewhat did, but not entirely. Most of these kitties were quite young and some were kittens. You hope they were older kittens, but no kitty should have been forced to be out in such cold weather.

As with the different cats in the wild (sometimes called wildcats), some kitties can withstand the cold better than other kitties can. It's all relative, but as noted before, no kitty can withstand supra-cold weather. They can easily freeze to death, especially when temperatures dip at night. When the weather is not good, kitties will not find sanctuary until there is a break in the weather and if they are forced to be outside, there may not be a break from cold temperature for some time. If it is raining, they will likely go to a covered area. If it is snowing, they'll go where there's protection from the snowfall. But the temperature will still be the same wherever they go, and for small kittens, it wouldn't be long before they would freeze, if the weather was really cold. The more north an area is, the more there will be frozen kitties (when they are forced to be and to stay outside).

<u>People should rescue all outdoor and stray kitties certainly before the first freeze, and bring them inside.</u> <u>Even sooner than that would be better.</u> <u>The first freeze comes faster at night than it does during the day</u>. Don't wait until the <u>first-day freeze</u> because by then, most likely, there will have been night freezes.

Even just wind can be harsh on a kitty outside. Kitties don't weigh as much as we do; they weigh from around five to ten pounds when they're fully grown. They can be tempest-tossed during high winds. Most kitties will try to find immediate sanctuary. Debris from high winds can get in their eyes, and down in their ears. Heavier items can hit them, square on. Quite often, high winds bring rain with them, which adds to the cold and inconvenience for outdoor kitties. Long-furs get terrible mats because of the wind. Wind twists their fur round and round. Over time, they'll have mats all over. Rain packs these mats down, which is also what happens when they lay down to rest and sleep. Mats become permanent and they can be a nuisance for a kitty, and can even cause them pain. Wind is a major cause of mats and this is why indoor-only long-furs don't get mats (or get very few of them), even if they aren't regularly combed or brushed. Some indoor kitties will get mats, especially when the temperature is more humid. The fur gets more pressed down, but at least if they are indoors, they can be combed so the mats can't form. If they do form, a caretaker can try to comb them out or carefully clip them off.

If you do not feed outdoor cats, they have to wander around in the cold or heat, trying to find food, and they never know if they will. That is real stress. They may have to go miles to find food. In desert areas, it's just too hot for them to roam around very much. Someone has to feed them or they will starve. If no one puts water out for them, they will die from thirst. Again, both hot and cold weather can kill any sized kitty.

In desert areas, the warm/hot season is a long one and a female cat can go into heat late in the warm/hot season and have kittens early—fall or mid-fall, when it is cold and the kittens will still be young during the winter, which can have some cold days and nights. The cold can kill the kittens. It can get below zero even on the desert, at night. No kitty should be outside in below-zero weather. The mother will try to keep her kittens warm when it is cold by using her own body heat as much as she can, but she will have to leave to try to get food into her body so she can keep nursing her babies. That is when the kittens can die. It's a catch-22 for the mother because when she leaves, she has to suspect that her kittens can die from the cold. Most areas get even colder than desert areas do, so many kittens have died because of the cold.

The mother absolutely has to eat so she can keep nursing her kittens but she has to leave her kittens for a while. She has to leave her kittens because she is hungry. The ordeal is so stressful on mom cat and she well understands the dilemma. Her kittens are tiny, tiny creatures when they are first born. It doesn't take much at all for them to get too cold and to get hyperthermia. Cold fronts can suddenly come in, too, if weather has been warmer. Many people saw the movie *March of the Penguins* (2004). Many penguin eggs froze because of the cold, and many chicks died because they weren't able to withstand the cold. Sometimes, a parent wasn't around to keep them warm. They were out trying to find food.

If it is too hot outside, kitties can get heatstroke and can even die from excess heat, especially if there is no water around for them to drink. Kitties have to walk around in the heat sometimes and it is difficult for them to have to do that. They are sensitive to the heat and they are not comfortable unless they are in a climate-controlled environment. In that way, they are just like us. Pavement and landscaping rocks get very hot, and kitty's paws can get very hot, as can kitty, as heat rises out of the pavement and rocks. In desert areas, some areas are hot even in the shade. Hot weather slows kitties down just like it does people. The darker, furrier cats become hotter, faster, but the light, short-furs are more vulnerable to harm to parts of the skin. Kitties can get sunburned, mainly on the ears and some facial areas, particularly the nose area and around the eyes. The lighter kitties are more vulnerable to this. In fact, the cells in the ears can die if they get too much sun exposure. The bottom of their paws actually get burned and some paws have needed ointment and bandages put on them. No one is around to help the outdoor kitties or to even know about any burns, when a kitty is always outside.

When kitties experience heatstroke (and this can happen even in the spring in some areas), they salivate excessively. Their body temperature can jump to 105 degrees Fahrenheit (about 40 degrees Centigrade), and, sometimes, to even higher than that. Over-heated kitties get disoriented, their tongue becomes red, and their breathing is significantly affected. They pant and breathe in quick, but meager breaths. They can go into convulsions.

They may vomit, as well. It isn't a very pleasant experience for kitties to have to endure, especially repeatedly. They walk clumsily, and they're also very anxious. They could die if where they are gets too hot for too long a period of time. Kitties must get to a shady and cooler area, fast, and also drink some water. Some people have been known to shave or sheer their kitty (or kitties) when it starts to be summer. Pet groomers will do this for a price.

You never want to shave or shear a kitty for the summer if the kitty is to go outside because their bodies can get sunburned. (This happens more with dogs because it isn't very often that kitties are sheared.) Any of the hairless or semi-haired (semi-furred) kitties should never be put outside because of UV rays. Kitties can get sunburned even in the fall and winter if the sun causes enough warmth. Always keep in mind that kitties can wander off if they are put outside. You may not be able to bring them in when you want them in— like when it is too hot and sunny. Some sun is good. Too much sun is not good. In any season, kitties that are outside need shade and water. If it is cool outside, many people don't stop to think that kitties need water, like they do when it is warm or hot, but they absolutely do need water. They always have to have enough water. Kitties always have to have shade if the sun gets to be too much. Enough shade has to be available for them, like it does for dogs. Caretakers have to be on top of such matters, all the time.

The cold and the heat that kitties must experience hour after hour is what will reduce their lifespan considerably. Remember, the nights get very cold and chilly. We may not feel that cold, night after night, because we are inside. We don't think about the cold that our small domesticated kitties must endure, but enduring, they are. Some will be chilled to the bone, hour after hour as they huddle somewhere—possibly with another kitty, possibly not—and they all get very stressed. Stress happens when any living creature is too cold. <u>Continual stress will shorten lives.</u> Kitties get stressed when it gets exceedingly hot, too, and some days, in certain areas especially, get very hot . . . hour after hour after hour. When it is real cold, kitties may, or may not move around much, but when it is real hot, they are in jeopardy if they try to move around and they could even end out dying. They have to wait for the sun to go down before they are safe or comfortable when they move around.

Because of temperature dangers and discomforts, bring all kitties inside. But there are so many other reasons why kitties need to be inside. Remember 'the list' at the start of the book. Always remember the list. I purposely made it all one sentence so it would grab people's attention.

3

Natural Disasters

As with earthquakes and volcanoes, hurricanes, tsunamis, tidal extremes, monsoons, floods, tornadoes, dust storms, thick smoke, fires spread by breezes and winds, blizzards, rain, and wind extremes can harm and kill kitties. All outdoor pets should be brought inside as soon as caretakers hear weather-danger warnings on the News, or from a relative or neighbor. Kitties shouldn't be outside in the first place so when any of these extremes hit, they would be protected from being right in the thick of it (if they are living inside).

Volcanoes usually don't affect a very large area, but they can and kitties can die but so will the caretakers unless they can get away in time and take any pets with them. If a kitty is outside and loose somewhere, the caretaker won't be able to grab the kitty before they evacuate (and so, too, when evacuating because of any natural disaster). Lava flow and ash is what kills, but all total, compared with other natural disasters, volcanoes have killed very few kitties. Heavy smoke from volcanoes can be bad, too. It can kill people and pets.

Earthquakes have killed outdoor pets. Many have died because of earthquakes—from the shaking, the falling rocks, and the crumbling of buildings. There's been so many of them around the world. One very bad earthquake occurred in Haiti on January 12, 2010; it particularly affected the

Port-au-Prince area (the capitol city). Because the quake occurred way deep in the ground, there was little tsunami affect. 316,000 people were on record as having died. 1,000,000 were made homeless. Around 250,000 homes and 30,000 commercial buildings collapsed or were damaged from the shaking and ground movement. Many cities and towns were impacted besides Port-au-Prince. All the homeless people went to temporary camps. Not too many pets were rescued. The country was so poor to begin with. Then, it became even poorer. All the looters didn't help, either. If 316,000 people died, how many animals died? Haiti is a poor country and it is very dependent on domestic animals. Millions of animals were harmed, killed, and affected. Many were farm-related animals, necessary for eating and/or for survival. There is always chaos after a huge natural disaster and because of the chaos, many pets end out starving. Many get separated and lost from their owners. Many got injured, sometimes really badly.

Dogs and cats always suffer in any natural disaster. Many of them starved soon after this horrible quake, if they were able to live through it. The houses and buildings all tended to cave in because of what they were made of and because of how they were built. The heavy rubble that collapsed killed many and it caused limbs to be so damaged that they had to be amputated. There was little help around, for the people and for the animals. Many people (and animals) suffered a great deal before they died, too. Haiti also got hit by a hurricane in 2008; 800 people died, and again, animals also died, were displaced, and horribly deprived. Hurricanes hit Haiti later on, too—several times—but they hit all the Caribbean islands. It's what they do. If all pets get put inside and a wet wind swirl hits, some homes are strong enough to withstand the winds and rains, so they would be safe.

The April 25, 2015 Himalayan earthquake, mainly around Nepal, killed around 8,200 people. (Some countries have more dogs than cats around, as pets.) Whenever people die from earthquakes, at least two and sometimes three times as many are badly injured. Even more than that is more moderately injured. This principle also relates to the many affected animals. So often, it is farm and ranch animals that get killed. Damage, and harm that is done, is relative. It was mainly this first 7.9 magnitude-registering quake in Nepal (et al.)—or it could have even been 8.1, depending on the seismograph and reportage—that killed so many, but there were a number of aftershocks, too, and they also caused casualties and injuries. There was a 6.7 magnitude aftershock after the first big one (and it was only one day later). People and animals die with some of these aftershocks, too. They can register high, and destroy ground areas and near-by homes and buildings.

Following those first two, around forty aftershocks, that did little damage, came around relatively quickly. Much went on underground, and much could still happen in the future…at any time. There are earthquake zones all around the world. Science measures the magnitude of all these aftershocks. Dates for them are recorded. The forty-some aftershocks occurred in Nepal, Tibet, India, and China—all a rather broad range. The other large aftershock quake occurred seventeen days later (but was it an aftershock or another earthquake?). It was 7.4 in magnitude. That aftershock (or new earthquake) killed around a hundred and twenty people. Two less-strong aftershocks followed that. Relative to all these shakings, buildings were toppled and homelessness soon abounded. When there is homelessness, nobody can take care of any pets. There was so much damage that relief efforts had to go slow (so people were homeless, longer). Sanitation became a problem, which is the case with all after-effects of all bad earthquakes and other natural disasters. Pets and domestic animals are affected by the poor sanitation, too.

It isn't just the pets and the domestic animals that suffer whenever there are earthquakes, but it is also the wilderness animals. Getting to helpless animals anywhere can a problem. Vet care is never enough because there are so few local vets for the number of harmed and suffering animals. Vet clinics get destroyed during natural disasters, too. There never are enough doctors for all the people, either, when big disasters hit, nor are there enough medicines and medications. Frankly, sometimes any available local vets end out helping people who need medical care, depending on what the problems are. Pets, if they do survive these natural disasters, can lose the people who have cared for them—either permanently or temporarily. After such disasters, humans almost always have medical priority over pets and farm and wilderness animals. When the time comes and the human situation has generally been managed, the animals will then get some care. Some are lucky and are in the right place at the right time and are rescued and get some care, but this would be few because humans are the focus.

Sometimes, animal rescue groups come in from other places. It's so wonderful when they do. These people are dedicated. They volunteer to go in, for no pay. Some of them have been trained to seek out and get what animals they can and care for them or find care for them. Sometimes, the animals have to be taken elsewhere. Catching frightened and loose animals can be easier said than done, however. Usually, those in these rescue groups have animal-capture training that can make all the difference. They have equipment with them that enables them to catch loose animals, but the larger animals can be more difficult—to both catch and transport. Blood banks are always needed for humans but there is less blood available for hurting or dying animals—quite often, there is essentially none. Search and rescue goes on for both people and animals for weeks after most natural disasters. Search and rescue is quite a job.

A tsunami is different from a hurricane. Some people spell tsunami, sunami. A tsunami is sometimes hurricane/typhoon/cyclone-based, but not always. A hurricane, typhoon, and cyclone are one and the same. Each is found in a different part of the world—that's the only difference. I call them all wet wind swirls or just wind swirls, just to keep it simple. A tornado is a dry wind swirl but tornadoes don't have three different names and they ae always referred to as tornadoes. Generally, tsunamis are earthquake-based. A wet wind swirl occurs when wind force goes in a circular direction and moves along a path. (This is also the movement trend of wind in tornadoes.) Wind swirls are always started by high winds and they eventually become circular winds. They start off as straight-moving or blowing winds. A typhoon is a word used in connection with wind swirls in the Philippines or the China Sea areas. It is a tropical cyclone there, when wind swirls occur. The cyclones in those areas have been forceful and lethal.

Because of <u>all</u> the many types of natural disasters and acts of nature all over the world, it is easy to assume that people and animals have suffered because of them, and sometimes grievously, over the years. Many animals that were inside a home or building when certain of these disasters hit were spared. When there are tidal waves and debris is falling or being blown around, animals don't stand much of a chance and there can be fires, too—don't forget the fires.

Tsunamis occur when there is a major disruption in ocean or seawater. A meteor can fall, some kind of underwater land slippage or upheaval can occur, and/or there can be an earthquake in the land underneath the water. There are fault zones under the ocean (and seas), which slip and slide and can cause an underwater thrust and water rush, which, of course, includes the top of the water, as well. Big waves form and rush to shores. Ripples, eddies, and waves go out for miles and miles and when they hit coastal shores and land areas, they can be so forceful that they cause immense damage, and a number of deaths. Generally, more than one giant wave can hit but it is usually only one. Tsunamis take terrible tolls. An earthquake that is on land and not under water can cause a really powerful tsunami. When there is a land earthquake not too far from water, it can shake up any nearby water.

Whenever there is a tsunami, more people and animals die. Tsunami is a Japanese word—tsu means harbor and nami means wave. Japan has been the brunt of many tsunamis, more than any other country. (They have many domestic kitties.) Any under-ocean earthquake that registers 9.0 or more on the Richter scale is highly destructible to land areas—especially to those nearby.

An earthquake occurred one hundred miles off of west Sumatra, around six and a half miles under the ocean. It was, final determination, a 9.0 one. This December 26, 2004 Indian Ocean earthquake caused tsunamis that went out in several directions, causing devastation of several coastal regions of India, Sri Lanka, Thailand, Malay, and Sumatra, principally, but also of island groups in the Indian Ocean, and beyond—even on over to Africa. It affected around a dozen nations, which means that a dozen nations lost many people and many pets. One huge wave would come in to a coastal area, then retreat out to the ocean, then another wave would hit, and then retreat. Both the hit and the retreat action caused devastation and deaths. Approximately three hundred thousand people died (around the same number as with the Haiti earthquake in 2010). Quite a few tourists were included in that number. Many were never found. Obviously, many animals died, too. They were never found, either. Quite a few were forced out into the deep part of the ocean area and out from shore, and they drowned. Afterwards, disease and hunger affected some of the people, and the animals. Relief food packs came in from many countries, for the affected people; only some of the animals got care. Quite a few animals had cuts that got infected. Many had been bruised and battered. That's how some died, although most died by drowning.

Two very bad earthquakes hit the world, in 2008. One was in Myanmar (formerly Burma) and one was in Sichuan Province in China, around the city of Chengdu. There are many earthquakes in parts of China and South-East Asia, in general. Earthquakes can originate as far down as six miles below the surface. Earthquakes cause awful devastation when they are under cities and towns because they destroy so many homes and buildings and kill the people, and the animals, that are inside. With the Myanmar disaster, around one hundred and thirty thousand people (or more) died. With the China disaster, around sixty-nine thousand people (or more) died. Animal loss is generally proportionate to human loss; disaster was quite far from Beijing, the capital. There is always destruction of the land, homes and buildings, and infrastructure. Harm that is done to the people and animals will range, from disaster to disaster. You have to factor in the larger ones and all the ones that are less large to really get the full loss impact. Business buildings (and jobs) are harmed and lost. A country's economics will be hurt and crippled for some time. The area's crops get ruined with some natural disasters. Replanting can take time, which is another reason why there is starvation for people and all the animals.

When a cataclysmic natural disaster occurs, any previous work stops. New work (clean-up) starts up. Many end out being jobless. With no income, no one has money to care for very many animals and this would include any vet care, which is always sorely needed. The time when people get around to giving proper care to animals is greatly delayed, in other words, and in the meantime, many animals that are in captivity or are displaced or are strays, will end out suffering and dying. In some places, certain animals will be killed (and not euthanized, which is the more merciful method). Some countries do not euthanize animals because some countries have very few vet clinics.

The less equipped a country is to rescue humans, then, most certainly, the less equipped a country is to rescue animals. Around China, where their 2008 earthquake hit, it is estimated that five million people became homeless. Homeless people cannot take care of animals. Not very well, or at all. Some of them may want to and will try to, but it is very difficult due to lack of resources.

One earthquake in China, around Tangshan, near Beijing, caused from two hundred and fifty thousand to six hundred and fifty thousand deaths, depending on what report you read. It registered at 7.6 strength. It occurred in 1976. It is the most devastating earthquake in modern history, and perhaps in all of history. Large rivers can get messed up, with earthquakes, and rivers are needed for agriculture. Rivers can get clogged up, or re-routed because of an earthquake. Rivers can get flooded with high rain amounts; which happens when there are wet wind swirls that go on around the world. Damage along river edges can be severe. Many homes can be along river edges and banks.

Another bad tsunami hit North-East Japan on March 11, 2011. The Tohoku Earthquake was under the water out from North-East Japan and the tsunami waves came in from that area. The quake was a 9.0 magnitude. Some of the waves got to be 133 feet high (or 40.5 meters). A tsunami can travel from 300 to 500 miles per hour. Waves of a tsunami can go in more than one direction. Quakes can cause areas to move, slightly. The town of Honshu shifted from four to ten inches. There were 15,850 deaths, 6,000 injuries, and 3,300 were believed to be missing. (One year later, there were still 350,000 homeless people and unemployment corresponded since businesses had been destroyed and homeless people had trouble becoming employed). Several thousand people were still missing. Damages were many and costly. Needless to note, many animals died—many in awful ways. The Japanese people tend to be pet owners but there aren't as many multi-pet homes there, compared with what you find in America. Still, natural disasters always end out killing pets (and domestic farm and ranch animals), no matter where they hit.

Two more earthquakes followed in Japan that were 7.1 magnitude—both were in April. There was a 7.0 one the next July. In January of 2012, Japan even had two more earthquakes—one in central Japan—a 5.5 magnitude quake on January 27, 2012, around the Yamanashi area, and a slightly earlier 6.8 magnitude quake on January 1, 2012, around the Izu Islands. Around March 13, 2012, there was yet another earthquake to the east and slightly north of Tokyo, under the Pacific Ocean. This caused some damage to Japanese shores but not to Tokyo. Depending on where the earthquakes are and the severity, my suspicion is that earthquakes can shift the Earth's poles and even cause them to tip a little and get out of sync and thereby contribute to Global Warming. A slight change at the Earth's poles can alter the temperature, relative to when and where the sun hits. Earth's axis can be minutely altered. I thoroughly cover this and other views and rationale in my book *Global Warming Causes and Solutions (and Theories)*.

One outdoor peril for kitties that ties in with Global Warming is the periodic heat wave. Days of extreme heat can come in like a wave. Whoosh, suddenly it is there. Europe got a big one in 2019 and it went up north and caused additional snow and ice melt in Greenland and other areas up there. You particularly notice heat waves when you live in warmer areas (which includes high and low desert areas). All living creatures need extra protection and sanctuary when heat is exceptionally high. For one thing, they need to have more fresh water available because water evaporates faster. It can completely evaporate rather fast when the temperature is hot. Caring people must keep this in mind when there are any outdoor and stray kitties around where they live, assuming they put food and water out for them (and I hope they do or will start to do this).

Kitties may eat a little less when it is hot, too, and this is good to keep in mind. Food should be out for them day and night because kitties tend to 'graze' and eat only every so often anyway. (They have small stomachs.) They'll especially come around early morning, before the heat sets in, and then they'll come around again when the sun is almost down or when it is down. They'll also come around in the middle of the night. Unfortunately, kitties that are outside are not usually able to graze because what food is out for them gets eaten up fast. Not enough people (or any people at all) might be putting food out for them. You never know if more dry food is out for them so you must put food out for them, yourself. Many kitties may only be able to get a portion of a whole feeding every so often and this is one reason why so many of them end out getting so thin. People might think they're getting enough food but they likely aren't. More food needs to go out for them. Food <u>always</u> needs to be out for them. The less roaming they do, the safer they will be.

It is not wise to put out wet food for them because wet food is not enough substance for them. Dry food is better for them, all the way around. It cleans off their teeth better than wet food does. Wet food particles can stay in their mouth a long time so they get gum disease and tooth decay. Wet food doesn't have all the vitamins in it that the dry food has. It is only meant to supplement dry food. It is an incomplete food. A little wet food is OK every so often, especially if it is mixed in with the dry food. Dry food for cats has to have taurine in it so if you feed outdoor kitties, check the print on the bag and make sure that there is taurine. Again, bad weather can keep kitties away from needed food.

When there's a natural disaster, life becomes chaotic and distressing for all loose outdoor animals. Any food or water tends to be eaten by animals that are bigger, stronger, and more adept. Where there are loose dogs and cats that are disoriented and displaced by a natural disaster, the dogs will get to any food and water first. They will even drive off any kitties that are also looking for food and water. Sometimes, any kitties around where there is food will get maimed or killed by the dogs. Therefore, the kitties can starve or die of thirst first and well before the dogs do. Both the dogs and the cats need help and intervention as soon as possible, however. All their lives need to be saved. Domesticated animals do not like upheaval and do not cope well when it happens. They are going to need special attention and care. Many of them get lost during harsh-weather upheavals. Fences get knocked down, and fear drives them elsewhere.

In November of 2007, a cyclone or wind swirl hit the Bangladesh area and caused twenty thousand plus deaths, but the Bhola Cyclone, in that area and that occurred in 1970, took about five hundred thousand lives, over a period of time. Death statistics are often difficult to complete. Death statistics often include after-deaths, from starvation, disease, exposure to the elements, and even suicide. Japan's cyclones are too many to list. Some areas around the world seem to get more cyclones (or typhoons or hurricanes) than other areas get, but the wind-swirl patterns can change, and have, at times. Again, where humans are affected, animals are, too. In many countries, there is considerably more concern about livestock than domestic pets, since livestock is livelihood. Wind swirls will always be, and so will all natural disasters always be. With Global Warming, there seems to be an increase of natural disasters and therefore, more people must extend themselves outwards, and help the helpless animals that are affected by natural disasters. They need <u>immediate</u> help, too, so people have to jump in right away. More protection is needed and the biggest protection is keeping domestic animals well sheltered.

There are times when weather can be so extreme that people just aren't safe. Nor are the animals. During the summer of 2004, for example, when Florida got hit by four hurricanes in a row—Charley, Frances, Ivan, and Jeanne, there was devastation and a number of deaths. The island country of Haiti got hit, too. Then, who can ever forget Hurricane Katrina, soon after these hit. This one hit in 2005, in Louisiana and Alabama. When levies were downed, water took over New Orleans and this became a second, major problem. Hurricane damage can take a long time to repair. Many animals were hurt or died during these hurricanes. A number of animals ended out being homeless because they became displaced and, in some cases, they permanently lost the home they once had. No one could take care of the animals. If the animals were outside, it was hour after hour of trauma for them, as the wind, rain, loud noises, and flooding overtook them. Not to mention all the flying debris—that hurt and killed many of them. Some animal shelters were damaged or slowed down so it took a while to even get a little help for the hurt and displaced animals.

So many homes were downed or partially downed. It's very hard to take care of pets when a home is partially downed, or completely downed. Quite a few pets died, whether they were inside or outside at the time. They drowned or they had something crash into them. Many animals were unable to get food for quite some time. Some were forced to starve because people were forced to evacuate their homes and were forced to leave their pets (which is now a very controversial subject because people did not want to have to leave their pets but were told to do so, at the time). Since that time, there have been many other wind swirls, earthquakes, and fires all over the world. Animals always suffer during and after every natural disaster. If people have to rebuild, it's hard for people to be able to afford to take care of pets and this has been another problem. It helps to think, in advance, how you will leave an area before the disaster gets to your area. Make a plan and be ready to put your pet or pets in your vehicle and take food and water with you, and old newspapers and baggies. You may end out at a rescue center for some time.

During 2005, there were several hurricanes that hit America. Some hit in 2006, but none were all that bad; the next year, 2007, was bad because of the cyclone/typhoon that hit the Bangladesh area of India. That wind swirl was really bad. Around twenty thousand people died and many more were injured. Whenever people die, we know animals die. Many groups go in to help with rescue and clean up, after natural disasters hit an area. Some are tied in with the United Nations or the Red Cross, but most are supported privately. Sometimes, individual volunteers, not a part of any group, will mobilize. This happens quite often, but again, people are given rescue priority over animals, as a general rule. It can be hard to know when or if any animals will be saved. When these volunteers go out, they usually rescue many animals but they need special equipment, cages, and food for the animals when they head out. They may need wading boots and some good row-boats. Quite a few hurricanes hit in 2017, 2018, and 2019, too. (Fires hit then, too, but not so much in 2020, which is when people were quarantined because of the coronavirus.) Hurricanes got the Caribbean areas and the USA. There were tropical storms in 2020, more so than hurricanes. There is a whole chapter on these natural disasters in my Global Warming book.

Hurricane Katrina was very hard on animals all over the Gulf Coast areas. The wind swirl got many areas. Animals were harmed, bantered about, and deprived of basic needs until they got some help. Before help got to them, many animals died. Animals around the New Orleans areas were especially in peril because three levies broke and water flooded into the city and settled there. In some cases, the water level was right at or even above people's attics, which is why people and many animals drowned.

All this happened in just a few days. Early September of 2005 was the worst time, and the consequences were lasting. During the hurricane itself, winds caused building collapsing, and debris flew around, helter-skelter. Animals inside of a home were more protected from the wind and rain phase but animals that were outside of a home were not. The experience outside was hellish. Then, the rushing water from levy bursts was a horrible blow for both outdoor and indoor animals around parts of New Orleans. That is when many drowned. Animals were separated from familiar areas, too, and became displaced. When water got inside all the houses, pets went up to the next floor and even up to the attics with their caretakers(s) (if there was an attic). Some went up on a roof with their caretaker(s), but more were stuck in attics and couldn't get out. A few attics actually got flooded. If people and animals can't get out of an attic, they can drown. If there was a way to get out, they, of course, did, only to come into contact with a number of other perils.

When there is about to be a natural disaster, the National Guard gets called out. They do search and rescue as do local authorities. During the ordeal, most people did what they could to save their pets. When evacuations took place, however, a number of people were forced to leave their pets behind so we know that many of the pets died. Many pets were simply not allowed to go with their caretakers. Some animals were airlifted. They were the lucky ones. Dogs were shown being rescued but kitties weren't, in large part because kitties can be hard to catch but also because if not in a carrier, kitties get very frightened when being airlifted (and so they weren't) and also, once put down on the ground, kitties, out of fear, tend to want to get away. Most kitties don't come when called, either, like dogs do; a few will, but most kitties don't, especially when there are precarious, uncertain conditions. Also, dogs swim better than cats do, so more kitties initially drowned. Kitties will hide from strange people, too, especially if they've been going through an ordeal. They'll be very frightened.

In time and soon after the calamity subsided, eight animal shelters were set up in the State—one at Louisiana State University (in Baton Rouge)—so this was helpful. Some shelters that were for people allowed pets in, but others didn't. It was hard to get pet food and to keep the animals from drinking water that was outside, which had been going bad. People were so pre-occupied with their own survival and the survival of other people that pets, in general, had to take a back seat.

The water all around became dank and putrid, for a number of reasons, and it became undrinkable. Pets became ill from the bad water, but medicine for them was not around for them, not for some time. It was quite hot, too, and pets needed a lot of water. Some bottled water was brought in, but it usually went to people. Meanwhile, pets left in houses languished and some died. Start to finish, the ordeal was piteous for pets. Some made it through part way, then didn't make it the rest of the way. Some did make it all the way through, though. The S.P.C.A., Humane Society, and other animal groups went in to rescue as many animals as they could. They worked very hard to rescue every animal that they could. They had many successes because of their hard work and dedication. They took charge. They did much of the rescuing by row-boat. All flood-prone areas should have row-boats around for flood emergencies.

After foundations to homes dried out well enough, people went back to what homes were still there. Any formed mold had to be destroyed. Much was salvaged, over time, but much had been lost. People couldn't afford pets for some time. A lot of people never saw their pet, or pets, again. Sadly, many could not afford to take them back because they'd lost their jobs and homes. New Orleans and surrounding areas were a mess.

As a result of Hurricane Katrina, one of the conclusions made by animal organizations is that people should be able to evacuate with their domestic pets whenever there is a natural disaster. In other words, pets should be included in the evacuation. This became a new law. Domestic pets are part of the family and this is the premise and perspective. Many people were forced by officials to leave their pets in their home or their yard. Several were left on porches and patios. Again, a number of them ended up on roofs because of water surge. It's difficult to count how many domestic pets died. Some pet owners didn't leave enough food out for their pet(s), thinking they'd be back soon. So, too, with leaving water out. One pet owner left water in the bathtub (water did not end out rising to that area), and they put a heavy object in front of the bathroom door to keep the door open. They put all the pet food they had in the safest place of the home so their pet could get to it. They cut the top off of one of the bags of pet food so it would also be accessible. It had previously been closed up in a closet. Fortunately, a number of homes had an upper floor. To pet lovers, pets were more important than what was material. Quite a few pets were unable to get to drinking water. In some cases, the water their owner had left for them ran out and/or evaporated so they got dehydrated, which can leave a pet very sick and can even cause their death. (There could be organ failure if there has been dehydration for too long a period of time.)

There were finding centers where people could come around and look for their pet(s). Volunteers went around and picked up as many of the abandoned and stray domestic pets as they could get to, and they took them to these centers. There were some reunions. A number of pets had to be sent to other states because the centers were overcrowded. But photos and descriptions were on record so if an owner did show up, the pet would be given to the owner. Little by little, the volunteers got more organized, and they set some new precedents for the future. Several vets and other volunteers came in from other states, at their own expense. They saved the lives of a number of animals. One organization that is contacted when there is a natural disaster and pets are in peril is the International Fund for Animal Welfare at ifaw. com. That is a good one to put in your address book or on file somewhere. Often, when hurricanes hit, pets never get back together with their original owners. Owners always go back and try to find them, though.

The 2008 hurricane season was bad because there was a hurricane every month, from July to November. Bertha was a particularly long-lived one. It was the third hurricane of the season that was particularly bad for Haiti. Eight hundred people died. There were four hurricanes that actually hit in a row—Fay, Gustov, Hanna, and Ike. It was Hurricane Ike that got Cuba that year. Cuba has been a pet-oriented country for some time. They also have many domestic animals around Cuba. Therefore, when a hurricane hits Cuba, animals die and/or suffer. Most countries that are Latin-American have many domestic animals; they have to have them, so they can survive. They depend on them. Pets tend to be utilitarian, but not always. They are often, mainly, companion animals.

If domestic animals die from any natural disaster, the people of that country can starve. If they are weakened in this way, animal breeding to get more animals can take some time. It can take years before animal numbers get back up. If countries are 'really' starving, after a natural disaster, some of the people might turn to eating dogs and cats. (Sadly, this happens in certain countries around the world anyway, even if the people aren't starving.)

Hurricane winds can get to be as high as 250 miles per hour. Anything over two hundred miles per hour is in the highest mile-per-hour range. Quite a few hurricanes have had winds that exceeded 200 miles per hour. Sometimes, hurricanes don't come over to land. They are out in the ocean areas. When they do affect land, lives of people and animals can be devastated, and devastated for some time. They can be so set back. Restorations can take years. Some countries get hit by them more than once, over a period of time, or they'll get hit by a strong tropical storm soon after a hurricane hits, which causes set-backs.

In 2019, Tropical Storm Barry hit New Orleans. It had been a hurricane that made landfall with 160 miles per hour winds, which slowed to 75 miles per hour. It put 20" of rain across Louisiana but the levees stayed intact. Whitecaps were seen all over the Mississippi River. Louisiana also got hit hard with two hurricanes that became tropical storms during the latter part of the hurricane season of 2020. Again, rains caused flooding; flooding is awful for humans, and animals.

Typhoon (Wind Swirl) Haiyan, known as Typhoon Yolanda in the Philippines, hit six central Philippine islands on November 8, 2013. Samar Island was also hit pretty hard. At first, it was believed that ten thousand people in one city alone, died, but figures ended out being less. This city was Tacloban, on Leyte Island. Another city hit was Guiuan. Winds were up to 150 to 170 miles per hour. The typhoon hit the eastern seaboard of the Philippines and then went across the mid-islands and did even more damage. In some areas around the world, houses are not built so well and they aren't sturdy and so indoor pets are not safe, in that respect. Tacloban was flattened in that so many buildings were completely toppled. Eleven million people were affected and homelessness was rampant. Food and supplies, including medical supplies, were in short supply. Needless to note, thousands upon thousands of animals were adversely affected, if they did not directly and soon after die. Some people were blown into nearby water by the winds. Most died under collapsing and broken-up buildings and debris and if people died that way, we know animals did, too. It is all part and parcel.

The Philippines is in a typhoon belt and they have been known to get around a dozen of these a year. Five are usually really bad ones. They get many earthquakes around there, too, including under the ocean, so they get tsunamis that way, too. Because of these larger natural disasters, they get landslides and floods, as well. All the islands around there are vulnerable and they always have been.

Many natural disasters are nothing new. That some natural disasters have increased or increased in intensity may have something to do with better instruments, now, for measuring and assessing. Some of them 'could' read a little differently than previous instruments for measuring and assessing, since they've never been standardized and since there's been new technology.

The area around the Philippines is Typhoon Alley. Tsunamis cause waves and water surge to come against all the islands. Some world areas are more vulnerable to specific natural disasters. This is all mapped out. In other words, certain countries should establish better disaster-control plans and rescue plans, for people and animals. They should make those efforts, before it is too late.

Typhoons hit many more poorly-developed areas. Shelter, sanitation, and safe and drinkable water became extremely problematic after the Philippines typhoon in 2013. Obviously, many boats and ships were destroyed, as were people's homes. Outside countries rallied to help and food and supplies were brought in. Many people needed help. Many animals needed help. Whenever people cannot help themselves, they cannot help the animals. It's just like that. Animals need able caretakers.

Around 7,300 people were eventually confirmed as dead because of Typhoon Halyan (Yolanda). Some were confirmed as missing, which means they are likely dead. Many people get taken out to sea (especially when there are tsunamis and high wave surges. They drown because of highly turbulent waves (as do many animals). When a caretaker is dead, and can, no longer, take care of any animal, or animals, their animal or animals must be re-homed, which is not always easy to do and if local people are not able to manage that and the animal(s) do not get re-homed, guess what happens to them. Many Asian areas were damaged, in varying degrees, so many homes were not available—to people, or pets. Realize, again, that kitties are extremely vulnerable in these forceful disasters. They're just so light-weight. They get bantered about, horribly.

Super-storm Sandy (that had been a hurricane, but slowed down) hit the American coast late October, 2012, and it caused devastation in several states, especially New Jersey and New York. The wind swirl hit from the Caribbean on up to Florida then on up to Maine, which is a pattern for Caribbean and Gulf of Mexico wind swirls. They even go up to the Maritime Provinces in Canada. Some will hit southern states from Louisiana on eastward (to Florida and the Keys), and some will hit the east coast of Florida and Georgia, and will usually hit some of the states but not all of the states, depending on the routing of the wind swirl, which can be both predictable and unpredictable. Sometimes, different states only get one edge of a hurricane or tropical storm that hits a coastline. The rest of the hurricane is off-shore. Still, that edge can be devastated. Giving hurricanes human names makes the specific ones easier to remember.

Hurricane/Tropical Storm Sandy hit the North-East coast and mid-Atlantic areas with full force. It's rather coincidental the name is Sandy because the hurricane sure brought in a lot of coastal sand into coastal towns and cities. There were many tidal surges. There are two types of water damage with winds swirls—rain, and wave surges. Afterwards, sand cleanup was difficult, plus, there was horrendous wind damage, and, water damage. Electricity was off for thousands upon thousands of people (which happens a lot). Again, Sandy began as a hurricane and when it hit the east coast and even inland areas (and was forced to slow down), it became what is known as a super-storm, which was predictable and occurs because of resistance to the wind, because it hits land or makes landfall. Land causes it to slow down, especially hilly land. Once it makes landfall, humans and animals are clearly at risk. Some people do not evacuate the areas that are vulnerable to the brunt of the wind swirl, nor do their pets (since they don't). Farm and ranch animals, put in a barn or similar building, can be vulnerable because roofs get torn off and buildings can be blown down. Fifty million people were affected and inconvenienced by Sandy.

When Sandy hit, many animals were harmed and displaced and this included both the domestic farm and ranch animals, and the pets. Many outdoor animals were physically hit by debris and some of it was rather large. There are always a number of tidal surges along the coastline when wind swirls make landfall. Because of the overall disruption to people's lives, some animals starved or died of cold before anyone could get to them and take care of them. No electricity was available, for one thing, and that always sets everyone and everything back. Streets were flooded, too, so vehicles couldn't drive around. Some animals drowned because the water level was so high and in some places, it was very turbulent. It became a spread-out tragedy of large proportion (as happens with all forceful wind swirls). It took months before everything became livable again, which had been the outcome with Katrina, too.

Even when natural disasters are not so bad, many animals can still be displaced and end out far away from home and from help. They can be harmed and even killed during their ordeal. High winds, excessive rains, floods, snowstorms, sandstorms, fog, fire, and smoke, even when more minor, can cause kitties to be lost, or harmed or killed. For example, there are many of the more minor earthquakes that take place. Just as on example, there was one in August of 2013 around Mexico City, and it was just a little over 6.0 on the Richter scale (or seismic scale). That would be enough to wreak havoc on the local animals and to cause them physical damage, some set-backs, and disorientation and displacement. Even some earthquakes with less intensity than that can cause harm and loss and hurt animals and there are always quite a few of those going on around the world. Some natural disasters, no one ever hears about because they are minor ones. The whole area around Mexico City gets low-registering shaking and some of it occurs after other shaking because of an underground network of faults and related shifting.

Again, all these deaths from natural disasters add up, and so do the deaths of animals. There's been such excessive accumulation. Droughts are very bad for animals, too, though you don't often hear so much about droughts because they are slow acting, not sudden calamities. Lack of food comes from droughts because food either doesn't grow or it will die in the ground, during droughts. Humans and animals end out starving, and, they can also die of thirst and dehydration, as can any and all animals. Agricultural workers can do very little when drought hits, unless they have an irrigation system in place and water can come in from a different area—one that is less affected and has more water.

In April, 2011, a cat named Rascal was forced away from his home and he stayed lost for ten whole weeks. He'd been in a natural disaster. The faithful kitty returned to his previous home and only weighed two pounds. The kitty's life had been in jeopardy and its life had been interrupted by a tornado. With vet care and good food and nutrition, Rascal was nurtured back to health. Rascal, a beautiful gray long-furred kitty, was one of the fortunate kitties. Hopefully, the lack of food and the wrong kind of food didn't cause Rascal any permanent damage because vitamins, and enough of them, are consistently needed for kitty's maximum health. In Alabama, right around the same time, there was an outbreak of tornadoes, all in a row, which was stressful and traumatic for all who were affected. Then, Joplin, Missouri got hit by a big tornado, the next May; the City was pretty much destroyed. The tornado had been a mile wide and it tore up the southern part of Joplin and killed one hundred and fifty people and injured at least a thousand. Flying debris from tornadoes kills people and animals, too; so do downed trees. Animals have been horribly hurt or killed by both. Even if animals live through a tornado, tornadoes are traumatic for them, especially the outdoor farm and ranch animals. They are so out-in-the-open. Barns don't always protect them, and you can't fit them all down in a cellar. They can't all be rounded up in time, either, even to put in the barn. Pet owners will round up their outdoor pet(s) and make an effort to keep them safe, if they are able to get a tornado warning in time, and they sometimes don't.

Tornadoes are extremely high-wind disasters. Winds can sometimes exceed 300 miles per hour around the circle area of the funnel, and the force of the winds diffuse outwardly. The further away an area is from the tornado, the less the wind velocity will be. Anywhere near the funnel can be devastating and the tornado funnel area has to pass over somewhere. Whatever is in a tornado's path is vulnerable to being demolished and swept away. Domestic farm and ranch animals, and pets, have been known to be picked up by the wind action of a tornado, and then dropped elsewhere.

Tornadoes tend to form around certain areas so people who live in those areas know they are vulnerable. There are quite a few tornadoes in certain world areas but when one forms, they don't take up a lot of space. Still, they travel along and total area travelled can add up. They can jump whole areas, too. They can hop, skip, jump, and meander. Much depends on terrain type. When they move along and stay on land, they wreak havoc. They can spread out and get bigger and bigger, as the funnel is rotating. They can move very fast, or go slower. Dust gets sucked up and mixes with the water droplets in the funnel's center. Updrafts in the center can pick up and even uproot heavy objects, like trees, roofs, and even houses. Tornado Alley is a central United States strip of land and it is a rather broad area. In April of 1965, forty-seven tornadoes swept through central United States over just two days and they killed at least two hundred and fifty people, which is a much lower number than you get with most of the hurricanes and larger earthquakes. Tornadoes also hit the Mississippi Delta area. Sometimes, they hit unexpected areas and places, too. They can come about after a hurricane hits, too—they are as spin-offs.

Nowadays, there is Doppler radar to detect tornado formations and pathways. Warnings can go out fast to threatened areas. Other natural disasters are also detected by Dopler radar. More people and animals have been saved because of it. People are able to get to shelter and take their pets with them because of this technology. It is very hard to get larger, domestic animals into a shelter, regardless of the type of natural disaster, and so, sadly, they are the more vulnerable and exposed. Tornadoes are often spawned by wet wind swirls and tropical storms. The numerous wet wind swirls and storms in 2008 caused many tornadoes to occur. Tornadoes occur every summer, in diverse places. They occur in several world areas. They especially occur in southern Canada, Europe, and Australia, in addition to certain areas in the United States.

In 2012, there were destructive tornadoes in Bangladesh and East India. There are way more tornadoes per season than is generally known. Just in one season in the United States, there can be 600 confirmed tornadoes. Some are small and generally powerless. Japan gets them, and so does Indonesia and Turkey. Again, some areas around the world get hit by tornadoes more frequently than others do. Texas gets more tornadoes than most of the other tornado-prone American states. Some areas only get relatively harmless tornadoes. Still, these less powerful tornadoes can hurt outdoor animals. Dust devils are a form of a tornado but they generally don't do much damage. Sometimes, they pit windshields of cars (with grit and sand being blown around).

Forest fires are sometimes considered to be natural disasters. They happen naturally, but sometimes they are planned, and these are not natural fires. Forest fires are, of course, really bad for the animals because so many of them cannot get away. The older birds can fly away, a few animals can get into caves or go underground (though some of those can still die from the heat and, in some cases, from smoke inhalation), but most of the animals get burned alive, and this would include even the tiny and small insects. We should be caring about all life, including the life of insects. We need insects. They are a part of the cycle of life. We do not want them burning, in a fire. Stray and feral kitties sometimes get caught in these fires, but no one likes to think about that. It is sad to think about that.

Fires increase recorded temperatures around the world. Fires, be they forest and/or ground, kill many cats. When kitties are taken out and dumped in the country, or dumped around a forested area, if a fire starts, they can get caught in it when it spreads. They wouldn't even know what direction to run in. Many animals don't. Smoke inhalation can be debilitating. It can and will kill. Jumping up in a tree will not save a kitty's life in a forest fire. It may, if there is ground fire. Kittens are, of course, very vulnerable, and fires often start around the kitten season. Some areas are plagued with occasional brush fires. California, in areas, gets a number of fires. The Malibu, California fires of October, 2007, affected many animals; only some were able to be saved and evacuated. There were also fires around San Diego at the same time, but northern California gets several of these fires, too. Colorado gets quite a few ground fires and so does Wyoming and Montana. Some of these fires are arson induced. California gets arson-induced fires, as well as natural fires.

When there is a fire, kitties may get so disoriented that they end out running into the fire area, accidentally. A mother with kittens will try to rescue her kittens, but she may not be able to get them all away (or any of them away). She has to try to rescue them one by one. If they are already mobile, they can follow her, but again, kitties can get disoriented and not know which way to go and they could go in the wrong direction. All animals panic when there is a fire near or around them.

Ground fires have increased in America over the last twenty-five years. These are fires that don't, necessarily, occur around forest areas but occur away from forests and on plains and prairies. There have also been more forest fires over the last twenty-five years. As the population has increased, more people are careless about campfires, and about tossing cigarette butts. When brush and vegetation is dry, there will be more fires, and more severe fires. During the summer of 2012, there were fires in Montana, Wyoming, Colorado, Idaho, Utah, Nevada, and New Mexico, which were particularly noted on the News. The range of burning area was 150 to 7000 square miles per fire, but there was more than one large fire in some of those states. For example, New Mexico got hit with quite a few fires, which makes one wonder about arson. You wonder about arson with some of the other ones, too. Smoke was around for many days; some smoke drifted over to Albuquerque and stayed around until fires finally stopped burning. When fires are started by lightning or because of dryness and heat, the fire will be considered a natural disaster. Many fires started by lightning, however, are dowsed or put out by the accompanying rainfall, depending on how a rain cloud travels.

A relatively new phenomenon is that several fires will start and each one won't be all that far away from the other fires. This has been happening more and more, which makes one think of arson as being a strong possibility. Fire-starting individuals are responsible for killing many living creatures that were dependent on the environment that got destroyed. These concurrent fires have been especially noted in California—both north and south but especially around Southern California. There's been ground and brush fires as far up as Napa, though. Some fires have been around more mid-state, like around Santa Barbara. Some have been around Los Angeles, more to the south. The forest fires are more up north. The one that destroyed Paradise, California was particularly bad. It occurred in November of 2018, but there were many wildfires around the State the year before, in 2017. The fire came on so fast that evacuation was difficult. Some pets were not taken with the evacuees. The whole town burned down.

In the case of <u>some</u> natural disasters, having a pet indoors isn't going to save the pet because the devastation can be so harsh and awful. Sometimes, if a pet is inside, this may save the pet, and you hope it will, but it may not. In poorer areas, pets don't generally stay inside, even though they should.

Many of the three hundred thousand people (or more) who died in the Indian Ocean earthquake and subsequent tsunami, in 2004, were poor. A number of the dead were fishermen. Whole families died. Clearly, quite a few children died. Many of the areas hit were dependent on tourism, too, so that industry was ruined for some time. With no money coming in, animal care gets put on the shelf. Generally, wild animals aren't that close to oceans. They live and roam around more inland because they don't drink salt water. Many of the affected people lived and worked near the ocean, around beaches, so their livelihood terminated, which also stopped the money flow. With so much devastation, domestic animals were horribly affected by the tsunami—i.e. the farm animals, and the cats and dogs were. Survivors mentioned seeing way more dogs than cats around, afterwards, but cats are small and hard to see. They also like to hide and do not like being out in the open. As they are smaller, they are less able to contend with moving water, too, so more of them died. Many dogs can swim. Most cats can't.

Dogs were numerous, and were very hungry. Any loose cats were killed by some of the dogs, quite frankly. A number of cats had been indoors, and many of these cats drowned and were not seen, like the dogs were. People are always sad when they lose a pet. Cats were hard to catch so workers were limited, when it came to helping them. Many animals starved. Animals would comb the ravaged areas for food, but it would be decayed. After a natural disaster, some governments go around and kill a number of stay animals. They 'claim' a fear of Rabies, when often Rabies was not the problem. Feeding and caring for the animals was the problem. Many survivors are quite relieved and comforted when they find their pet(s). Some who lost a pet or pets might get a new pet or pets—i.e. from the pool of any that were found roaming and loose.

Quite often, there aren't enough people to retrieve the strays, give them medical attention, and adopt out the animals. No matter what, if relief workers are able to get in, they will go in and do whatever they are able to do, relative to saving lives of animals. Humane groups for animals are not commonly found around poor areas, where people barely eke out a living. There can be some, however, and some can come in from other countries, to help any wandering and needy animals. When there's a disaster, animals are usually not considered to be of much value, in the poorer countries. People have priorities. At the onset of a disaster, there may not be enough immediate resources to give animals much help so that any animals that are still living may still end out dying. Again, some are even purposely killed. In some countries, many pets end out being euthanized but this usually does not make the News.

Relative to hurricanes in the United States, after 1979, they added male names when naming hericanes and himicanes. There had been only female names since 1956. A couple of good-sized, well-known ones were Camille (1969) that affected Mississippi, Alabama, and Louisiana, and Andrew (1992) that affected Florida. Considerably later, came the ones that hit the U.S. in 2017 and 2018. These were Harvey, Irma, Maria, and Florence. Hurricanes in the U.S. seem to affect the Gulf of Mexico area or the U.S. Eastern coast. They often go all the way up the East coast. In 2004, Florida got four hurricanes in a row within a six-week period of time so obviously Florida can get hit rather frequently. Usually, they tend to hit one at a time, and infrequently, and they are spaced apart. Big ones don't come around all that often but when they do, it's like a power punch of a several hurricane force. Hurricane Katrina displaced a million people (in varying degrees). Hurricanes hit shorelines and seaboards. Many pipes got horribly busted. Again, many animals were displaced and animals drowned, starved, got sick, or were hit or crushed by debris. Some of them had no place to sleep if they were stranded somewhere, especially if they were surrounded by water. If they tried to sleep, certain of them could drown, and probably some did because rescue was not all that fast and if you fall asleep, you drown.

Countries all around the world must contend with wind swirls. Wherever there is an ocean or a large body of water, there can be a wind swirl. A hurricane that affects the United States will often wreak havoc in some countries that are around the Caribbean (of which they are all islands), and are on the Atlantic side of some Central American countries and some more northern South American countries. Many wind swirls start over to the east area of the Caribbean, come through the Caribbean Islands and continue to go west over to Central America and Mexico and the Gulf of Mexico; not all will go up to the Florida area. South America gets the brunt of a few hurricanes, but not too many. Coastal areas get hit the hardest. Whole seaboards get hit. Some hurricanes start off the coast of Africa.

Many believe that El Niño has been the cause of Global Warming, but why El Niño exists is up for debate. Is it caused by Global Warming or are there other reasons for El Niño? One thing we do know is that upheaval in just one area can cause problems in surrounding areas and even in far-away areas. It is cause-and-effect from one area to another. It is as a domino effect in some places, and animals (and our outdoor kitties) are around when those dominos fall.

As noted earlier, one type of upheaval is earthquakes. Earthquakes under oceans and seas (some that may even by minor) can cause tidal shifts, which can affect both wind and weather, in general. Temporary weather changes in certain areas can be the result of underwater earthquakes. Even earthquakes under visible land can affect ocean currents and flow, and change weather patterns. They can be less-forceful earthquakes, too, even some that nobody on land feels. Some earthquakes go undetected because proper measuring equipment is not available. Earthquakes way under the ocean are not so easy to measure. It can be hard to know their exact point of origin. People living on islands and along coasts have to be ready for huge waves. Many have been caught unaware.

Many did not get to higher ground, or did not take their pet or pets with them, if they did. People who are pet owners should own a carrier. Dogs will walk, and obey commands, but kitties will probably need to be put in a carrier as people are evacuating an area that is about to be hit by a natural disaster.

4

Too Many Problems and Perils

Outdoor and stray kitties also get more fur-balls. They are out in the heat more, so they shed more. When they groom themselves, they ingest more fur because of the heat and their shedding. Because of more shedding, dry and arid areas cause more fur-balls than humid areas do. Some kitties eat very little (or nothing) if a fur-ball has formed inside of them. Wet food is good for fur-ball-prone kitties because the oil in it helps loosen the fur-ball so it can more easily be expelled (vomited out). However, people who put food out for outdoor/stray kitties usually don't put wet food out for them because it spoils easily and because of the cost. Therefore, outdoor kitties have fur-balls for longer periods of time compared with indoor-only kitties that get a little wet food every day, every other day, or on occasion.

Getting fur-balls can be a miserable condition to have for a kitty. It can even be painful for the kitty. Fur-balls cause suffering, in varying degrees. Some dry cat food is formulated to help a kitty expel fur-balls. If you feed outdoor/stray kitties, you might consider buying that type of dry food (that helps with fur-balls), as cost is the same or maybe just a little bit more (but not much more). Remember, too, that outdoor/stray kitties need more food than indoor kitties do, on average, because they burn more calories by running around outside. A stray mother cat that has kittens somewhere outside will definitely need more food, and she'll need to eat the food more often.

Another peril for kitties occurs when kitties swallow something that gets stuck in their trachea. Swallowing things that get stuck in the throat happens because a kitty's trachea is narrow. If no one is around to take the kitty in for emergency vet care, the kitty can actually choke to death or die of starvation if they cannot get food down. Because of what outdoor kitties are sometimes forced to eat, trachea obstructions occur. Regular cat food—the dry—has pieces small and crunchy enough to easily chew and it is never too hard to chew—but it isn't always available for outdoor kitties and in some cases, it is never available. If you ever put your leftovers out for outdoor kitties, make sure all pieces have been cut up or sliced, to be small, like the dry cat food pieces are. Remove all bones. Make sure it is not spoiled and doesn't spoil and if it does, remove it promptly (again, it's prone to spoil fairly quickly if it is outside).

Dry food is also better for outdoor and stray kitties' teeth. Chewing it helps to remove tartar on their teeth so they are less prone to have dental problems, including gun disease, which can be so painful for kitties living outside and that have no caretaker. Consider putting dry food out for kitties in your area. It is a good deed to do.

One somewhat latent peril has to do with the change of behavior a kitty will experience if forced to be outside. Because of what the kitty sees and experiences outside, the kitty won't be the same kitty as the kitty was before the kitty was forced to be outside. And keep in mind that even though a kitty may willingly go outside, the kitty is still being forced to be outside. The kitty does not know what is good for it. Also, the kitty may think that you want him/

her to go outside. The kitty may think that you don't want him/her around. The kitty doesn't know what to think or what is best. The kitty may think it's nice to roam around and get a sunbath, but no kitty realizes all the perils, many of which will end out taking a kitty's life.

The unrealized peril, which is not easy to immediately see or realize, is that if kitty becomes more skittish, fearful, aloof, anti-social, insecure, and unpredictable because of all that the kitty sees and experiences outside, then the caretaker will no longer find the kitty to be as friendly, affectionate, and approachable—to the degree that the kitty had previously been. There could even be a litter box usage problem if the kitty comes inside at times. As a result, many caretakers may not even want the kitty in their home anymore, and some owners will even turn a cold shoulder to the kitty being outside and will just leave the kitty outside all the time. They may even abandon the kitty. Now, whose fault would that have been—i.e. that kitty's personality and behaviors changed? Not kitty's fault. Kitty would have been the innocent. It would have been the owner's fault and no one else's. This kind of thing is a tragedy and it has been happening all over the world and for many years. This 'eventual abandonment' is a peril, then, that relates to kitties being put outside. For people reading this part, <u>if</u> the shoe fits, will you please wear it? Do not let your kitty be outside and if the kitty is, bring the kitty inside right away and keep the kitty inside all the time.

For all kitties that are outside, but particularly for unneutered males, abscesses are common and are generally treated with antibiotics, from a vet clinic. Some people will dowse rubbing alcohol or diluted hydrogen peroxide (HP) on the wound, once it is open. You can use a small bottle syringe to squeeze the rubbing alcohol or diluted HP right on the wound. Hold the cat firmly down by the nape or scruff of the neck with one hand and squeeze out the rubbing alcohol or diluted HP with the other. You should keep at least one of these products around all the time, if you are helping kitties. The kitty will not like this, but it kills the germs. Put lots on, to be safe. Usually, the abscess will break open and that is when you realize that there is a wound. Until then, you may not know that a wound is there. The abscess fills with liquid, raises the skin and fur as a result, and when it bursts, the area is a circular open-wound area, without fur being on it. You can't miss it. It is exposed open skin, and it won't bleed unless kitty scratches it or bumps the area on something. Most abscesses heal. Scabbing helps protect the open skin.

The wound part of the abscess will be where the teeth of the other cat went in and punctured the skin. Claws have bacteria on them, too, but abscesses are usually caused from bites. Open-wound areas can heal faster if the kitty gets some sunshine on the area. If they get into another fight, the wound may, of course, be compromised. No unneutered males should ever run loose outside. They need to be brought inside—trapped if necessary—and taken to the vet to be neutered. Some pounds or shelters will neuter (and spay) strays for free if kind people will bring them in.

Outdoor kitties get into fights over food, territory, and mating rights. Almost always, abscesses are around the neck area or very close to the neck, and they tend to be on one side or at the back area. Again, abscesses are from bite wounds but they can be from a claw scratch or from anything that scratches and breaks the skin open. The scab forms, but bacteria and germs that got inside the wound can keep spreading in the area underneath the skin, which is why you douse the area with liquid antiseptic. Eventually, an abscess can become larger and can get to be bothersome for a kitty. A vet can lance an abscess because it is filled with fluid, but they will break open on their own and then the fluid will come out. Once the abscess ruptures, the kitty feels better about it being there, but before it ruptures, the kitty may be a little stressed. Kitties are known to break open their own abscesses. They may clean the area themselves, by licking. Most abscesses break open on their own, however.

The abscess any kitty gets often heals up without human intervention. Quite often, there is no scarring and the fur grows back over the area. What happens to the abscessed scab is anyone's guess. Once an abscess dries up, I wonder if the kitty eats the scab off its body. I suppose that wouldn't be too harmful, but it seems gross. Also, I have yet to find an abscessed scab (the size of a fifty cent piece) around my home when a kitty in my home has had an abscess. They could pull it off their skin in pieces? If the kitty cannot get to the abscess it will eventually ball off but it may be stuck in the kitty's fur for a while. Eventually, it may ball out on its own.

The kitty can gradually become ill from an abscess, because of infection. But, most of the time, the top area dries, crusts, and scabs. The area can scab more than once. Meanwhile, there is that non-fur area that is about the surface area of a fifty-cent piece. It's always round. The longer the cat's fur, the harder it is to see the exposed round area because the fur covers some of it because of the length.

Again, rubbing alcohol or diluted hydrogen peroxide (half water to half hydrogen peroxide) can serve as a disinfectant and will kill germs. Even if you poured beer or wine, etc. on the wound, germs will die. If you use a regular alcoholic beverage as a disinfectant and have nothing else, you have to rinse the area off with water soon after. Since beer, wine, etc. is not a pure disinfectant, it is only somewhat effective. I suppose some people have resorted to using wood or grain alcohol topically (on skin), but I have never tried that because I don't keep it around. I don't recommend it.

Everyone should keep a container of rubbing alcohol around for first aid, in general. It is an antiseptic that has 70% isopropyl alcohol in it; the rest is water. It's very inexpensive. I've seen abscesses heal up on strays on their own; even one that was about two inches round healed up. It is good news for the outdoor kitties because usually, no one ever takes these poor unfortunates to the vet. Again, sun exposure always helps open wounds heal and indoor kitties don't have this advantage (but they aren't so likely to get open wounds in the first place). An abscess area may get worse, though, whether a kitty is always inside or is a feral or stray and is outdoors. Someone's outdoor cat can get an abscess. An abscess may not heal up at all, especially if it goes untreated. All the ones I've seen healed up on their own and the fur always grew up over the space. If I can handle a stray that has an abscess, I will, but quite a few of the outdoor ones run away before a person can help them. Even though most abscesses heal up, quite a few other things that happen to outdoor kitties may not heal up. Much that is sharp and cutting can be found outside, and can harm a kitty.

It isn't always from fighting that cats will bite other cats around the neck area. This can happen from mating. One cat can get on top of the other and bite down hard. Skin gets punctured and perhaps even torn. The mouths of cats are not bacteria-free. Staphylococcal infections can result. This type of thing happens from just general rough play, too. Even though these wounds tend to heal up on their own, it is chancy to not take a kitty to the vet when there has been biting. Closely observe any related wound because it can worsen and become problematic. Some people mistake this round wound for ringworm, because it is round. When kitties have ringworm, you don't always see it. If you do, it forms a round ring. Just rubbing alcohol, could kill it?

Side-of-the-neck wounds occur when two kitties roll around together. Normally, the bite would have been on the top of or under the neck, but because use any alcohol other than rubbing alcohol, it will leave a sticky residue on the kitty. of rolling around, it ends out being on the side of the neck. If a kitty is biting at the top of the neck, it is for dominance and/or for mating. A male can bite the top area of another male, in an effort to establish dominance. A male will bite down on the top of the neck of a female, to hold her still, for mating. If a male goes for the bottom of the neck, it may seem like it is going for the throat because it literally wants to kill the other cat, but domestic cats don't usually go for the throat. They don't usually want to kill another cat. They just want to establish dominance, or chase the other cat away. (This no-kill fighting is quite common with many animal types around the world.)

This kind of fighting is done male to male. It doesn't happen often, but when it does happen, it is loud and fast and seems violent. I've been fortunate because I've been able to break these kinds of fights up. I've brought in strays before they were altered and that is usually when you see the fighting. If you've brought cats inside, and this happens, the runaway cat has nowhere to run from the attack cat, essentially, because of four walls. They'll go under furniture, rather often. With fights outdoors, a cat can run away and get away from an attack cat much easier. Attack cats don't always chase, once they see the other kitty running away.

It's also rare that one domestic cat would ever kill another domestic cat because cats have a powerful defense instinct. If nothing else, they break loose and run away as fast as they can and usually the attack cat gives up the chase, once the runaway cat is far from where the confrontation began. Jealousy is often a reason for fighting. It ties in with their dominance desire—to establish or keep a desired area.

Again, a cat that gets on top of another cat does so for dominance. As they mount, they hold the skin on the neck of the other cat with their teeth. Even kittens have done this, and so have neutered males. Such a positioning is done by males on other males and males on females, but it is for dominance (unless mating is the intent and that is really dominance, too). A male that does this but is only rough playing will not be trying to mate when he does this, though an onlooker might assume that he is trying to mate. It is really a dominance stance and effort. I have never seen an abscess on a female cat after she has mated. Males generally try to be firm but gentle, when they hold the female down for mating. I've never seen an abscess on a female but that doesn't mean females don't ever get them. They do. I've only seen a few on males and again, they all healed up quite well, and healed up relatively fast. Males also get clipped ears. A claw goes though the ear tip and tears it. The ear tip splits apart.

Regarding any kitty fights, if you are ever outside and two stray or outdoor cats start to fight, yell really loud "hey, hey" or something similar, and immediately walk over and get between the two kitties if you can. Break up their fighting so neither kitty can get hurt. Startle them so they'll stop. Clap your hands, maybe. Drive one (or both) of them away. Take this action seriously and try very hard to split up the two kitties. Scoot one of them off if you can. They are usually too fearful of the person breaking up their fighting to want to continue their fighting. They won't scratch you, unless you try to touch them. You don't want to touch or handle an agitated kitty, even if you are familiar with the kitty and know it has a nice temperament.

With a cat fight, especially if fur is flying, it is a kindness to physically go out and chase one or both cats away so the fighting will end and the kitties won't be harmed. Sometimes you will hear yowing, which is a sound made right before two cats engage in serious fighting. You go out when you hear this, and rush to do so. When you go out, take a broom with you. Grab one fast. You can also toss a towel or small blanket on one of them (if you are able to think fast enough and have something like that on immediate hand). This startles them, and ends the aggression. If you toss a soft throw pillow at one of them (particularly at the aggressor cat), that will also end the fight. Never throw anything hard and especially with edges or points at any kitty (like a book or piece of wood). If you just yell and clap your hands as you go towards the dueling kitties, this overture is most likely all you will have to do. It's all I've ever had to do. Not a one ever turned on me. The larger or more aggressive kitty is startled, which gives the other kitty a chance to run away.

Fighting usually isn't all that lengthy, however, and there is first hissing and posturing. You'll hear that yowing. The two will angrily call out to each other, as a way of warning the other cat of an impending fight. This may be enough to cause the two to not want to fight, but if there is a fight, one will attack the other, you'll hear a lot of quick and loud growls, and there'll be some quick biting and clawing. But this is quick and one of them generally breaks away and runs off to escape, very soon after the fighting began. Still, damage can be done, that fast. Blood can be drawn. Therefore, you want to rush in to prevent imminent fighting. Have that broom handy and only use it as a separator.

Kitties outside must often run. They may not have a choice. When they do run, they can run into problems, i.e., something can hurt them. They can get scraped, cut, poked, bruised, gouged, stuck, slammed, impaled, etc. On occasion, kitties run around as a part of play with another kitty, but, usually, when a kitty is outside, any running is done because they are trying to escape some kind of danger. Any running around outside can be harmful to a kitty. Kitties indoors run around and chase each other more because they know they are safe. They play more. Outdoor kitties don't play that much, including the kittens. They don't like to be distracted because there are more dangers.

There are many kinds of eye problems for the outdoor kitties. (CATegory 30 of my *I Care for My Cats* is about the eyes of cats, including all the eye problems of cats.) There can be eye abscesses as well—right next to the eye, affecting a cat's vision. Many things can get in their eyes and cause irritation and the desire for the cat to scratch. Permanent damage can be caused by any eye irritant. Thorns, quills, splinters, glass bits, and debris of any kind, can get in the eye. Winds and even breezes put debris into the eyes. Rubbing against something can also put debris in them. If the cornea is penetrated or scratched, bacteria can multiply.

There are many genetic or just general problems or diseases of the eye that outdoor kitties need vet care for but most of the contracted kinds of eye problems could be avoided if a kitty were to always be kept inside. There can also be problems with the eyelids, and as with the other eye problems, a vet would be needed. The problem, whatever it is, may take care of itself after a time, but, usually, eye problems don't just go away. Humans can use eye-drops. They can take showers (that clean around eyes), but kitties can't. From fighting, a dog attack, or a car accident, an eye can even be torn out of its socket. But where is someone to race the poor kitty to the vet if the kitty has no caretaker around? How often would a Good Samaritan come around, if an owner wasn't around? The kitty might want to hide. Outdoor and stray kitties can suffer grievously from these horrid calamities, which is why they need to stay inside, where they are safe, or at least much safer.

Kitties can get conjunctivitis. A bacterium gets in their eyes and into their nasal passages and eye weep starts and then it crusts over. This happens with kittens more easily than cats because they are so low to the ground, where the dirt and germs are. Kittens with conjunctivitis have been known to starve because they can't see to get over to their mother. They can get lost and disoriented. Some have been known to leave the rest of the litter, by accident, and then not be able to get back. Their eyes cannot open once they crust shut. <u>Never</u> try to open them when the crust is dry. You'll hurt the eyelids. Enough water over the eyes for a long enough period of time will loosen the crust and the crust can then carefully be wiped away, but if the problem is viral, then antibiotics are needed and who will rescue them and take care of them and get them the antibiotics? Without antibiotics, the crusting may happen again. If you bathe the kitten real well, over the head area, more than once (baby shampoo works okay and is not harsh), all the germs might be gone and the crusting may not happen again. This has worked for me a few times but if the eyes do not heal up within a short period of time and the problem is viral and not bacterial, you must use antibiotics along with doing the head bathing and rinsing.

If you put the kitten back outside, after getting the eye condition under control, would the kitten even find its mother, and would the over-crusting happen again? It may be best to keep the kitten, and try to oversee any future eye crusting and the kitten's feeding. You could try to get the kitten back to its mother but you would have to monitor that and be ready to bring the kitten back inside if there are problems. True, kittens need to be with their mother to feed so if you can, put the kitten back with the mother. But they may not be able to get back to the mother so you have to get food into them, one way or another. You have to know how to feed a kitten, and some people don't know how to do that. It is good to learn how to feed kittens—with feeding tubes and by way of a schedule but it is best to keep kittens with their mother. She takes complete care of her kittens. They need her milk—big time. Once they eat dry kitten food on their own, they can probably survive but it is still best to wait for any kittens to be weaned because kittens still need the milk to grow their best. They need it until mom cat shoos them away.

Conjunctivitis is a continuous eye weep, which again, on occasion, will clear up if the kitty is well bathed several times in a row around the head area. The area can be rinsed with a pitcher. The area around the eyes has to be rinsed well with water. You can use the baby shampoo around the head. Some of it will automatically clean around the eyes as you rinse the shampoo off the head. Once rinsed (by pouring water over the area), all the crust around the eyes will gradually loosen and can, then, be wiped away. Make sure it is totally gooey before you wipe it away. It can harm the kitty's eyelids if you try to wipe it all away when the crust or eye weep is dry or part-dry. Water will soften and loosen the crust but the water has to be on the area (by constant rinsing) for long enough for the crusted area to <u>completely</u> loosen all the way through.

After the eye crust is softened and removed, you can use regular sterile, wash-out eye drops, too—a redness reliever type that just washes out eyes. (A vet once told me you could use such drops. You still might need to transition to prescribed antibiotic eye-drops, though, if the condition is viral.) You may need to wash and rinse the head area at least two or three times before the eye weep and crusting around the area completely goes away, but it can and may go away sooner than is expected. If the eye weep doesn't clear up after a week, and the eyes crust back up and are shut because of the hardened crusting, then the kitty very definitely has the Upper Respiratory virus and will need prescribed antibiotics as well as the eye drops (that are not all that costly).

If the kitty is eating OK, you can wait a little longer to see if the washing/ rinsing clears up the eyes (because the problem could just be bacteria in the eyes and the kitten may not have the virus). However, if the kitty is not wanting to eat, then vet care may be needed unless you can figure out other ways to get food down into the kitten. The kitten might be fine, and end out eating OK, but you'll eventually need to have the kitten examined by a vet. If you have more than one kitten with eye crust, you'll have to do the same with all of them.

Really young kittens cannot defecate on their own. The mother licks and stimulates their anal area and will even eat the kittens' waste. (You just rub that area with a tissue and the kitten will go on its own and you use a tissue to clean it up.) If you don't know how to do this, the kitten can die even if you feed them—perhaps especially if you feed them, which is another reason why you need to get kittens back to their mother. Kittens should never be separated from their mother too soon. Once they eat solid food on their own, at five to six weeks or age or longer, they will defecate on their own. <u>People have separated kittens way too soon and all too often from their mother.</u> Children are prone to doing this if they find kittens outside and, of course, the kittens often die. Train children to leave kittens alone so they cannot be separated from their source of food—their mother.

<u>If</u> a person can bring in afflicted outdoor kittens and take over their feeding and, clear up their eye weep and crust, then that person will be rescuing the kittens but don't permanently separate the kittens from the mother, and the kittens may need to be returned to the mother. If you can fix the kittens up quickly and can quickly get the kittens back to their mother, then great. Again, the kittens could either have the Upper Respiratory Infection or the Upper Respiratory Virus. With the first type, the condition might disappear with proper care and washing; with the second type, prescribed eye drops and antibiotics will be needed. Most vets insist you get and fill both prescriptions for the second type (the viral one). You will need both.

On the subject of mothers and kittens, and bringing them in to care for them, if a female growls at you when you are outside, there's a chance there is one or more kittens nearby. Cats just don't growl for no reason; frankly, they almost never growl at people. They might run away, or even hiss, but they don't growl. A growl means 'stay away, don't come any closer.' It generally doesn't mean the kitty plans to attack you, it just means 'stay away'. A kitty may attack another kitty, however, if they first growl. A kitty could strike against a human hand if it gets in the way of what the kitty is being territorial about, but then again, it may not do that. When I note 'strike against', I mean 'bat at' with claws unretracted (and sometimes retracted). I've never had any kitty ever attack anywhere else but my hand and so I have never found kitties to be dangerous. Claw scratches could be dangerous around the face and eyes but I always keep my face away from claws. I wish <u>certain</u> people would start saying more good things about domestic kitties. Kitties need our help. Scathing words about them makes certain people want to do them in—that is so off the mark. I recently saw an ad for insurance that ran kitties down and had no understanding of kitties, whatsoever. What can you do? The ad alienated many women, and women influence their children. Quite a few men feel protective towards kitties, too, so the ad alienated them, as well.

The other times when I've heard kitties growl is around a food dish (the growl is intended for any kitties near the food) and also, if a kitty has something in its mouth and does not want another kitty that is nearby to have it, it will put out a growl, even with something in its mouth. Growling relates to territory and possession, in other words. It means 'leave be'. If you get close to her kittens, a mom cat might, then, hiss, but she'll growl first. Kitties do not usually attack humans, though. They might bite or scratch a hand, however, if they're upset or afraid and the hand is near-by.

One thing that most people don't think about is that outdoor kitties don't get near as much sleep as indoor kitties get. Many of them don't even have a regular place to sleep. They sleep whenever and wherever they can, but their sleep is interrupted quite often. They have to be on the alert to dangers so they don't sleep for long periods of time and they don't sleep well. They can't always curl up and get comfortable, either. Most outdoor kitties are sleep-deprived and this actually shortens their lifespan.

Kitties are oftentimes frightened by noises when they are outside. Noises don't hurt or kill kitties but they can add stress to their lives. Noises don't always have to be loud, to scare a kitty. Some noises could cause hearing problems for a kitty, but such a situation would be rare. The odds of this happening would be similar to lightning striking a kitty. Noises can be sudden, or incessant. Jackhammer drillings, dynamite blasts, loud motors (moving or in one area), honking horns, loud construction hammerings, thunder, fireworks, and the barking of dogs are just some of the noises that can frighten and/or stress out a kitty. Kitties are also frightened by sudden movements or even movements that seem unusual to them.

Outdoor kitties get very dirty, too, and this is unfortunate and likely bothers them but they can say and do nothing about the plight. Until you bathe an outdoor or stray kitty and look at the dirty water, you won't know just how dirty they can get and really are. On the surface, they may not look very dirty (although at times, they certainly might), but the dirt and dust particles get caught in-between all the cat hairs. When they groom themselves or other outdoor kitties, they ingest dust and dirt particles on a regular basis and this is not good. When an outdoor or stray kitty is well-bathed, their coat will end out being so much lighter.

At times, outdoor kitties roll around in the dirt. Many times, they do this to relieve their parasite bites or to get rid of parasites, but not always. They just enjoy doing this, and that's reason enough. Then, they have to groom themselves and they lick up all those dirt and dust particles (not good) and they also lick in parasites. Of course, if a kitty is always kept inside, all the kitty can do is roll around on the carpet or the furniture, which is so much better for the kitty.

Outdoor kitties, when they roll around in the dirt, can look like they're powdered in dirt, and their fur doesn't feel very soft until you bathe them.

One stray kitty that I recently gave a bath to was so dirty that I had to bathe him twice. Dirt and grime or grease was stuck on his face and tail but it was especially on his lower legs and upper paw areas. I had to put soap on a toothbrush and scrub those areas, and I did this on a couple of other areas, too. I had to soap up stick swabs to clean inside his ears real good. (Never put them in the actual ear canal.) I used several swabs, because the inside of his ears were so dirty, mainly from dust. He tried very hard to get out of the water and his back claws accidentally dug into my hand as the frightened kitty was trying to get away. I should have held him down more securely. Sometimes, you have to put more effort into bathing a kitty. You also might need two people.

When I picked off the kitty's fleas when his fur was sopping wet, I was able to hold him down securely. I go into considerable detail about my wet-down-pick-off method for flea removal in CATegory 28 of I Care for My Cats. Holding kitties down is for their own good. You may also need to wrap them securely up in a towel and weigh them down with the towel when they are in the water when you bathe them, so they cannot move. You use sudsy water and you bathe the kitty as best you can. Kitties feel so good after the bathing and flea removal from all over their head and body and after they're dried off. They know they have no more fleas. They groom themselves and walk around like normal kitties, once they're clean and their fleas are gone. They know you did them a good turn, too. They don't like being held down as you pick off the fleas and put the fleas in water, to drown, but it has to be done. There is no choice in the matter, if they have fleas. Again, I have a whole chapter about parasites (and fleas and flea removal) in my I Care for My Cats book.

And by the way, reference fleas, realize that if you put your kitty or any kitty outside during flea season (it lasts approximately six months in some areas, but less in others), the kitty is going to get fleas and there is no way around this because flea collars and spots don't really work 'to perfection'. A spot is a flea repellent you put on the back shoulder area of a kitty and the repellent gets rid of fleas. (Most outdoor kitties obviously don't get to wear flea collars or are given spot flea-inhibitor treatments.) Fleas will get on the kitty's body somewhere. Some fleas may die with flea collars or spots, but some don't and besides, others jump on. Fleas are, at least, kept to a minimum. The scratching and itching can be tormenting, especially when they're all over a kitty. You, of course, can't see them if the fur is dry. Even when it rains, if kitty gets wet, the fleas will still live and not drown because kitties never get real wet outside. They find shelter. Plus, many kitties have an underfur which doesn't get wet real easily. The fleas are under the underfur layer. When kitties are given a bath and get sopping wet, you can pick the fleas off. They cannot move well, or jump.

People will say, "oh, our area doesn't get fleas", but any area can get fleas at any time—if it is warm enough. Many and perhaps most areas will get fleas from late spring through to early fall. They just aren't always seen. Sometimes, shelter workers will say fleas are not present at the shelter, when they really are. They'll say "we haven't seen any", but fleas are hard to see, especially if there aren't too many of them. It only takes one pregnant flea to start an infestation. Fleas live outside and they're a yearly (seasonal) occurrence. It is false to think your area does not get fleas. It may appease the conscience of people who put their kitty or kitties outside to think there are no fleas, but that is a rationalization that has no valid basis, when the weather is warm. A kitty will eventually pick them up; fleas can hop great distances, fast. It's not a question of, 'if' your kitty will get fleas, it's a question of 'when' your kitty will get fleas, if your kitty goes outside from time to time or stays outside.

Think of how you'd feel if fleas were hopping and moving around on your body and biting you all the time and you couldn't get away from that, day or night. That's how it is for kitties during flea season when they're forced to be outside. Flea bites are extremely distracting and so is the itching. Flea bites are, at first, inflamed and they can be sore for some time. If many bites are on an animal, it's very traumatic. Animals have died from shock, when they've had too many flea bites.

One problem centering on outdoor kitties has to do, mostly, with children, since they are most apt to get cat-scratch fever. If a kitty is outside, it can pick up the bacteria, bartonella henselae. It's believed that the bacteria are transferred to cats from fleas and that this bacteria can be in a cat's saliva. When a kitty grooms itself, it often uses its paws to do so and so the bacteria gets on the paws. A scratch or bite can transfer the bacteria to a human. It is rare, that this ever happens and that people get these bacteria, so it generally isn't too worrisome but it is another reason why kitties need to be inside. After the scratch or bite occurs, in one to two weeks the affected person will have a fever and swollen lymph nodes. They will not want to eat. It takes antibiotics to treat this, but it is easily treated. The kitty will need vet care, but if the kitty is without an owner and living outside, the kitty won't get the needed vet care. This is always a problem for outdoor kitties.

Other parasites besides fleas can cause torment, too. Ear-mites are another example. The mites of Mange cause itching and scratching, too, so that bald areas on an animal become apparent. Skin flakes are also seen. Cats and dogs that get treated for Mange must be treated with special skin salve that is prescribed. Sadly, with cats, many don't have a home or a caretaker so some of them are driven insane by parasites. Ticks can be bothersome and tormenting, too. Fleas, ticks, and mites are the more common external parasites that plague outdoor mammals but there are so many others, too. Actually, tiny bacteria that gets all over their skin bothers them, too.

Ringworm isn't a parasite, it's a fungus, but it can be hell-on-Earth for a cat and for humans. If your kitty brings home ringworm because you've let your kitty go outside, the kitty will need cortisone shots, but also topical treatment that a vet will have to prescribe. Could just rubbing alcohol kill it? There's a special shampoo you can get from the vet that you can also use, as needed. Kitties can't get rid of ringworm on their own. You'll know ringworm by the circular patches on them and the loss of fur on those patches. You may have to look for them. Any fur loss will eventually grow back once the fungus dies.

Another fungus that can affect animals relates to the fungus that causes Valley Fever, which tends to occur in dry desert areas. Winds blow dust around that gets breathed in by the animals. This fungus can be in that dust. Spores that grow in the soil become airborne and these spores are as spears that get into lungs and implant there. Areas don't have to be entirely desert to generate these fungal spores and Valley Fever. With Global Warming, more world areas are becoming dry.

Often, if the kitty has ringworm, humans in contact with the kitty will get it. A whole family can get it. Humans can use Tinactin®, which is used for jock itch, more commonly. Ringworm has the same effect as parasites have. It reddens a skin area and it itches. I've used rubbing alcohol combined with a dry powder (Mexsand®) but you can get a prescription from a physician for it

(Nizoral Cream). I put it on top of it but I do not know if ice killed anything under my skin. The rubbing alcohol may have killed the virus that formed the ring. Parasites are all too common and outdoor and stray kitties run into several types. Parasites are all around the world, just like kitties are. Another contracted problem is Valley Fever. If you see lesions on a kitty that do not appear to be ringworm, kitty could have Valley Fever and will need to have a blood test and be checked.

Just about any insect or animal that a kitty catches and eats while outside can transfer parasites or disease to the kitty. Parasites can go into their system, or get and stay somewhere on the body. Whatever is already inside an eaten animal or insect goes into the kitty and usually stays in the kitty and doesn't leave by way of a bowel movement. Parasites can lay eggs inside an animal, which can become so many in number that there is no way all of them can come out the other way. Eggs hatch inside and the new group of parasites live on whatever they can, inside of the kitty. They eat stomach food, which goes into the kitty. Often, the parasites can be worms. Worms inside of a kitty will constantly eat the stomach's contents. If you see a really skinny kitty outside, chances are, it has internal parasites. And who will help the poor kitty?

Kitties can also get stung or bitten by insects while the kitty is going after or eating them. They may or may not eat some or all of the insects they kill, but even if they don't, some insects are dangerous and can pass on problems for the kitty. Sometimes, kitties only eat part of an insect, but that may be all it takes for them to get parasites transferring in and living inside them.

Are you beginning to see the bigger picture? <u>The list of outdoor perils goes on and on.</u> <u>Kitties are more helpless, on the whole, than is usually perceived, and certainly kittens are very helpless.</u> In this perspective, kittens are actually babies just like human babies, who are helpless and dependent on those who are there to take care of them or who have gone before them. There is nothing more helpless, in fact, than a newborn baby—they must be taught everything and they have so much to experience and to learn before they are even borderline sufficient. Babies must have all of their basic needs met for some time, as do kittens. Each and every day, kittens need care and protection every step of the way. But cats need protection too, and are like human babies, as well, reference their inabilities to defend themselves, to make themselves safe, and to keep themselves healthy.

<u>We intentionally domesticated kitties so now they are tame and very small</u>. Claws and teeth are just not enough to keep them alive when kitties are outside or in the wild. We bred kitties down to be small and generally docile and tame. So what do we do? We put them outside, where they shouldn't be. Some people are more a part of the problem than are others. Some are part of the solution, or they are in process of becoming a part of the solution. Kitties are not wild animals, at all, because we've bred them down to tameness and general docility. You cannot lump them in with wild animals anymore. That is not what they are. You cannot expect them to survive outside, like wild animals tend to do. All kitties need to be protected inside, by people who will go the extra mile for them.

To believe that it is not good to keep kitties inside because they shouldn't be cooped up is a wrong or short-sighted belief. It is not a need for kitties to live outside. They are just fine inside and they're better off inside. <u>Kitties actually like being inside</u>. Kitties are happy inside. They roam the home, and roaming the home, I find, is enough roaming for them. Even if they've been outside, they will still settle down inside of a stable and organized home.

Sometimes, settling in to a new home takes as little time as a week. Certainly, once they're cared for medically, and given love and are cared for in general, their outdoor wandering ways will fade away. Time changes things. Their habits and routine changes. They become as a family member.

Because kitties have been domesticated, we really have to start bringing the outdoor ones in, and fix them up medically and give them consistent love, security, and food and water. Granted, if they had been outdoors, they may be cautious and skittish at first because being that way was what kept them safe and alive outside, but after they're captured and cared for, they'll mellow out and their demeanor will change, if given <u>enough</u> time. Some people give up this project way too soon. Even if such kitties stay a little skittish, they can still make nice pets. Such kitties will come around to a caretaker some of the time, which, I find, is enough. After a time, they'll come around more. They learn to trust their caretaker.

<u>Perils for outdoor kittens and cats really do add up, all in all, creating helplessness, no matter what the age or the intelligence level of the kitty might be.</u> <u>There are just too many circumstances beyond a kitty's control when a kitty is outside.</u> <u>Kitties living outside have a much shorter life span than kitties living inside haveP</u>

The average outdoor kitty is lucky to make it to their sixth year. An indoor-only kitty usually makes it to their fifteenth year. Can you not see why? Some even believe that the average lifespan for the outdoor kitty is only two and a half years. When you factor in kitten deaths, this makes some sense. If no one feeds the outdoor kitty, they eventually starve to death. Starvation shortens their lifespan quickly and kitties just wander off and go somewhere to die when they know the starving is taking their life. When kitties do not get enough food, their resistance is down and they can get sick. It can become cause and effect. Perils are around every corner for the outdoor kitty. Kitties are not safe outdoors.

Not long ago, as I was driving and had just entered the freeway, I saw a dead kitty lying at the side of the road. It had obviously been hit by a vehicle as the kitty was trying to cross the road, possibly in an effort to find its way home, if it had a home. Perhaps, it was trying to make its way to one of the commercial Dumpsters® in that area so it could get some food, who knows? I was heartsick when I saw this kitty— absolutely heartsick. If only people would keep their kitties indoors, then cars on any road couldn't run over them. Such an outdoor peril cars and other vehicles are for kitties, whether the outdoor kitties have owners, or whether they are feral cats or strays. I felt so powerless and sad when I saw that dead kitty on the road because there was nothing I could have done to prevent what had happened. If I could have, I would have.

Not too long after I saw that dead cat on the road, I saw another dead one, squashed as flat as a pancake, on a busy street. Actually, I see dead cats around or on roads all too often. Every time I do, it deeply saddens me. I get a sick feeling in my stomach. The other day, during broad daylight, I saw a very young black cat sprint across the road I was going down and the road that was going the other way. It was a busy two-lane street and, by some miracle, the cat missed getting hit by all the moving cars. It was running as if its life depended on it. I don't think I've ever seen a cat run that fast. This cat was lucky. Usually, in such dangerous situations, cats get hit and hit more than once. There have been way too many dead cats on roads over the course of time and this is somewhat because of population increase. Roads get traveled on more often, by more people. This puts outdoor and stray kitties in even more peril.

There are a number of people who do not live directly on busy streets. They may live several streets away from a busy road, or they may live in an apartment building, duplex, mobile home complex, or a military-base housing complex that is far from a busy road. Some of these residents will reason, "I can leave my kitty or kitties outside because there aren't many cars in my, or in this area". Two problems are present with this thinking. First off, all it takes is one car to kill a kitty, and it doesn't have to be going very fast. Cars are around even uncongested areas. Second, kitties are roamers because they are curious and independent creatures. Because they are roamers, they will roam over to any and all busy streets that are within a several mile radius of where they are used to being. Even if you just put your kitty out on your patio or front stairs, the kitty is apt to leave, and go roaming.

Cats, by nature, are afraid of cars. When a car is moving, they are threatened by the car and will not venture out on the street if they have seen a moving car. The problem is, they don't always see the car. Cars can move fast. Also, a kitty may dart out in front of a moving car, from underneath a parked car. Very often, kitties will rest underneath parked cars because of the shade. When they go to leave, they can get hit because they don't see a car coming. So often, when kitties cross the road, they could be halfway across the road and a fast-moving car can get them. A car rounding a corner can come around unexpectedly and run over a kitty, too. On occasion, something in the way can blind their sight. Kitties that get run over on fast highways and freeways are not able to judge speed well and they can get hit for that reason, too. Also, if other cars are in other lanes, if the kitty tries to outrun one car, another car they were unable to see ends out getting them. Kitties are extremely vulnerable on any busy road, especially the ones in towns and cities that are heavily populated. We all know how busy these roads can get, especially during certain hours. Kitties that must roam for food often have to cross busy roads and so they are continually vulnerable to getting run over.

I saw yet another dead kitty on a road, recently. This one was a white kitten—just a little one. Had the kitten been born outside and somehow lost its mother or got lost from her? Perhaps, a coyote got its mother and its siblings? This kitten was several miles away from a town or a city, and it was dead along a highway. It likely never knew what hit it but we can never know how long an animal lays somewhere before it dies, after it has been hit by a vehicle. An animal could be laying there for hours and hours, before it finally dies. So often, nobody stops. I'd seen those other dead cats along a road (city and highway) in the fairly recent past but the City and the County people are supposed to come along and remove dead animals promptly and they don't always. I suspect citizens sometimes do that, and then put the dead animal in the nearest garbage bin. A dead animal along a road (road kill) can be a health hazard, though. They require expert handling.

Quite a few cars go over the speed limit. Kitties don't realize the dangers related to speeding vehicles. The coast may be clear, they dart out, but a fast car can come upon them quickly. Again, many times they have no choice but to cross the road. Some of them get run over by cars backing up from an area, too. A kitty doesn't know what's going to happen, if they've been resting or sleeping under a car or behind a car's wheel. Accidents happen fast.

Many a slow-moving car has killed many a kitty. Backing up accidents are common because the driver may not see the animal. There are blind spots.

The smaller the animal is, the more likely it is that it won't be seen. Cats are such tiny creatures when compared to vehicles, and really, dogs can also be very small. People who run over a cat or a dog are going to feel badly about it, whether it is their pet, someone else's, or a stray. One case I heard about, a man who ran over someone else's cat, took the dead pet and put it under the owner's car, at night. This was a sneaky and deceptive trick. Rigor mortis set in and the next day, the cat's owner drove out of his carport and one of his tires went over a big bump, whereupon he stopped the car, got out, and discovered his cat. He had seen his cat the day before, over on the neighbor's lot. He suspected that the neighbor had somehow caused the death but he couldn't prove it. But he knew that he couldn't have possibly run over the cat because of the timing and the rigor mortis. For one thing, he had not taken his car out since he had seen his cat over at his neighbor's. There was no way his own car could have run over the cat. But, was he the one who had been negligent, by not keeping his kitty inside all the time?

Vehicles should all slow down if they ever see a cat or dog near a road and they should be ready to brake. Kind people might sometimes park and try to get the cat or dog, and then try to find their owner so that their owner could come and get their pet. This has happened with outdoor animals. Some would say the pet was abducted, when someone does that, but is it an abduction if the pet appears to be a stray? Then, if a dog or cat can be picked up and put in a car, that kind person would try several ways to find the owner and if that didn't happen, they would try to find a home for the animal. In the case of a dog, especially if that kind person happens to have a fence, removing a cat or dog off the street might be considered to be a theft, but was it? Do citizens have the right to do this? It is very iffy, but if you took the animal to a shelter, and they allowed you to adopt the animal, after so many days, then that would be looked at as being less iffy and perhaps even legally acceptable. You could also put up a few 'Found a Kitty' signs. If you genuinely believe the kitty is a stray or a feral, any just-found cat can always be kept inside, once supplies are purchased. <u>Dogs and cats need interception and help. More people should start to see themselves as animal protectors and rescuers.</u> You do not want to ever take a dog or cat that you know or strongly suspect belongs to someone else, though.

Always keep in mind that you can take just-found dogs and cats to a shelter or pound. I've seen many a dead dog along a road or highway, too; my heart sinks whenever I see any dead animal along a road. All in all, I've seen more cats that are dead along a road, than I have dogs. The local County pound will usually pick up roaming dogs but not roaming cats. Roaming cats are harder to catch when they are out in the open, which is the main reason why they do not go after cats, other than there are no laws in place noting that they have to.

You may never know that the kitty you were responsible for was hit by a car because local government comes around and picks up dead animals off the streets, mainly because the dead bodies become a health problem, as the bodies decay. Citizens remove such bodies, too, because they don't like to see them in the neighborhood. I know I've picked up dead turtles and frogs off my street, and dead birds that fell out of trees, and I then bagged them for the garbage bin, but I live on a privately-owned street. I couldn't stand to look at them and was worried that a dog or cat might try to eat what was left—all decayed and parasite-laden. You should always suspect that if you leave your kitty outside and the kitty turns up missing that the kitty could have been run over, since that is a possibility. You may think your kitty was stolen by someone who wanted to keep your kitty, or was taken in by someone who thought your kitty was a stray (and these would be the more comforting thoughts), but really, your kitty may have been run over by a slow or fast-moving vehicle and subsequently, was removed from the street.

You may think your neighborhood is a quiet, safe place, but kitties can get run over, any time, any place. Kitties will often rest or sleep under cars, believing that they are safe under a covered protection. They may need the shade when they're under a car. Sometimes, they go to sleep right next to one of the wheels. Again, they get run over this way. They can get run over just by walking in front of a car that goes forward or by walking behind a car that goes in reverse. It could be your car or a neighbor's car that does this. People can pull out really fast from a parking spot, too. People can be in a hurry. But slow or fast, a kitty can get killed if it is under a car and in the path of a wheel. There are no cars inside of a home.

If you know you have kitties in your area, condition yourself to remember to pull out of your parking area slowly. Look under your car first, preferably. Especially if you see little paw prints on your vehicle's hood or trunk, know that a kitty could be under your car (or even resting in the engine area). A kitty could be in a deep sleep, under your car, so that even your slamming the car door when you get in may not be enough to wake the kitty up and cause the kitty to move. A kitty waking up out of a deep sleep may be in a stupor state for a while so they may not move away from the car wheel in time. Again, a car does not have to be going fast to run over and kill a kitty. Honk your horn if you think a kitty could be under your car.

Kitties wander off to where busy streets are more often than is believed. All outdoor kitties, sooner or later, can become roaming kitties. They get hungry. They may roam far and wide, looking for food—in a dish or otherwise. Kitties don't stay in one area even if food is out for them somewhere. They leave the area—to explore, to do their business, to find water, to find a place to sleep, or to find a safe place to have kittens. They're just plain roamers. If something scares or bothers them at one place, they will go to another place. If they're bored somewhere, they'll go off and explore. Anything outside can get them. Cars and traffic, in general, get more kitties than most people realize. Kitties just are not safe outside. One of the dead kitties that I saw along the road was a black kitty, with white paws. I felt so sick inside when I saw that poor little, defenseless, and unprotected dead kitty. How can a kitty defend itself against a heavy, moving vehicle if the kitty is in its direct path? It just can't.

Certainly at night, many kitties are run over by vehicles. They have good night vision but again, they can't judge speed or react to the speed of a moving object, fast enough. This is the case with other animal types at night, as well. Again, a car can suddenly back up, round a corner, or even go forward unexpectedly, and thereby run over a kitty. Drivers just can't see very well at night. If headlights shine directly into a kitty's eyes and the kitty is on the road, guess what's probably going to happen to the kitty. Kitties are blinded by headlights. The vehicle will run over them.

If a kitty ever does survive being hit by a car, the kitty is so small and lightweight that both external and internal damage could have been done. So many kinds of surgeries may need to take place to save the kitty's life or to restore the kitty back to some kind of normalcy, if surgery would even be possible, which usually, it isn't because even if there is an owner, how are you going to find that owner? If an owner is found or is present, they may not be able to afford the medical costs.

The whole ordeal from being hit by a car would be so painful and difficult for any kitty—start to finish. The kitty will probably gradually die on the road, if it isn't killed on impact. People don't usually stop because they assume the kitty is dead. Most people are usually in a hurry these days, too. A rare person will stop and take such a kitty to a vet right away. This is what should be done. Such kitties can, at times, be patched up and restored by medical treatment and surgery. Even a kitty that looks really hurt may be able to be saved, treated, restored, and still live a decent life.

Some vets will fix a kitty up for free if a Good Samaritan brings in a kitty that has been hurt. They may try to place the kitty later, too. In any event, take a kitty in to a vet if you perchance come across one that has been hurt, whether the kitty is along a road or is somewhere else. At the very least, the vet will put the kitty out of its misery and euthanize the kitty, if the kitty is too far gone and is suffering.

Sometimes, kitties that have been hit by moving vehicles end out having their organs go out of place because what had held them in was torn. The torn area may heal, but the tear itself will not be repaired so a stomach can be pressed over to a different area, inside of the kitty. This puts pressure on other organs and can move them out of place. Kitty will be uncomfortable, and, sometimes, in pain. Kitty will have problems eating. But, who will even realize this? A fall or the impact from being hit by a vehicle can cause this kind of problem, and other similar things can also occur. This is why x-rays are needed after a kitty has fallen or been the brunt of some kind of impact. I know about this because this happened to me, after a car hit me.

If someone has an outdoor kitty, they may never see the kitty fall, or be hit by a moving vehicle. Even a farm or wild animal can kick a kitty, and cause this 'hidden' damage to be present. Poor kitty will have to live with this until death. The kitty may still be able to eat and drink, but the food may not go down real fast or very easily, and the kitty may only be able to eat small amounts whenever the kitty does eat. Internal organs can be out of place.

Another problem that results when kitties are hit or run over by a vehicle is that if a stranger picks up a broken-up kitty after the kitty has been hit by a car, and then takes the kitty to the vet, the vet may euthanize the kitty because there is no owner around, unless the kitty does not require very much mending. In that case, the vet may tend to the kitty, if there is space at the clinic or if a vet clinic employee, including the vet, can take the repaired kitty into their home, which they often can't. (Occasionally, animal shelter employees might take in such a kitty, but if there's no one who will, the kitty has to stay there and then be taken to a shelter or a pet store to be adopted, as soon as possible.) (Most pet stores do not take such animals, to sell.) But, if the kitty is too battered and broken up, the vet has no choice but to put the kitty out of its misery. (A few vets will repair the kitty anyway, if they think the kitty may live, but some vets will automatically euthanize such a kitty.) Had such a now-dead kitty been safe indoors, and genuinely loved and cared for, it would still be whole.

Before I finished this book, I saw four more kitties, dead on a road or next to a road. Obviously, they'd been run over. For every dead kitty I happened to see, I knew that there were many, many more that I didn't see. I thought, "I've got to get this book out, fast, so people will make more of an effort to keep kitties indoors." This is one reason why I extracted the content out of my long cat book compendium. The content had priority for publishing.

I also heard about an outdoor kitty that lived in Michigan. He was outside, minding his own business, when all of a sudden he was hit hard by an arrow. The arrow went way into his body, and the poor kitty somehow made its way home. He was taken to a vet, who spent some time removing the arrow and repairing the internal damage. The kitty is still alive and they probably never found the perpetrator. Clearly, someone out there intentionally shot this innocent kitty, and assumedly, God has the number of that person. Many believe that God makes a record of such bad deeds. I wrote a poem about another kitty, named Lucky. Lucky had an arrow shot through his head and neck area. The poem includes for both kitties, though it had originally been written because of Lucky. The poem is titled *Lucky's Message* and it is in my third (of eight) poems and short works books and it relates to outdoor perils. I've written a number of animal-related poems and short works. Certain ones are presented here, in the last chapter.

Some hunters think they can use kitties as target practice for their bows and arrows (cross-bows included) or their guns. How hard is it to shoot a sleeping kitty, or a sitting or slow-moving kitty? You may as well go into a meadow and shoot a grazing cow, which, of course, is also illegal. That outdoor kitty that was shot with an arrow for target practice had been someone's pet, but even if it wasn't someone's pet, there would have been the potential for such a kitty to be taken in by someone or adopted out and cared for and loved. Not much is too much easier to do than suddenly shooting an innocent outdoor kitty (which should never have been done). <u>What should be done, instead of trying to kill kitties, is to make efforts to rescue outdoor kitties.</u>

Bringing a kitty in to a home and giving it full care is a noble endeavor. Shooting a kitty is repugnant. It is admirable to rescue kitties. Certain hunter-type men (and boys) would scoff at that because they lack knowledge and because some of them can be insensitive, uncaring, and even depraved (not all, just some). We can all breathe a sigh of relief that not all are like this and also, that the law is around. Not all would use loving and needy domestic pets or potential pets as target practice. We, as a culture, domesticated kitties to be small, and tame. They should not be outside. We domesticated them to be house pets. They are not, at all, on the same par as legitimately hunted animals (kitties are not wilderness animals, not even close), and to think that they are is to be and stay in ignorance and to be and remain unenlightened.

Because kitties are small and tame, they need our help, care, and protection. I can't emphasize this enough. Because of domestication, even feral kitties can become someone's pet, given <u>enough</u> time, love, and medical care. Most feral cats can, anyway. I've experienced this, myself. Very few feral cats are what I call deep feral. Even some of the ones that seem deep feral can be rescued, fixed up, loved, understood, and spared. They may never come around full measure but they will come around close enough to being acceptable in-home dwellers. <u>No feral is so far gone that they cannot be spared and rescued.</u> It will take special care, treatment, and know how. It is a step-by-step process. People can be specially trained to do this. They can learn to do this. Centers should be set up and constructed in such a way that feral kitties can go through rehabilitation. This should become an all-world goal. It should become an all-world goal to rescue every outdoor kitty (and of course, all stray dogs).

Sadly, kitties are secretly used as target practice by ignorant young people (usually young men) who don't yet realize how wonderful kitties are and that we are here to protect and rescue them, not hurt or kill them. Whether they use a bee-bee gun, a rifle, a handgun, or a cross-bow and arrow, or bow and arrow, it is wrong and illegal to harm and kill such domesticated animals, and to even kill many species of wildlife, which would include certain birds. There are other ways to practice any kind of shooting. Get yourself a bunch of tin cans and use them. Blow up some balloons and shoot at those. Go out on a shooting range and zero in on material targets. Etc.

<u>All kitties deserve to live out the course of their natural lives. This needs to be a new world goal. People everywhere should prioritize these animal issues so there are fewer kitties born, none living outside, and better, consistent care and protection given to all kitties, everywhere.</u>

5

Dangerous Animals/Cruel and Thoughtless People

Another problem for kitties, found in the more southern areas of the United States, are coyotes. If you go up more north, the problem will be wolves. You can substitute the words, wolf or wolves, for the words, coyote or coyotes, as you read along if you want to (especially if you live up north). Up north, there are also mountain lions (cougars) and bears. In the South-West, many people have homes that are more on the outskirts of desert towns and cities. At night and even in the early morning, these residents can occasionally hear the coyotes howl and see the coyotes wandering around. The coyotes are out looking for a meal. Coyotes even come in to a town or city. Many a kitty owner who put their kitty outside or let them go outside ended out losing the kitty to a coyote. One lady who lost her kitty that way said to me, "I was just too lazy and cheap to get the kitty litter so my cat could stay inside". She blamed herself, which didn't bring her kitty back but gave hope—that any of her future kitties would be indoor-only ones. Learning can come hard.

Coyotes are very stealth. And they're much faster than little kitties are. Coyotes can even walk about during the day, looking for food. They're often mistaken for dogs. If they have to, they will go in to a populated area to find

89

food. They'll especially go along a ravine, river, canal, or stream because they think it is safe for them to do so, and, they like to take some drinks. Then, at night, they'll hunt for prey around the houses or buildings that are near the water area where they had just come over from.

Coyotes easily get cats and certainly, kittens, but they can also get small dogs. Small dogs cannot run fast enough and cannot spring up into a tree or get up to a high place, like cats can. Sometimes, there can be more than one coyote travelling together and so together, they can get larger dogs. They may even know where a large dog might be and they may come in to the area, specifically, to get that larger dog. In other words, even large dogs are not safe from coyotes. Even large domesticated farm animals can get killed by coyotes. Pets get picked off, one by one, in areas where coyotes live. Again, coyotes can travel down a waterway that goes right through a town or city and get pets that way, and they can also hunt pets that live around the outer rim areas of a town or city. Country pets in certain areas are always very vulnerable to coyotes, both day and night.

A real strong fence helps to keep dogs safe. It has to be regularly checked and made to be coyote-proof. Usually, wolves are stronger than coyotes. They are more apt to bust down a fence, as are bears. A mountain lion (or cougar) can jump over a fence. Some dogs, in some parts of the country, have to be put inside a home or a shed of some type during the night, when everyone is sleeping.

With small animals, coyotes pick them up in their mouth and carry them to an area where they can relax more and eat their meal. The poor animal (that's in the mouth) is horribly frightened while being in the coyote's mouth. It is powerless. Then comes the kill. It's an awful way for the smaller animals to have to die. Often, animals that become prey to certain carnivores start to be eaten before they're even dead. They're maimed, but not dead. This is a really horrible way for animals to die but it happens far more often than people realize (or like to think about, so they suppress the thought). Many outdoor and stray kitties have been killed, this way, which is another reason why they should all be indoors.

Caretakers of all pets have to be diligent when protecting pets from coyotes (and all other carnivorous animals in the wild). Keep dogs inside whenever possible and as much as possible, and, always keep kitties indoors. Some people chain or tie up dogs. Keeping dogs chained or tied up can actually prevent the dog from running away from danger or getting to a place where the attacking predator can't get to it. These attacks can happen very fast, many times before a caretaker can even react (and prevent horrible mutilation or the death of their tied-up pet). This can happen even if the pet isn't tied up.

Any person who lets their kitty outside and who knows that coyotes are not very far away are essentially feeding their kitty to the coyotes. They'll innocently say, "oh, my kitty just disappeared" and I feel like reading them the Riot Act. They very well know that they were responsible for the kitty's death, which nine times out of ten came about because of the coyotes, but some will completely dismiss the whole thing. Their negligence was plain wrong. They're out a kitty. The kitty is out a life. Even a kitty that just goes outside for short periods of time will eventually get picked off by a coyote, if coyotes roam the area.

I heard of another kitty, found on the open desert, and it had had its rear leg eaten off (possibly by a coyote). The leg was torn off from the hind so there was no part of the leg left, at all. The people who found him took him to a vet right away. No one knew, for sure, what had happened to him (though it looked like a coyote got him). Obviously, whatever did get him got him out of doors. The people kept Très (which means three, i.e., three legs) and Très lived to be fifteen years of age and he finally died of cancer. Très still did many things, despite his handicap. He jumped (somewhat), played, and roamed about the house just fine. When Très died, the people got another cat, to pal around with the other cat that they had had when Très died. It's always good to have at least two kitties so the kitties won't be lonely at night when a caretaker is sleeping, or during the times when a caretaker is out of the home for whatever the reason.

This story proves that handicapped kitties can still live long and happy lives, and also that kitties should always stay indoors. It also proves that kitties that are outside in desert areas can be killed and eaten by coyotes or other predators. Coyotes can be in other areas besides the desert, though, so if coyotes live in your area, outdoor pets will be in danger. Vets treat more dogs than cats for coyote bites and this is because kitties never make it into a vet clinic because they're usually killed. They make quick prey for coyotes. Odds of getting away on a flat desert with few trees are slim to none. Kitties can't outrun coyotes. And kitties can't climb up a saguaro or Bird's Nest Cactus, either. The quills prohibit it. If they try to, they're in big trouble. They can get up your average tree, easy enough, but it can be hard for them to get down it, later on. It's rare they ever get up on a roof somewhere, to be safe, unless they climb up a tree and then jump on the roof.

Keep in mind that roaming dogs will maim and kill kitties, too. Dogs can be roaming out in the desert, or around any urban or rural locality. Dogs should not be allowed to roam. Ordinarily, if they do, they slowly starve. They eat bad food and little food. They may not get any water (or just get dirty water). People don't usually feed them because they assume they belong to someone. Plus, dog food is a little costly. A bag of it does not last as long as a bag of cat food does. Also, dog food costs a bit because you have to buy a large bag. Who wants to buy a large bag to feed a roaming dog that will probably go elsewhere and go elsewhere soon? Besides, when a roaming dog is sighted, rarely does the person seeing the dog have dog food in the home right then and there. They have to make an extra trip to the store to buy it. Hence, the poor dogs forced to roam generally starve. In any event, roaming dogs often kill cats. The dogs don't even have to be all that big, either.

Dog attacks sometimes cause a kitty to be lame or partly lame (but sometimes kitties born outside can be born with such a defect, and so they can be lame from birth). Still, if you ever see an outdoor kitty limping or only using three limbs to walk, this could be permanent for them and if you do not bring the kitty in (or catch it), a dog could easily get to the kitty and catch it and kill it (or severely harm the kitty). The kitty would not be able to run very fast or jump up to safety somewhere because it is lame. Many types of animals could harm such a kitty, actually. Somehow, get the kitty and take the limping or affected kitty to the vet before the kitty gets harmed by a larger animal. Even other cats could harm such a kitty, though this isn't likely. A vet can determine why the kitty is limping and if the leg can be fixed in some way.

It is particularly not good to allow dogs to roam during the kitten season. Kittens that are born outside are very vulnerable to dog attacks. Dogs can sometimes get in to where kittens have been born. A dog can wipe out a whole litter. When kittens go wandering around after becoming mobile, dogs and other animals can hurt or kill them very quickly. The kittens won't be too agile or very fast. As noted before, quite a few kittens get conjunctivitis and their eyes are forced shut because of the eye weep that hardens. Kittens are so low to the ground that their eyes get exposed to dirt and bacteria. If their eyes are crusted shut, they absolutely can't get away from anything dangerous because they can't see anything; they are totally helpless. Even if they can see, though, they are still easy prey for roaming dogs or coyotes.

Even though I know dogs can harm cats, I still love dogs—always have and always will. I have fed stray dogs, around where I live. I buy inexpensive dry food for them because they don't stay long (and I may not ever see them again). I put the bowl down but I sometimes have to hold it down for the dog as it eats. Otherwise, the bowl shifts and moves around. I give the dog enough for it to lose its hunger. I usually put a lot of water in with the food and always fill up a bowl with water for the stray dog. That way, the dog will get enough water just in case it happens to be dehydrated, which stray dogs so often are. They can't tell you that they are but they usually are.

It is hard to know if a roaming dog is one that's been dumped, permanently, or one that just got loose and the owner is looking for it. It is always good to take a roaming dog to a shelter or the local pound if the dog is friendly enough to handle. If you keep the dog, yourself, as some people do, then the owner that might be looking for the dog is out their dog. This concept applies to stray kitties, too, which is why some owners who allow their kitty to ever be outside put an identifying collar on the kitty. You can have a phone number put on a small metal tag and put it on a kitty's collar. You can have a vet put an identification disc under the kitty's skin. Some caretakers have this done when the kitty gets altered. It can be scanned, for the identifying and home information.

Recently, I was talking with a neighborhood girl of around ten years of age. I had been wondering what on earth had happened to all the tiny and small dogs that had been running loose, around where I was living. At one time and close in together, I had recalled seeing ten or twelve loose dogs but at different times and on different streets. (They were not on a leash, halter, or inside of a fenced area.) Several were Chihuahuas. There were others, though—two of which had long curly fur that was never combed or clipped. One day, I'd happened to go over to the home where those two dogs were being kept because I'd seen a little boy crying there and no adult was home, and I happened to notice that the dogs' water had been knocked over due to an insufficient bowl type, and so had their food been knocked over and it was all over the dirt/ground. The boy was obviously not conscientious or mature enough to mind the dogs. But, back to the story.

The young girl I'd spoken with told me that several dogs in the neighborhood had been run over. This was no surprise to me. The dogs I'd seen loose and running around had no caretaker with or even near them when they had been running around (and they were outside most of the time). Most of them didn't have a collar on, but some may have. The dogs were not walked, or at least, I never saw any of them being walked (and certainly I never saw them on a leash). What may have happened was that the owners of the dogs let the dogs out so they could 'do their business' and they left them out way too long and did not go out to supervise them, at the time. Dogs are in peril, too, when they're loose outside. Like cats, many things can harm them if they run

95

around loose, outside. Moving cars and dogs in streets especially don't mix. These loose dogs may have hurt some of the local cats, too.

What I am indirectly noting here is that the caretakers of the run-over dogs were negligent and probably even abusive if they left their dog out most all the time so that its odds of being run over was greatly increased. Some dogs I saw were always out in the street, hanging out with some other loose dogs, so who can be surprised that those dogs got run over? I called the local pound about one of them down the road a ways and gave them the street number and street but still kept seeing the dog outside. I called the pound, again. Still, I kept seeing the dog. (Well, maybe they were understaffed?) The pound doesn't usually come around to pick up stray cats, unless a stray cat is real sick and acting like it could have Rabies. For healthy and public-danger reasons, they have to come out.

Another outdoor peril is that an outdoor kitty can run into a porcupine. A porcupine has thirty thousand quills that range from a half an inch to four inches in length. The quills have backward projecting scales that keep working their way into the body so the quills must come out fast because they will become even more torturous for a kitty, the more delay that there is to remove them. Kitty will need an antihistamine, as there will be an allergic response to the quills. Immediate vet care is urgent. The kitty needs to be in a calm atmosphere. If you are not near a vet, some people have tended to such a kitty on their own by following a specific procedure. (It is better to have a vet help the kitty, however.) A quilled kitty will need one milligram of the product, Benadryl®, per pound of weight. This product is an over-the-counter medicine. Double-check this with a vet, though.

The kitty will need to be restrained when the porcupine quills are being removed. It's quite an ordeal. Pull each one out, straight and gently, and use pliers. Do not pinch the quills too hard with the pliers. If any quills break off too short, a vet may need to surgically remove those imbedded quill parts. Put the pliers down close to where the quill meets the skin when pulling out the quills. Wash the area afterwards with an antiseptic soap. Look for all hidden quills; the blunt ends will stick up; you will need to carefully feel all over the kitty because some quills could be in unexpected spots. Double-check for quills more than once. Use a magnifying glass, if necessary. Monitor the wound areas for several days. If there is redness, swelling, or a discharge at any time, the kitty will need antibiotics, prescribed by a vet. In fact, the kitty may need to be put under anesthesia in the first place and a vet may need to pull out the quills. You (and a friend or relative because two people will be needed) may not be able to work with the kitty and the kitty may be too frightened and in too much in pain from the quills. If restraining works, after as many are removed as can be, the area may need to be clipped or shaved to check to see if there are more quills. You don't want a one left in the skin.

Many a kitty has had to be anesthetized after running into certain kinds of cactus. Some cacti are totally filled with quills—for example, Cholla and Prickly Pear Cactus. Mean children have been known to throw kitties into cactus, or, kitties run into them when running away from danger. Once stuck, kitties try to roll around the cactus, in an attempt to get free, only to get even more quills all over their head and bodies. Too many quills, and a kitty can go into shock. If you ever see such a helpless kitty that is stuck on a cactus plant, do the right thing and immediately take the kitty to a nearby vet clinic. You may have to cut the quills on the cactus plant so you can separate the kitty from the cactus. If the kitty is already separated from the cactus, you can take the kitty to the vet clinic right away.

If there are just a few cactus quills on the kitty, maybe you can get them out, yourself, but if the quills are barbed (curved) at the end, you have to remove them a certain way. Cactus quills are like needles. Porcupine quills are thicker. At a vet clinic, the quilled body area on the cat will be shaved after most of the quills are removed so <u>all</u> the rest of the quills can be seen and removed with tweezers. It is not good to miss any and this is the problem with trying to remove quills, yourself. Vet people know how to do these kinds of procedures. You have to get them all, even the little ones. Running away from loose, unfenced dogs is a principle reason why kitties run into cacti, but kitties run away from other kitties all the time, too. Outdoor and stray kitties can be territorial and so chasing happens.

Keep in mind that neighborhood dogs are just as dangerous as coyotes are. They don't usually eat the kitty, though, like coyotes do. In some areas, there are too many loose neighborhood dogs. Some are allowed to be loose around a block or neighborhood, for a time. Some get out of their fenced or penned-in areas. Some are walked, without leashes. Some are suddenly let out of a house when a kitty might be sleeping in their yard or going about their yard and outdoor area. Many, many kitties are killed by neighborhood dogs, and in horrible, brutal ways. Both dogs, and vehicle impacts kill many a neighborhood kitty.

Dogs roam loose in certain neighborhoods, especially. Some dogs have been dumped and abandoned, so they obviously roam. Or, they just, somehow, got loose from a yard or from being tied up. These dogs also need help and protection. Again, some of these dogs become prey to desert predators, whether they are big or little dogs. It is not easy for these roaming stray dogs to find food. If they see a kitty at an area where a bowl of food is, they may kill the kitty, if they can. They'll shake it by the neck until it is dead. Certain dogs might viciously attack the cat, and bite it and tear it apart. It all depends on the constitution of the dog. Leaving one dead cat is an example to near-by cats that the food dish or bowl of food is not theirs but will now be the dog's, so in case the dog comes around again, they'd better not be anywhere near the dish. Roaming female dogs are less likely to kill cats than roaming male dogs are, but female dogs have killed kitties.

Some roaming dogs will only maim a kitty. If no one is around to help a maimed kitty, the kitty will suffer. If you ever find a maimed kitty, put it in a car and take it to a vet clinic, right away. You will be doing the right thing. The clinic may or may not charge you. They shouldn't. You can call a local shelter, too, to see if they'll come out. Usually, they won't—you have to take the kitty to them. However, more time will be lost and that will not be good. By then, the kitty could be dead. Immediately rushing a maimed kitty to the vet's is the best action. Most of the larger shelters and pounds have medical facilities. Shelters almost never come out to get kitties, unless there is a hoarder case. Some shelters are hard to get a hold of on the phone and they only have answering machines. When you get to the vet clinic, you'll have to convince the vet clinic that the kitty isn't yours. Of course, if it is yours, then realize that the inevitable has happened so get your kitty fixed up and keep the kitty inside from that time on.

Again, many kitties have been meals for outdoor pawed predators that roam around—coyotes, wolves, bears, mountain lions (cougars), et al. There will <u>always</u> be some of these predators in certain areas. Kittens born outside don't stand a chance. When people dump their unaltered female kitties outside, any kittens they might have can end out dead—sooner, rather than later. Some people even dump kitties out on the desert. How heartless can a person be? That kind of horrid deed is lower than a salamander's belt buckle. Of course, a forest isn't a good place to dump a kitty, either; they become prey very quickly, to something or other. Birds with talons, poisonous snakes and spiders, wild animals, and other predators can be around. Any one of them can eventually get a dumped kitty, wherever it is dumped.

Again, in some areas, wolves have been a big problem and outdoor kitties have often been a meal for them. They usually can't outrun them, but at least, in a forest area, a kitty can climb up a tree. Way up north, in polar bear country, kitties can be dead meat quickly if they are dumped outside or they accidentally get out. Up north, in general, kitties should not be outside in the cold, anyway. Never, ever, should they be out in the biting, low-temperature cold. Some are forced to be in the cold all day and all night, when temperatures are intolerably cold.

Also, kitties can actually be prey to foxes, wherever foxes are found. Most of the older kitties can get away from them and can even defend themselves against some foxes, if they must. They can jump up to a high place, too, while foxes have to stay on the ground. The problem is with the real young kitties and particularly the kittens, of any size. They are too small to get very far if the run, and they haven't yet learned, in every case, what to be afraid of. Their reaction time can be too slow. No kitten should ever be outside and these very reasons are why they shouldn't be. They are easy prey to a number of animals, including wild dogs because sometimes they're around, too.

In some areas, there is a poisonous toad—the Colorado River Toad—and when a kitty takes on such a toad, as kitties will do, the toad emits a poison. (These toads are not just found in Colorado, they are in several states, including Arizona.) Dogs are vulnerable to this toad, too. (So are people, for the record.) Just touching this toad can cause death, and certainly putting one in a mouth means certain death and the death is an awful one. The dog or cat (or other animal) will not be able to be saved. Vets cannot, ordinarily, save them.

There is also the Cane Toad, which originated in Hawaii but some are in mainland America. Some are in South America, too, and also, Australia. This toad, when touched, also puts out a deadly poison that is in its glands. It causes a fast and awful death, in other words. There are other poisonous toads around, too (around rain forests and otherwise). Some are not deadly ones but they can cause awful irritation and/or pain. Any poison can cause great irritation and pain around a mouth area. With some toads, such an experience may not kill the kitty (or dog), but it can end out being painful, and then stressful as the area is healing up because the kitty (or dog) has to eat and drink water. Every time it opens its mouth—ouch.

The Colorado Toad comes out when it rains, or right after it rains. Sometimes, they end out being around ponds, even a man-made pond that's in the neighborhood or on the lot of someone's home. Be very careful about all toads; if you see any, do not assume they are safe to touch. Children like to pick them up, just like they like to pick up turtles. Keep all your pets away from all toads. Frogs look like toads so it's best to keep them away from frogs, as well. Cats will play with frogs and toads. They'll touch them with their paws. They might put a frog or toad in their mouth and carry it around.

Often, people have ponds constructed as a part of their landscaping so they can keep attractive-looking fish. It is good to have a strong wire mesh put over this area so no kitty can get to the fish but, more importantly, so a kitty won't drown. Most of the older cats won't drown, but kittens could. If there's a real large pond, though, an older kitty can drown in it. They can try to catch a fish, for example, and accidentally fall in. Some cats can swim—one breed in particular can, known as the Turkish Van—but if a cat doesn't know it can swim and doesn't try to swim, then the kitty can drown. Their fur can become weighted down when wet, and this can add to the problem as a kitty is struggling in the water.

Quite a few kitties that are outside get shot. So many guns are in the hands of people, these days. Gun ownership has increased. If someone owns a kitty and they happen to notice a wound, they may not realize that the kitty's wound is from a gun or rifle shooting. They might think the wound is from fighting, from a barbed-wire fence or nail, or from running into something, and so, the gunshot wound may heal over but the bullet, shot, or bee-bees will still be in the kitty, which will be painful and distracting for the kitty.

Stray and feral kitties suffer this stress, pain, and discomfort more than is realized because uncaring and insensitive boys and men shoot at innocent kitties. Small shot and 22-caliber bullets, in particular, are sometimes found in kitties when a vet is consulted and a kitty is checked over. Vets have been known to remove one or more bullets or the numerous tiny pellets from a shotgun or bee-bee gun. Any pellets can stay in the body and an x-ray would show that they're there, but stray and feral kitties don't get such vet care. They have to live with this metal being inside them. Also, an outdoor or stray kitty in pain will usually stay away from people so it will be hard to catch such a kitty for that reason and also because the kitty will now be afraid of people because someone shot it.

It is against the law to shoot kitties, but these insensitives get away with this because nobody sees them doing it. If you ever see this being done or if you know someone has done or is doing this, report it to authorities and try to get the kitty (or kitties) to the vet. When there are bullets or shot in any living creature, infection can occur and so can death, so act fast and do not be afraid and think the vet could suspect that you shot the kitty (or someone in your household did). Get the bullet or pieces from the vet, too, so authorities can find the culprit and prove an animal-cruelty case in court, especially if you know who shot the animal. The authorities will interrogate the suspect and perhaps the suspect's family.

Insensitives kill cats for no logical or valid reasons. It is always better to somehow catch outdoor and stray kitties and take them to a shelter, or take them to a vet, have them altered, put them back outside, and do what is kind and put food out for them so they don't have to starve and lack water, too, and so they don't die of thirst. Always use tin cans or boards for target practice, never cats. Take care of cats. Protect cats. What is always best is to keep them inside.

It used to be (and still is, in some places) that drowning cats, particularly litters of kittens, was commonplace. In the days before there were vet clinics in every community and even neighborhood, where kitties could quickly and easily be spayed or neutered, litters simply weren't wanted. Cats were used as mousers, rather often, and if they have mated and the female had any litters, they were literally put in a bag that was tied, and drowned in water. This still happens but it is against the law and considered animal abuse. For many years, most cats that were around were not brought inside. They had to live outside, or in barns. Because they weren't altered and were outside, they mated outside on a regular basis and therefore, many unwanted litters were born and then killed. It was all too commonplace for people to put them in bags and tie the bags and throw them in a river or lake. It was generally known that this occurred. There are a number of ways litters are killed today, besides drowning. They are all pretty cruel.

Today, you can take litters of kittens to a shelter or the local pound. You should wait until they are older, though, so they do not need to suckle and get milk from their mother. This ending suckling time ranges from seven to ten weeks—six weeks, minimum, and that is chancy. As noted previously, you should not separate kittens from mom cat, absolutely. You can take both mom cat and the litter in at the same time, if the kittens are still suckling. That would keep the kittens alive but as noted before, they will die if they are separated from their mother too soon. Even at a shelter or pound, they may have to be euthanized if mom cat isn't around for them to suckle.

Many people have taken in litters too soon, and separated the kittens from their mother, and the kittens did not make it. Shelters and pounds don't have enough employees to hand-feed litters of kittens. There have been cut-backs. Foster care isn't always available, either. It may be implied that it is, but it may not be and so they may be euthanized. Foster-care people don't always know how to care for really young kittens, just the older ones that are able to eat commercial kitten food. With some kittens—the weaned or almost-weaned kittens—they might be eating mashed-up commercial kitten food that has water added to it. Kittens want to live. They'll fight to live. But sometimes it is hopeless for them to live. Too much goes against them, too fast.

Usually these drowned kittens would be very young—possibly just-born because when they are older they can be hard to catch. Even today, there are places where there are no animal shelters nearby and so unwanted animals cannot be taken to one. Some litters and solo cats are killed in this way in a number of other countries. It is wrong to do so anywhere. In America, people could drive to the closest town or city where a local shelter can be found.

Back in time, if unwanted animals were born, it was often the father of a family who would see to their drowning. This was sometimes upsetting to the rest of the family, especially the children. This practice has always been prevalent more in rural areas (of all countries). (Never dump a kitty in a rural area and this is another reason why this should not be done.) Being drowned by humans is actually an outdoor peril for outdoor and stray kitties. Today, some of these unwanted kittens might be captured and sold at the marketplace when they are old enough, but for years, many of them were drowned, lest they continued to multiply.

Some time ago, it was also commonplace to take an unwanted domestic animal, or pet, out to the country or wilderness and just dump it. Some peril or other would always get them, sooner rather than later. Sometimes, they were dumped near farms or ranches but they may or may not have been taken in, or even made it over to where any people were.

Animal cruelty laws have tightened up since those days. Around forty states now consider any form of animal cruelty to be a felony and not just a misdemeanor. Anything at all that can be construed to be animal cruelty is presented and prosecuted. Animals have been persecuted too long as it is, so stricter, tougher laws have been more than welcome. Juvenile's cruelty to animals is well-known. Juveniles will not get off lightly if they hurt animals.

Even throwing rocks at animals is against the law. Young boys will sometimes do this to people's pets and they should be reported to authorities for doing this or doing anything else that relates to animal cruelty. Throwing rocks at animals is a criminal offense, but so are so many other things now. Shooting at kitties is sometimes done by undisciplined kids, especially boys. Whether throwing rocks, or shooting, the intent is to hurt a kitty, and this is what causes criminal acts.

Certain bee-bee guns—that have ammo having several bee-bees or the larger single ones—are common, and young boys can and do use these guns to harm animals. Often, their parents don't even know they are doing this. Some of these guns are not loud but are fairly silent and this can make detection fairly difficult. Many a kitty has been shot. Even with one bee-bee in their body, a kitty has died because of internal bleeding. One bee-bee can cause slow death and no one would even know the kitty had been shot. A bee-bee can go into an organ, which can cease to function. The kitty may even have time to clean the area and lick off any blood, before it dies. Grown men use these bee-bee guns, too, if they don't like cats. Many grown men do not like cats. Conversely, many grown men do like cats. Some have even become hoarders and have taken in a number of kitties. (Women are more prone to be hoarders, however.) I know an eighty-two year old man who gladly takes care of twelve kitties that have come around as strays. That is what these grown-men shooters should be doing, in the view of many. Get a special kitty trap, and catch outdoor and stray kitties; then, work at rehabilitating them. Try to keep them all inside.

Cats deserve protection—they are really so small and helpless. They're dependent on humans. They have no one else but those who cross their path.

Again, they've actually been bred down to be dependent on humans. They aren't vermin. They do not deserve to be shot. They deserve to be helped. Like dogs, cats are good, not bad. There aren't any bad dogs or cats; each one of them is good.

Parents have to teach their kids to be good to animals and to treat them well and even lovingly. It has to get ingrained. This cannot be surface or flip teaching. It has to be focused teaching. Parents are responsible for what their kids learn and don't learn and do and don't do. <u>Kindness to animals is something that has to be shown and demonstrated, by the parents.</u> Older people just cannot harm or neglect animals. Furthermore, fines for doing so can be high. Sometimes, the criminal will have to go to jail, or even prison, if they harm animals. Certain new laws are here to stay and they are on the increase, as well. Kids should be taught these laws, early on. They need to see good examples of animal treatment. They should also be encouraged to turn in other kids if they know that certain kids have been hurting an animal or animals, in any way at all.

There are a few people 'out there' who think that people should have the right to shoot outdoor feral cats. Feral cats is a subject that few really know very much about. The reason they give for shooting cats is that these cats are killing valuable, small wildlife, both endangered and non-endangered. Small mammals, and birds, are at-issue, in other words. Often, statistics regarding the number of feral cats are exaggerated. Usually, also, they're considering and including outdoor and stray cats that belong to or have belonged to people and these kitties are not really feral. A feral cat is born outside and knows nothing else.

Do not shoot cats. Feed cats. The biggest problem with shooting outdoor feral cats is 'how can you tell unowned feral cats from owned outdoor or previously-owned strays? You cannot tell, is the answer to that question and you shouldn't really be shooting them. Also, feral cats have a right to live, too. <u>Even feral cats can be rescued</u> and I cover this is in Chapter 9 of this book (and also in my longer book, *I Care for My Cats (and Other Animals)*. It's hard to know if a cat is more mild-mannered and friendly if you are shooting at it, from a distance. If a kitty runs away from you, that does not mean the kitty is feral or isn't mild mannered with the potential to be friendly. With the kitties that owners put outside and that have collars, people will steal collars off cats, a collar can slip off, or a collar may not be able to be seen from a shooting distance. People who go out and shoot cats are not doing what is right. Get the community to invest in a number of box/slam traps and capture the kitties and make an effort to fix them up and help them. Get organized. It should be an 'all hands on deck' endeavor. Do this on your own, if you must.

In my day-to-day experience (and observation), cats don't usually catch birds, unless they're baby birds that fell out of a nest, in which event, the baby birds would probably have died, anyway. The point is, birds almost always fly away before a cat can get them. Small mammals are another thing. They aren't airborne creatures and unless they can quickly get into a hole or a safe nook or cranny somewhere, they'll be outrun, assuming the cat is larger than they are. Many mammals have means of protection, though, so the types of small mammals cats can overtake and kill are limited. In other words, kitties really can't depend on any of these birds or animals to be regular food and they are in great need of receiving dry commercial cat food on a regular basis.

It's been reported that more birds die from flying into glass and windows than die from cat attacks. Still, there have been occasional cat attacks on birds, all around the world. Bird lovers may sometimes turn on cats because of that, and bird lovers can be a force that cause kitties some problems. In some areas, some of the people want cats to be shot. Some of these people will kill cats on the side because they do not want local birds harmed. But, cats do not really kill that many birds. You are not supposed to do anything that causes kitties to suffer—like poison them, use inhumane traps to trap them, or shoot them. If you shoot them, you may only wound them, causing them grievous pain and even a slow death. Poisoning, and using certain kinds of trapping methods can also cause kitties to slowly die, and both are in the arena of animal cruelty because the animal will be in torment and will be being tortured as they are dying, in both cases.

Some shrews, smaller rats, squirrels, etc. have, perhaps, been killed by cats. So have rabbits. Outdoor cats don't often eat such mammals. They only kill them because they're in their territory or along their path. They might eat them, if that is all they have to eat and if they can get to the meat, which they can't always do. We have actually bred cats down (to tameness) so they do not like to have to eat birds and rodents and the like. They want and need to be given commercial cat food, because they've been <u>so</u> bred down to tameness. If ever they do eat these animals, there's not much actual meat and it's hard to get through and past the fur and the feathers. Whatever meat they don't eat, spoils and insects crawl all over it. Usually, cats that are outside eat put-out cat food (that sometimes is not commercial dry food and so it spoils really fast). Cats roam around until they find food. <u>There are kind souls out there who do care about kitties, including feral cats, and so they put out cat food</u>

<u>on a regular basis for the hungry kitties.</u> <u>There's a shortage of these kinds of people all around the world, however.</u>

Any law authorizing shooting outdoor kitties/feral cats is not now so apt to happen but it has happened. The Wisconsin Conservation Conference vote authorizing this, on April 11, 2005, included seventy-two counties of which most were rural. To make shooting cats <u>an actual law</u>, though, the hurdles such a policy must jump over are several and they are awfully high. Cats have to be given an unprotected species classification but the fact that they're here to be our pets can never be ignored. The point that it was human beings who took time out to domesticate cats is the most valid argument because to now shoot them would be a maximum show of hypocrisy (and a show of going backwards, historically). Even feral cats should not be shot. In truth, had feral cats had a good start in life, always living inside a loving home, they would be completely different. This is not so with other animal types. We've taken the wild out of cats because we gradually domesticated them and the following is what I've seen and personally even researched: <u>all feral cats can be rehabilitated and calmed down, were we to care enough about them and give them proper care.</u> <u>Even the wildest of feral cats is still a domesticated cat, which can be de-conditioned and re-conditioned and given a second chance/new start at life.</u> I cover this point over and over in this book and in my large compendium book because I feel I must. It's one of the most important points. Feral cats can be rescued, changed or modified, and they can even end out living inside a home. There needs to be interception as of yesterday.

Outdoor cats of all types need our help and our intervention. Mostly, these people who want to shoot cats really don't want to take time out to feed them, take them in, care for them, or find good homes for them. They don't have the patience or the heart to go in the humane direction and climb up the good-deeds ladder. If they would just humanely trap them (not separating a mother cat from her kittens) and take them to a pound or shelter, that would be humane.

Shooting domesticated animals is one thing and it is a cruelty, but there are some even crueler people out there, who torture and kill animals, whether they are wild or domestic. Some serial killers are definitely in this group. (Not all serial killers harm and kill animals and some of them care about animals and prefer the company of animals to that of humans.) Still, some of these criminals have been sadists. Some cruel-to-animals people don't cross the line and become murderers of people but they hurt and kill innocent animals. Some of the animals that have been killed may have been trusting and loving towards the very people who hurt them. Certain of the animals did not know the abductors and were fearful, of course, and tried to get away, but couldn't. Sadistic people hurt animals. Screws in their brain are way too loose. In fact, they're missing. Not all of these types of people choose to hurt animals but sadistic acts by demented people is yet another solid reason for keeping kitties inside.

Again, it is a myth that <u>all</u> serial killers kill animals. Certainly, spree killers generally don't. Most serial killers start off with assault on people. There will be numerous assaults on people and this escalates. The few who do kill animals are <u>very</u> cruel and you always hear about them on the News. Usually, people around them know they have a cruel streak. They care only about their own life. People involved in the occult and black magic sacrifice innocent animals, which is blatant animal cruelty. They may kill farm animals right on the farmer's property, even though they don't even know the farmer.

Sometimes, they leave body parts of animals at someone's doorstep, if they are angry at the person. Often, they put curses on people. They are unable to love animals or people (other than themselves). They know this, too. They serve a master that is incapable of giving the right kind of love.

There are even some hunters who are sadistic or who have a sadistic streak. (Most of them are not this way, though.) Animals are helpless and defenseless, so some of these whackos go into a power mode when they hurt or kill an animal. They are unable to relate to the sufferings of animals and don't want to, either. It's too bad they couldn't channel their errant motivation into woodworking or building or repairing things. There is a good kind of power that comes from creativity and accomplishment. Some hunters see the other side of the coin, genuinely, and they are good men, all across the board. They need meat for the table, and <u>that</u> is why they hunt. Sadists can still change, if they want to. It takes an act of will and some compassion, on their part. There are many hunting and conservation laws, now, and plenty of rangers around to monitor those out in the country and wilderness and haul people in or fine them for violations. Rangers generally care about animals, including dogs and cats. They are the good guys.

Again, there are serial killers out there who go around killing other people's domestic pets—dogs or cats—and other animals, too. They are not kind when they kill them. Often, torture is involved. All it takes is one serial killer or prospective serial killer to grab a wandering pet. Many pets are friendly and trusting and will go over to anyone, even a sadist. <u>All pets deserve to be safe, in an enclosed yard (for dogs) or inside of a home (for kitties).</u> Again, not all serial killers or potential serial killers kill animals. As one of them once said, "Where is the challenge"? It was humans the serial killer was after (although, where is the challenge doing that, too—anyone can fall prey to a serial killer because they lie and deceive).

Cats and dogs are vulnerable to being picked up by anyone who has evil and cruel inclinations. Sometimes they are trapped, and then victimized. In China and certain other countries, cats are crammed into cages and loaded into trucks. They are then taken to restaurants and killed and cooked and eaten. Anyone in those countries who leaves their kitties outside risks this happening to their kitties. Actually, there are some people in more democratized countries who will, on the sneak, eat cats. This is done, more, by some and certain older and less educated men, including some that have been hunters. This is rather sick and is against the law.

Some kitties that are outside get picked up or trapped by people who sell them to people who plan to use them for animal research. Most people are not aware of how horribly cruel much of the animal research is. Much of it tortures animals. Much of it kills animals. The torturing of cats that fall prey to animal research can be way more harsh and painful than the average person can even imagine. The organization, PETA, has such pictures and proof of some of these torturings and you can barely look at them. Some people can't even look at them. Companies will not tell the public what is being done to these horribly victimized animals.

Animal research goes on at some and certain universities and at research-inclined companies and/or centers. What some of these heartless people do will more than turn your stomach, it will outrage people to the hilt. Kitties are more often used in animal research than people realize. If kitties are forced to be outside, they can end out becoming a victim of animal research (as can dogs). Do shelters and pounds sell cats and dogs to these animal research people? Some, unknowingly, might. It doesn't 'seem' like any of them would, knowingly, not in the more democratic countries if they are generally prosperous. Most people will put such notions out of their minds and just don't like to think that shelter animals go to animal research places. No one likes to think about such matters, but more and more people should. There should be so much more monitoring of these research places. The public should learn where these places get their research animals from. Very little animal research needs to even be going on and that is a fact. Animal research gets exaggerated and hyped, when results would be and are so obvious that why even do them? Results are common-sense to begin with. It is more than logical to assume, and even know that one plus one equals two and so why do the research and the experimenting? Also, there is way too much duplication, and repetition.

Even when a kitty feels fear, kitties cannot run that far in a short amount of time, like some animals can—certain dogs, for example—and so they can be overtaken by other animals that size them up as being prey. Kitties can suddenly spring, leap, or climb away from danger and get to a greater height than the ground, but many animals that see kitties as prey are sprinters, leapers, and climbers. From the ground, a kitty can jump up to many times its own height, but other outdoor animals can still end out catching a kitty. Kitties have to always be careful where they sleep.

Kitties can squeeze into tight and narrow places, but they can get stuck in places they've raced into, to avoid being prey. They can also lose at the waiting game. If they sneak away when a predator is still nearby, they can still end out becoming their prey. If one animal doesn't get the outdoor kitty, another one eventually will. This is the dilemma for outdoor kitties of any type.

Some people who put their kitties outside think, 'oh, they're just animals'. But, as previously noted, kitties are scaled-down Domesticats; they're not like your average animal in the wild. We've bred down their temperaments and natures to not be wild. Kitties are tame. The word, Domesticats, is one I've started up because, since kitties have been so wonderfully bred down to be domesticated pets, they not only can live inside or be brought in from the outside, but they should live inside or be brought in from the outside. Kitties may get defensive at times if they are outside because they have to, but they do not belong outside and they do not do well outside. They are not wild and 'just animals'. They are not like many of the animals in the wild that have never been domesticated. Years and years of domestication have produced tame kitties that belong indoors and it has produced smaller kitties that are in constant peril when they are outside. Even animals in the wild aren't 'just animals' either, though. Animals are unique creatures that have needs, and even desires. Many animals have emotions that can't be expressed in words. In that respect, they are 'as dumb'. Their behaviors will sometimes reveal their emotions, but many times, animals must suffer in silence when there has been deprivation, loss, and cruelty.

When kitties are forced to run up a tree to get away from a predator, it can happen so fast. Outdoor kitties will run up a tree to get away from humans, even if the people are just walking nearby. If they're frightened, kitties will even run up a tree that has thorns, because they are so frightened. Generally, the older cats are able to get down trees, even if they're real high up, but real young kitties, and kittens, may not have acquired the skills that would enable them to climb down a tree. Getting down a tree is a learned behavior. The young ones may not have the confidence to think they can get down the tree.

If kitties are treed, often, they cannot get down from the tree because they cannot climb down very far. They can, maybe, get down to lower branches. They get stuck and trapped. A kitty may have been chased up the tree by another animal, but when the animal leaves, the kitty cannot get down by itself. Kitties are only able to climb up but not down because their claws are in front of their paws, and not in back, facing the other way. (A very few kitties will climb backwards, down a tree; only a few will do this.) A domesticated kitty can sometimes jump down to lower branches, which is the way a few of them are able to get down. Some end out falling.

A big cat in the wild can get down from trees because they are larger and stronger than little domestic kitties are and they jump down from trees more easily, but if the tree is tall and a little kitty accidentally gets up too high, that kitty will not be able to get down. Humans (sometimes, firemen) have to come get kitties down from trees but if there are no humans around—for example, if kitty is in a forest or a grove of trees—what is going to happen to the kitty? Who will hear the kitty's cries? If branches are high up from the ground, kitty will be permanently stuck. Kitty is not a bird that can fly. Eventually, the kitty must sleep, which is when it can fall.

One kitty, noted on the News, was left up in a tree way too long. Do not wait more than two and at most three days to get your kitty down from a tree. This kitty was up in a tree eight days before anything got done. I'm not sure how the kitty could have slept. Her owners knew she had been in the tree, early on. Hire someone with a ladder who is willing to get the kitty out of the tree, if you absolutely cannot do so yourself. The problem was, the kitty was so afraid of the strange man trying to get her that she fell, very far down, from the top of the tree as she tried to get away. She could have died, but she fortunately survived the fall, or so it appeared. She was dehydrated and needed immediate fluids; she was quite hungry, too. It's hard to understand why action wasn't taken sooner. Sometimes owners may have to go up on ladders.

As soon as owners know a kitty is missing, they should diligently and consistently try to find the kitty. If they know the kitty is up in a tree, and obviously stuck, they should move Heaven and Earth to get the kitty down to safety right then and there. The kitty will be less fearful if it is the caretaker on the ladder, but this could be a dangerous job. Some people have been known to take a carrier up with them and they try to put the kitty in the carrier and then carry it down. A pillowcase could work so much better (a larger one could be used for a larger cat), but again, this job would be risky no matter how it gets done or who does it.

At times, kitties will run up trees because they are being chased by an animal that may also be able to climb trees. Kitties can be dead meat because they cannot get away from certain animals. In forested areas, for example, many a kitty turns up missing because a bear decided to have kitty for its next meal. It is never good to leave kitties outside in such areas, for sure. Bears get dogs, too—all the time. People put food outside for the dogs, or cats, the bears smell the food and come in close to the area and the next thing you know, a dog or cat is attacked or turns up missing. The pet becomes a meal for a bear. Dogs can't climb trees so they get killed really fast by bears. One bear swat and the dog can be dead. Bears can be overpowering of domestic animals. If a kitty is chased up a tree, it just gets trapped up on the branches as the bear climbs up to where the poor kitty is trapped. Certain cats in the wild kill kitties too. Cats in the wild are both large and small and they are all around the world. (Other wild animals kill them too, including snakes.) Again, some country areas and forested, wooded areas are not safe areas for kitties. The open desert isn't safe, either. Nowhere really is, except the inside area of a caring home.

6

Irritants and agitations/reptiles and insects

Some people have indoor/outdoor kitties that are inside some of the time and outside some of the time. For any kitty put outside on their own for any length of time, perils will still be encountered by the kitty. Even if they are inside some of the time, if they are outside, ever, they are technically an outdoor kitty. If the owner has a vet for their kitty, they should let the vet know the kitty goes outside so the vet can better diagnose the kitty when the kitty is brought in.

What happens if no one is around to remove glass, metal pieces, splinters from wood, thorns, insect stingers, or cactus quills from kitty's paws or body after kitty steps on or rubs up against or encounters these hazards in any way? If it were you, and your body, you would immediately remove the object and douse the area with rubbing alcohol or diluted hydrogen peroxide to kill any germs, but kitty cannot do anything like that. You would have to treat your kitty if such a thing happened to your indoor/outdoor kitty, and that's only if you notice a limp, some blood, or any other symptom, and you may not notice anything at all and so the kitty will suffer.

If you do treat a kitty wound, it is best to use the rubbing alcohol or diluted hydrogen peroxide to clean up the wound. Keep in mind that tiny pieces, as slivers, quills, glass, or thorns, can get lodged into kitty's skin and you may never see the tiny piece or pieces. If you wet the kitty down and the kitty's fur is light enough, you may be able to see small dots on the skin, and then be able to remove the agitations with tweezers. You might need to use a magnifying glass to find all the agitations and irritants in the skin.

Kitties shouldn't be walking around outside, period. Too often, they walk over fertilizer and/or sprayed insect or weed-controlled areas. They lick the residue off their paws and this is not good. Not only must you be careful about kitties walking over or around areas that have been sprayed for insects or weeds, but you have to be careful about any compost piles or layers because mold can grow on top of compost and can actually be deadly for a kitty.

Outside, kitties step on glass, nails, tacks, splinters, quills, thorns, and other sharp items. If a paw gets infected, a kitty can be in serious trouble. Infection, in general, kills many outdoor kitties. Infection is essentially the same as blood poisoning. It is similar to peritonitis. Kitties will get a high temperature and get sicker and sicker as their blood cells increasingly deteriorate.

Occasionally, I have seen a limping kitty outside. I always try to get such kitties so I can take them in and care for whatever is causing their limping. Usually, they have something in their paw but such a kitty could have a leg, hip, or joint problem. Something could even be broken. Sometimes, people can't catch wounded animals because such animals are afraid of being caught. Perhaps they think someone might hurt their sore area even more and so they run away. In any event, it's very frustrating to not be able to catch a kitty you want to help. You worry about them. If a leg is incapacitated for whatever the reason, they can't run very fast, but they still can move fast and get away. If it's a back leg, they can't spring upwards and this can be very bad if specific dangers are around. If kitties are inside, damage to a paw or limb is much less likely to happen. Again, outdoor kitties of any type get hurt trying to get away from a predator or an attacking dog or cat.

There is one grass known as prairie grass and it has arrow-like barbs on it. When an animal rubs up against it, and the barbs go into the animal's skin anywhere at all (including on or under a paw), the barbs can't be pulled out. With a kitty, they will try to pull the barb out with their teeth. This grass is found around flat areas and deserts. A kitty could walk through a field of these and get many of these barbs stuck in their skin. They work their way in to the skin, which makes it all the worse. This would be very painful and distracting for any animal, including a kitty. If something gets to be too painful for a kitty, they cannot commit suicide. They will just go mad, or go into shock. A human might commit suicide (not that they ever should) but kitties have to stay alive, in pain, unless a kind human intervenes…even a kind stranger.

The Foxtail can get caught and stuck in fur, too. It's 'a grass that has cylindrical spikelets, interspersed with stiff bristles' (Webster's New World Dictionary). These are not barbs. They are just a nuisance but no kitty should eat them. Some low-to-the-ground weeds put out horrible thistles and thorns, too. They not only get into fur, but some can get in to the skin. Also and again, they get stepped on and can stick into paws. Devil's Claw has some sharp edges, too. It's found around some deserts. This plant is not to be confused with Cat's Claw vine that I'm only inserting because of its name (a cat name) and am not inserting because of the danger-to-cats aspect. This plant is an ivy type of vine that can grow upward; it can hook onto the sides of trees and buildings as it does. It can climb very high if it has something that its hooks can attach to. This is not a peril plant, however, like the Devil's Claw is. It's actually an evergreen, but it needs an arid climate. If you have thorny plants on your own lot, you might want to get rid of them. You will need to remove any thorny weeds off your lot as soon as you see them so no pet will step on them. You can have thorny plants even in more northern, and more humid areas.

Nettles, thorns, thistles, quills, thorns, etc. are all in certain areas. They're a constant problem for roaming kitties. Some of these are multi-sided and kitties step on them or they get caught up and entangled in their fur. Some long thorns never end out coming out and a kitty can be in constant pain because of it. They may try to remove something that is in their skin, with their teeth, and they aren't always successful. Even with these small skin agitations, infection sometimes sets in. With most any kind of nettle, thorn, thistle, quill, or thorn, it is possible for bacteria to get inside the affected area. Keeping kitties inside protects them from what can be sharp.

Cactus quills, especially, can break off outside the skin but stay in under the skin. It becomes at least as irritating as a wood splinter does. Some cactus barbs are hooked at the end so if an animal tries to remove them, it will be near-impossible to pull them out with their teeth and if they pull part of the barb out, the curved part may stay in the skin. Cactus-laden areas are very bad for roaming animals. If an animal has paws, the quills or barbs can go in them. Large ones can go in deep and can sometimes even cripple animals. There are cactus quills and barbs all over various parts of the United States, and in numerous other countries, as well. Stepping on certain of these quills/barbs can be similar to stepping on a straight pin or needle used for sewing.

Again, Cholla cactus is a problem for kitties (and dogs) that are loose around desert areas. The Cholla is loaded with quills. The cactus tosses numerous little balls or groups of quills that blow with the wind. They can be anywhere. (So can other cactus quills that blow with the wind.) Kitties brush up against them or step on them. Certain ones have the barbed hooks. When a kitty tries to get rid of a ball of quills or barbs, more of the quills or barbs will stick in the paw or the face area (if the kitty is trying to use its teeth). Cactus quills or barbs can cause a lot of pain. Taking out barbed quills often tears the skin.

There are other kinds of cacti all over the desert. Some of the leafy succulents aren't too dangerous but the thorny cacti are abundantly quilled. They grow all over the desert, but many people use cacti to decorate their residence landscaping so even around the community, kitties can and do run into cactus. Kitties get chased and kitties back into cactus. They run into dangerous cacti or they step on quills and they very much suffer from these penetrating quills. Even just walking around, tiny quills are all over the place. Quills drop off of cactus, and winds blow them around. People can wear shoes. Animals cannot. And, by the way, it's not a good idea to combine cacti and kitties in the same home. Indoor kitties could have some kind of a run in with the cactus. People buy cactus plants for their home. Even people who don't live in the South-West order cactus plants for the interior of their home. If big potted cactus plants are around, that may not be so good if kitties in the house ever run around.

For kitties that are long-furred, any of these kinds of small agitations can get easily caught up in a fur area. They can get rolled up into mats that may have formed on a kitty. As noted earlier, if a kitty has no owner, who will cut the mats off? How is any kitty supposed to get rid of these sharp agitations that are stuck inside of their fur? An owner would have to routinely comb the kitty so no mats could have even formed, but if a kitty is put outside, owners are not so apt to comb the kitty. If a kitty is kept inside all the time, they tend to get more care and attention. Some long-furred kitties can get huge mats and quite a few of them, if they are always outside. Fur becomes thicker during colder months, but it can mat up at any time. If you are ever able to catch an outdoor, long-fur kitty that has mats, and then are able to clip off those mats, you'd be doing a good deed.

Large mats can't be combed out. Even some of the small mats can't be. I always cut off mats as close to underneath the mat as I can get, but you have to be _really_ careful of the skin when cutting off mats. Sometimes, I end out leaving some of the mat because I fear cutting in too close to the skin. I'll just wait until later, to get the rest of the mat. You can always cut off part of a mat. If I cut down to about a third of an inch from the skin, that's close enough for me. Then I try to separate what fur is there with my fingers. Some separates, but some may not, in total. Then, I clip off what I can after doing that. There's a bit of an art to mat removal. You don't want to cut off too much of the fur under the mat, unless you have to. I usually have acceptable success. Again, you can get the rest of a mat later on if you have to, after some of the fur has grown out. You can also cut upward on the mat and split the mat so you're essentially making two (or more) little mats. Then try to separate the fur and clip off what is easy to clip off. Just don't ever cut in too close to the skin—that's the main thing. It's very easy to accidentally cut the skin because it tends to be loose.

Some kitties are all right with this cutting/clipping effort. Some kitties will balk so you have to do mat removal at two or three separate times. I believe most outdoor kitties will be quite leery of the mat removal process (but it is worth a try). I've only removed mats off two of my own always-indoor kitties. You can try it with an outdoor kitty. You have to use really small scissors. A kitty can be in a warm to hot climate or a cool to cold climate and get mats and get sharp irritants and agitations stuck in those mats, and in their fur.

Even outdoors in more northern areas, there can be problematic plantings. Plants and bushes can be very thorny, and certain evergreen trees and bushes can have sharp edgings and if they're brushed up against, little tiny sharp points can prick the skin. This can cause irritation and, in some cases, itching. Some more northern plants have thistles, too, and thistles can be very irritating. And, again, anything sharp can cause harm to the eyes so if a kitty accidentally runs into a plant, bush, or tree that has sharp edges, thorns, or quills, great harm can come to the eyes, usually one of them, when such an accident occurs.

<u>Pity the kitties that are outside and that don't have owners.</u> They cannot remove these agitations with their teeth, or claws. Even the stinger from a flying insect will stay inside a kitty if the kitty is ever stung. This would include bee, wasp, yellow jacket, and hornet (and Giant Hornet) stingers. And, by the way, if your kitty is ever stung by a bee or similar winged insect, you do not pull the stinger straight out, you gently press it down to the side and side-sweep it out in the direction it tends to go, using a scraping motion because less of the stinger venom, still in the stinger after the bee discharged it, will enter the kitty's bloodstream. If a kitty is ever stung and if the kitty's breathing is then obstructed, take the kitty to the vet clinic right away. Wasps

and similar insects can keep on stinging and they don't lose their stinger like a bee does. Once, a wasp stung me on the neck three times in a row. It could have been a yellow jacket or hornet, though, I didn't have time to look real close. I was too busy trying to get away. Those Giant Hornets will sting more than once. Their stinger can be a quarter of an inch long, or more. To what extent these flying insects have already spread is not known. They came in from China—perhaps not so accidentally. The minute anyone sees them, they must be reported to local and state agencies. It is good if you can know where any nests are.

To emphasize, without help, kitty has to just suffer, because stingers, splinters, thorns, barbs, quills, etc. are apt to remain in a kitty's skin when no help comes from humans. Kitty can do nothing about them if they are lodged anywhere on a kitty. Some outdoor kitties (of whatever type) are loaded with these kinds of agitations. They learn to cope with these irritants that are in their skin, including stingers. Do they eventually absorb into the blood. Some do. Some don't. If they do, it may be a while before they do. Indoor kitties, of course, never get stung. They're very fortunate kitties. If stinging insects are mad enough, they will find a way to get past the fur and sting into the skin; they are able to sting a furred animal. If stung too many times, the trauma can cause actual shock, in the medical sense. Snake bites can cause shock, too. If a kitty is bitten by a known-venomous snake, rush the kitty to a specially-organized emergency vet clinic, and I do mean rush. Know in advance how to get to that emergency vet clinic.

Negligent people have let their pythons and Boa constrictors or Anacondas get out, or they've just flat put them out on purpose because they no longer want them. Such animals become difficult and expensive to feed so people don't want them after they've reached a certain size. In fact, one person told me to never give a cat out for free because an occasional snake owner will take that cat and feed it to their snake. A snake is a wild animal. They should never be pets. Many pet stores will not even sell them because they are so dangerous. By law, no venomous snake can be sold, but these other dangerous snakes are sometimes sold. Any dangerous snakes are sometimes sold on the Black Market. Certain kinds of snakes eat mice and rats and their owners buy live mice and rats and then watch them die as the snake eats them.

A kitty is a domesticated animal. Anyone who would feed a domesticated kitty to a wild snake is just not thinking straight. Anyone who would dump such a large, dangerous snake out in their own or another neighborhood is just not thinking straight, either. The Reticulated Python, in particular, will eat cats. Boas do not like cats over other kinds of food but they will squeeze them to death and, sometimes, they will have a kitten or cat for a meal. It's a cruel, awful, torturous way for a kitty to have to die. And again, a kitten or cat should be a beloved pet, and a snake shouldn't be. The kitty is domesticated; the snake is an animal that should be living in the wild and in areas where they <u>originally</u> lived. In the USA and even other countries, constructors are invasive species. Way more people than not believe that snakes are only happy and can only thrive in the wild. Why would any type of snake want to be in a tank or cage in a home or building? That is actually unkind to do to a snake. Snakes have to move around, considerable distances. They need exercise. Just because they don't have legs, don't think that they don't need to slither and wind and move around. Many snakes live in the jungle and they should stay in the jungle. Foreign snakes should stay foreign. Snakes belong in the wild.

People dump their oversized pet snakes outside so that the snake then resides in the neighborhood, as it grows even bigger. Such a misdeed can occur anywhere. These people also turn these snakes out because the snakes are hard to resell. Gosh, I wonder why. Doesn't everyone want an adult snake? Owning a snake was a novelty for these people, but when the novelty wore off, the snake owners got bored or frustrated with the situation. They couldn't find anyone who would take their now-grown, hard-to-find-food-for snake, and so they put the snake outside, permanently. I don't know what the legal penalties are for doing this but both the turned-out snakes, and the people who turn the snakes out (usually young people) are menaces to society. Such snakes have been found under houses and were spotted at night when they came out to eat because it was cooler. Outdoor kitties in areas where these snakes were caught had strangely turned up missing and so had some dogs. It's bad enough that local-living snakes are in areas where kitties are. More snakes are certainly not wanted.

The Florida Everglades are now loaded with pythons. They are considered to be an invasive species. Invasive species are animals not local to an area; they are brought in or dumped into an area where they are not from and they, then, invade this new area or space because they increase in number. They kill and feed on local species that are already present and this can cause ecological discord. Other species can be entirely killed off because of invasive species. Any tropical area can host these dumped snakes. Many thousands of pythons have been removed from different tropical areas around the USA, but especially from around Florida. Invasive species—whether animal or vegetation—can be anywhere around any country.

Worldwide, there are Coral Snakes, vipers, adders, cobras, mambas, mangroves, Massasaugas, Cottonmouths, Sidewinders, rattlesnakes, Gopher Snakes, Kingsnakes, Water Moccasins, and so it goes, and we want them to stay away from us and to not be able to hurt outdoor kitties. Even snakes that live in and near water can be dangerous to kitties if an outdoor kitty needs a drink of water from a lake, river, or stream. Some water snakes can come on land, too.

Kitties can't tell a Garter Snake, which is harmless, from a dangerous snake. There are snakes that crush and eat, and snakes that bite and implant venom and then eat. A venomous snake may or may not eat a kitty. For sure, they'll strike at and bite a kitty if they feel threatened. A venomous snake will strike at and bite a kitty if it thinks the kitty means to harm it, which, of course, this is exactly what kitties want to do when they see at least some snakes.

Snakes live in grass and in gardens. They're found on plains and in deserts. They live in forests, jungles, and in water. Some snakes even live underground. Snakes can be anywhere around a yard. They can be under wood items or rocks, or under anything, really. They can be in caves. They like to be under houses, porches, decks, and stairs which is where outdoor kitties love to go and be, for several reasons. So do dogs. Snakes have killed many a domestic animal. One strike and a kitty can be a goner. If a snake rattles first, the kitty may not know what it means or be able to get away fast enough. Sometimes, a strike is fast and there's no rattling at all. It's only when the rattler has enough time to coil up and poise for a strike that it rattles.

One state in particular, where you do not want any kitties to be outside, is Florida. You really don't want any dogs (or cats) to be outside—not without monitoring. In various places in the State, there are alligators, monitors, tuataras, Diamondback Rattlesnakes, water moccasins (they are as pit vipers), anacondas, pythons (there's a few different types), boas, Black mambas, and Coral Snakes. Coral Snakes, though smaller, have extremely lethal venom. Many people don't realize this so they are more vulnerable to being bitten. Many of these snake types were not in Florida originally but they were dumped outside or somehow got loose. The snake problem occurs in other states and countries. It's just that Florida already had quite a few snakes to begin with, which were native to Florida areas and so now, there's even more snakes because so many have been dumped. Snakes multiply fast. They have large batches of babies.

Dumping a snake outside is misanthropic because eventually, it will cause serious problems for people. If they find another snake, and mate, the misanthropy has been compounded. There are enough pythons in Florida to now mate and they have been mating and pythons are killing pets and people because they have multiplied. There are some anacondas around Florida, too. Snakes have been dumped in other states, too. Snakes generally don't do well in northern states where there is snow and ice, though.

Pattern is key to recognizing the Coral Snake. If red touches black, the snake isn't venomous; if red touches yellow on a snake, it is very venomous. If you think of a traffic light, you have yellow (danger) and then red (stop) and this is how you can also recognize a Coral Snake. Stay away from a yellow and red ringed or banded snake. Yellow and red might be pretty but it is pretty dangerous. You can also think of yellow and red as being fire colors and fire is dangerous. Coral Snakes also live in North Carolina, Texas, and Mexico.

They aren't all that large, compared to other snakes. They're smaller, but you can still spot them because of the two colors.

Try to keep all pets clear of any snake. The minute you see a dangerous snake, or one you are in question about, put the outdoor pet inside and call a company that is a pest-control one. State officials should also be called. If you see <u>any</u> snake, get the pet inside. Rarely does anybody know <u>all</u> the snakes that are poisonous and <u>all</u> the ones that are not. People may only be aware of a few. Most people know very little about the different snake types and even if people once knew, they can forget and maybe get confused.

People get venomous snakes on the Black Market and sell them, illegally. Therefore, venomous snakes can be anywhere. Owning a poisonous snake is against the law but in some areas it is not unlawful to own a constrictor snake. Such ownership is very controversial. Although constrictor snakes are not allowed in some areas, they, too, can be obtained by way of the Black Market. There are actually Black-Market breeders. No legal constrictor-snake owner should be breeding constrictor snakes. Both poisonous and constrictor snakes should be banned as pets (and as imports), in all countries as of yesterday and definitely as of today. Breeding any kind of snake should certainly be banned, except in centers where anti-venoms are being produced and manufactured.

Snakes strike pretty fast, particularly some snakes. They'll also strike more than once. Only some vet clinics treat for the specific snake bites. It more than helps if a caretaker knows what kind of snake has bitten their pet. Without that information, the pet can die. Extremities can be lost. Sometimes venoms cause organ failure, and some can cause internal tissue and bone damage. Therefore, the pet must be taken in to the vet immediately. Speed of injecting the right kind of anti-venom is of utmost importance. If someone cannot positively identify a snake, they shouldn't get near it to put it in a box so the vet clinic people can identify it. They should, instead, try to memorize the snake's markings, assuming they are able to see the snake. Also, unless someone is a trained snake handler, they should not try to handle any snake. Vials of anti-venom are extremely expensive. Sometimes several vials are needed.

Some strikes and bites from snakes may not have put in that much venom. Whereas one bite from the same snake on one particular person, could kill that person, another bite from the same snake, at another time and on the same person, might not cause death. This relates to animals, too, including domestic pets. To add, one bite could kill quickly, another bite might bring about death after a longer period of time. If you have poisonous snakes in your area, and particularly if you have seen them, find out where the closest vet is that treats for snake bites, just in case your pet ever gets bitten. Know the snake type, too. Take a photo of it if at all possible. Draw it, and include color and markings.

Some snakes like water and the humidity that comes with it. When there is storming, there is flooding. Flooding can sometimes mean that certain critters will be closer in to humans and pets. Critters are always hungry. In other words, when their meal digests, they are out looking for food, once again. Many Floridians own snake poles, slam traps (cages), and guns, because of different critters. Calling 9-1-1 can bring in help. Calling a critter-ridder company can also bring in help. Some snakes will go along canals and waterways and can end out populating new areas. They can also end out in people's backyards. Other states are somewhat oblivious to Florida's outdoor perils for pets, but Floridians certainly aren't.

Many areas around the world have critter problems—some more so than others. A few of these areas that immediately come to mind are India, South America, Australia, and Indonesia. The different critters found around those areas kill kitties. In some areas of the world, they can't even have cats because they disappear too fast. Some places can't even have dogs.

At least Floridians are generally equipped to deal with critter problems, in as much as possible. Some hospitals in the State are better equipped with dealing with venoms than others are. Generally, the first bite of a snake is the most venomous, but not always. Hospitals may or may not treat animals that have been bitten. In some cases, there may be special circumstances and they will make an exception and treat animals, but, they might not and so it will have been wasted time at the hospital when the pet could have quickly gone to an appropriate emergency vet clinic.

Where there are flood or tornado areas, snakes in captivity should not even be allowed because they've been known to get loose because of any related home destructions. Once loose, they can breed. Some snakes can produce fifty to a hundred eggs. Anytime an exotic snake escapes captivity, pets are in danger. People are, too, obviously, and if a pet loses a caretaker to a snake bite or to a snake crush, how will that help the pet? The pet may or may not be able to be put with another caretaker.

Certain types of snakes are considered to be exotics. Too often, these get released in the wild. Hurricanes bring about flooding but also very high winds so homes are vulnerable to destruction, which means that the indoor critter cages and the areas inside of a building where snakes are can be overturned or demolished, and they have been, many times. Venomous critters around any area cause people to be nervous, worried, and to even experience panic.

No one wants to live around such deadly animals, even if they are in cages. Now there are also the Africanized Killer Bees in Florida and storms can also disrupt their activity. Some people think that a government agency should go around and exterminate as many Killer Bees that can be found, and to go about doing this routinely. They believe they should all be exterminated here in America, and probably some other countries, too. It could be done. They are trying to capture certain snakes now, in the Florida Everglades. They have no choice in the matter, anymore, because they are a public nuisance. Killer Bees are also a nuisance. Killer Hornets are, too. Both are overly aggressive. Asian Killer Hornets have killed both animals and people, in areas where they are more common. Only a small number were spotted in the USA around 2020, in Washington State so, could they have already branched out?

Some people let their pet snakes wander around their home. They get loose and end out outside, or again, they are put outside. Certain types can kill any residents of that home when they're inside, or outside. Constrictors will go after babies and children, and even smaller adults. Pythons that are in the wild around Florida have now killed both adults and children as well as many a pet so it isn't just the alligators that get them, for a meal.

Please note that crocodiles are not found in America—only alligators are, and they are larger than the crocodiles. Alligators like being on land—this is the point to remember about them. They can be anywhere on someone's property, especially if the property is near water. They'll leave the water, to get to prey on land. They've been known to attack people who were standing on a bank, too, right next to the water the gator had just been in. If they get their prey to the water, they kill it by rolling the prey over and over, which drowns them. At any time, an alligator can rip off a body part. Alligators can be very fast. They often wait near a bank and if they spot land prey, they'll leave the water and go after it. People walking a dog next to water have lost the dog to an alligator. This is the main reason why they submerge in water right by a bank.

Crocodiles are in other parts of the world, like around South America, Africa, and Australia. They are really just like alligators and both will kill roaming or even resting animals. With crocs, you can sometimes see ripples in the water, or the top of their head and their eyes. At night, their eyes will be seen shining in the dark if any light is shining on their eyes. They're just waiting, and are temporarily hiding in the water, close to the bank. They always strike really fast. When they strike, they snap. Even on land, alligators will twist their prey around and around (this is known as the death roll); even on land, unlucky pets or people have lost a limb in this manner (because of the death roll), after they had been attacked.

Alligators somewhat walk-swim on the bottom of water areas, or they can swim in the water, mainly using their body and tail. Because they have four feet, they can walk on land and their moving is aided and sped up by the movement of their body and tail. Alligators wiggle side to side, when they move. Alligators are quick and strong, regardless of their size. Even baby or very small alligators can do damage. Special training is required to handle both alligators and crocodiles, and strength is needed when handling them. Alligators found around the South-East (they aren't only in Florida) can kill a kitty with one snap. They have forty teeth on the top and forty teeth on the bottom, and most of them are pointed. Their jaws are very powerful.

Many alligators are loose in the State of Florida because they live and breed in the wild. They get into towns and cities by waterways, including canals. Some have even slipped into swimming pools. Floridians never really know when or where one is going to turn up. Some people have dumped their iguanas outside. They buy one at a pet store when it's small, then it gets bigger and they no longer want it. Green iguanas have been the main ones dumped. Similar reptiles, even larger than iguanas, have been dumped outside. Another one is the large South American lizard known as the Tegu. This lizard kills and eats small dogs and especially kitties. They've been multiplying around the Everglades. All reptiles multiply quickly if conditions are right for them. The next thing you know, local pets turn up missing because of these reptiles. The more reptiles that are around, the more pets will turn up missing. Bones and carcasses are sometimes found wherever they were eaten. Pets will be eaten on the spot or they will be carried or dragged away and eaten elsewhere.

Most people who dump such animals outside <u>know</u> what they are doing, and they realize the danger these reptiles are to outdoor domestic pets. For this reason, they should be charged with cruelty to animals, <u>if</u> they are ever caught. They'll also be charged with animal abandonment. Some of these animals are a constant danger to people, too; this is a main reason why there are laws against dumping dangerous animals. Florida seems to get quite a few of these dumped animals, but they can be and have been dumped in any state or any country. Some of them die if the climate they are dumped in is bad for them or conditions are not right. Some are dumped during warm months but then the cold sets in and they don't make it through the cold months.

Again, there are Africanized Killer Bees in Florida, now; there's quite a few there, even in Miami. They'll go after dogs and cats that are outside. They are also critters, of a type. (Killer hornets are in Washington State.) A critter is a creature, be it large or small. Critters can be dangerous. Insects can also be dangerous animals. Killer Bees made their way up through Central America from Brazil. Negligent people in Brazil were responsible for a large group of them getting loose there. They multiplied fast, in part because they were able to find secreted areas so they could build their hives. The whole hive will attack a person or animal, full force. They'll also wait around for days, if who or what they are mad at hides or even jumps into some water. They are becoming a well-known public enemy because they keep spreading and they are lethal. They like to get into roof cavities of houses and sheds, to establish their hive. They sometimes build their hives closer down to the ground so coming in close to where they are is not that hard to do.

Chances of surviving an attack will depend on the weight of the person or the animal, on the number of stings incurred, and on how fast the person or the animal gets appropriate medical care. On average, after around five or six stings per pound, the person or pet enters the life-is-threatened zone. I write about Killer Bees in two other books I wrote—*Landscaping a Small Lot* and *Living and Travelling in the South-West*. I have a fear of Killer Bees. Realistically, they are to be feared. We never needed them. We don't need them now. I think we need to go to war against them. They terrorize.

Killer Bees are, sometimes, called Africanized Bees. Africanized Bees did not come direct from Africa. One bee type did and it entered Brazil, whereupon that one type was bred with a South American type. Therefore, Africanized Bees are a hybrid. For some reason, Africanized Bees—this hybrid—turned out to be very aggressive. They attack people and animals that get near their hive. There are, of course, beehives all over Africa but the bees there aren't Killer Bees. It is just this hybrid type. Cats are pets in Africa, especially in particular areas around the continent. They are also used as mousers. Cats get bee stings over there, too. Africa has a number of dangerous insects. Bees are always a problem for cats because they buzz around pollen plants close down to the ground.

The countries that have the most pet cats are larger and more heavily-populated countries: the United States, China, Russia, Brazil, and Turkey are included. All of the smaller countries have cats, in varying amounts. All countries have different perils. People who care for cats need to know what the perils are in their localities. Many other countries have shelters, even countries you would expect to not have them, have at least some. Some countries have very few shelters and shelter workers. It's pretty sad and sorry.

Bees are found all over the world. The Africanized Bees are found in quite a few countries and warmer areas now. They're in Mexico and around Central America, for sure. They made their way into the southern American states. They have been multiplying more and more in the Southern United States areas. They breed faster and more prolifically than regular honeybees do. One day, we are going to have to go out and exterminate these Killer Bees (like those Giant Killer Hornets). One wonders why other kinds of honeybees, in general, are decreasing. Are these more aggressive bees killing them? Some say yes. Bees are essential to human life. Even Killer Bees are, but non-attacking bees are much preferred and so can we not get back to that, more exclusively? Should war be waged against Killer Bees? Should they be exterminated—hive by hive? Many are saying yes to that.

Horses, dogs, cats, and various animals—both domestic and wild—have been attacked and killed by these Africanized Bees. Some animals were found dead with hundreds of bee stings in them. It doesn't make the News if cats were killed, and it rarely does, if dogs were killed. Horses make the News. People always do, if they were killed by Killer Bees, but it is usually the local and state News, not the national News.

It's estimated that well over a thousand people have been killed by these bees, from all the way down in Brazil and then on up to America. (From Brazil, they spread to other countries in South America, too, even western and southern ones.) These bees entered America around 1990. It's never good to be near any of these bees, most particularly, to be near any of their hives. You want to be going in the other direction from their hive. Unfortunately, you don't always see a hive or know where it is. You can't usually tell a Killer Bee from the other bees, either. That's another problem. If you notice an unusual amount of bee activity anywhere, realize that a beehive may be nearby. Watch where they go, if possible. Consider calling in Bee Removal. They'll go in (well covered), and remove a hive. They'll also know if they are Killer Bees.

<u>Many kitties have already been killed by these Killer Bees.</u> Kitties can run, but a swarm of these bees fly very fast and can sting faster than a kitty can run. Any outdoor kitty is particularly vulnerable. They are naturally curious and sometimes playful. They see a bee and follow it, right to a hive, which becomes even more interesting to a curious cat. This would be one incident where curiosity will very definitely kill a cat. Any and all outdoor kitties are vulnerable in any area that is known to have Killer Bees. The hives of Killer Bees aren't just out in the country, either. They are in towns and cities and in and around houses and they've already killed many yard pets, and horses. They don't live in real cold climates but they can live in areas where there are occasional frosts. They only go more north if they like the weather. Past a certain northern point and you will not find them.

If a kitty happens to get near any beehive, anywhere, the bees may group together and go after the kitty. Beehives can be found on trees, on rafters of houses and buildings, between walls, in sheds or infrequently-used buildings, under stairs, under homes, and in many unexpected places. Average Honeybees can be like Africanized ones if they perceive a person or an animal to be a threat to a hive because they'll attack, too (but not as vehemently as Killer Bees will). They're just not nearly as aggressive. Always be on the look-out for beehives, like you would for insects on or around ground areas (like stinging ants).

Again, kitties may see individual bees, but not be aware of a hive. They can easily become subjected to an attack by bees. Bees instinctively want to protect the colony, even if they must lose their own life. When they release their stinger, they die. Bees have, of late, been decreasing, but this is not good. They are needed to pollinate plants. Africanized Bees are hardier, so there are more of them now and there will be more of them in the future unless the government kills them and bans them. Again, one wonders if Killer Bees have anything to do with this decrease in regular Honeybees that has been going on. Many a kitty has been stung by a bee of any type and the stinger stays in their skin unless their caretaker sees it and carefully slides it out for them. If the kitty is dark in color, it can be hard to see agitations in a kitty's skin because where the fur is darker, the skin will be darker.

Wasps, hornets, and yellow jackets build nests, too. They aren't hives because these stinging insects don't make honey. With wasps, for example, most of the time their nests are higher up, but sometimes they aren't. They build nests in sheds and on or around patios (higher up). They also build them on tall-growing vines, shrubs, and in certain trees. They like palm trees so when you cut off any dead fronds, they will attack the laborer if the laborer is close enough to their nest. (Kitties don't usually climb up palm trees; I've never seen a kitty do that or even seen one up in a palm tree. The ends of where the fronds were cut off stick out too much on the trunk of the palm tree.) Sometimes, you have to wait to trim off fronds, tree branches, vines, and shrubs until the flying-insect season is over. Wasps will vacate their nest or the nest will be inactive because it is colder. When that time is clearly present, get rid of any old insect nests you see. Wasp nests are almost always brown or gray, with numerous round openings on them. Hornets and yellow jackets are very similar to wasps.

The Giant Hornets could be irreversible. They started on Vancouver Island, British Columbia, Canada. They came in from Asia, likely from Manchuria (Dongbei Province) and from B.C. went down to Washington State. They may be spreading eastward in Canada and going down into American states, unless it gets too cold for them. This hornet likely is now around several Asian countries. North Kora borders Bongbei Province. The hornets would have gone down to North and then South Korea. They don't attack people and animals aggressively like Killer Bees do but they will attack people and animals if their nest seems threatened, or they will attack, separately, when they are out and about. They kill Honeybees at their hive, or if they are solo. They have killed whole hives, too—down to every last bee. This is why they need to be purposefully hunted down and eradicated, along with the Killer Bees. The government should go in and look for <u>both</u> of these stinging insects at the same time, to save time. Giant Hornets will kill all Honeybees, in time, and are a threat to people and pets. Giant Hornets have such a long stinger that they can even sting through the long fur of cats, and certainly the short fur. The Giant Hornets could gradually spread east and south. They could, in time, become dominant in the USA and Canada. They could, in time, get into Mexico, then Central America, and then, South America, though this would take years. In the meantime, they would kill a lot of people, and especially animals. After several stings, there can be medical-related shock and heartbeat irregularity.

Repellants or poisons against critters can also be lethal for pets. Poisons can accidentally be eaten, sprays can be breathed in. Pets should be removed from any area where repellents or poisons are being put down or sprayed. Outdoor pets can be put in the home, with windows and doors closed, and then kept inside until it is safe. They can even be taken elsewhere. Bee repellents (as smoke, sprays, or foggers) can cause bees to seek out people and pets, to attack them. Therefore, people and pets should be away from the area before a spray or fogger repellent goes off in an area. Professionals wearing protective clothing and masks should be in charge. Kitties can outrun Killer Bees _if_ they have enough of a head start. Most of the time, their fur protects them from bee stings but not so much around the face, which is where Killer Bees zone in on. They will go for the face, and, they can get in to the skin in some areas on a cat.

The problem for outdoor kitties is that kitties are very curious and because of their curiosity, they can get in trouble. Kitties may see something dangerous and will try to chase it, paw at it, or go over to see it. Whereas indoor kitties have safe kitty-appropriate toys to play with, outdoor kitties do not have this luxury. What might catch an outdoor kitty's attention can be quite dangerous. Outdoor kittens—the younger ones and the older ones—are particularly vulnerable to what I term 'play danger'. They want to play with something because they are high energy and unaware of dangers. Sadly, some people put older kittens outside, thinking they will be safe because they are older. Older kittens play on a somewhat regular basis, and they can, therefore, be in peril if they are put outside. Plus, they would have no mother around to help teach them anything, and protect them. They simply do not know what is safe and unsafe.

Kitties that are outside get stung by insects more often than is realized, especially during certain times of the year. Certain insects can get their stinger in through any fur, on down to the skin. Some insects have a long abdomen. Tarantulas are dangerous. Some children and even older people go through a stage and choose to keep a tarantula as a pet. They aren't pets in the traditional sense of the word. A kitty may paw at a tarantula and can get stung. Kitties should not be near tarantulas, outside or inside of a home. Nor should they be near scorpions, Black Widows, or the Brown Recluse spider.

Kitties actually go after insects. They chase after them like they are enemies. They want to kill them. A kitty can get one or more stingers in their paws or around the face and head area, very easily. A kitty can get venom in their bodies, from spiders, bugs, various other insects, and, as noted earlier, from snakes. It's not like kitty can use a mirror to find a stinger, use a pair of tweezers or a sewing needle and remove any stingers, pull out any stingers between two fingernails, or sweep any stinger out with an index finger. Unfortunately, winged insects often go for the head and face area when they sting and, usually, no one is around when this happens and so a kitty would end out suffering a great deal, especially if there were several stingers left inside the kitty. After a bad experience, an outdoor kitty will be more leery of insects and won't be so apt to run around chasing after them. Keep in mind that some bugs or worms actually bore into the skin, and cause pain and suffering that way. Some lay eggs inside the body of mammals. Insects are dangerous and they are all around the world.

Different spiders and all ants can be a real problem for outdoor kitties. Certain spiders and all ants actually bite and leave some toxin. All the mosquito types suck out blood. Mosquitoes will bite kitty around the face area. Kitties don't get many such bites because they are so furry, but they can get some. Whereas fleas can get in between the fur on the skin, mosquitoes are too frail to do that. They have to land on open skin. Where fur is thinner or scant, mosquitoes can get to. Mosquitoes go for the nose and ears, particularly. Some areas have so many mosquitoes that kitty cannot get away. Certain flies will also bite. Diseases can enter a kitty because of mosquito bites.

Certain spiders can easily kill a kitty. Their venom can be deadly or debilitating. Black Widows, tarantulas, scorpions, and the Brown Recluse are some examples. Because kitties are covered with fur, it is impossible to notice welts and round bumps from any bites, even if there is discoloration of the skin. A kitty can die a slow and horrible death because of some spider bites, or they can die a quick and sudden death. In Australia, where many feral kitties live in the Outback (thanks to man's folly), the Funnel-Webbed Spider has killed people and certainly many kitties. They actually have fangs that are a quarter of an inch long. This spider is extremely dangerous.

Certain ants will bite, too. Some ant types can be annoying, harmful, and even lethal. Ants live in colonies (like bees do) so a kitty can get several stings at one time. In Australia, there are hordes of Jumper Ants. They're called Jack-jumpers and they are very dangerous. As a group, they will jump up on a person (or an animal) and sting. A number of them will do this at one time because they travel in a large group. On a person, the stings and welts are usually going to be on the lower legs. One colony can have two thousand ants. A person can go into anaphylactic shock from the stings, which are venomous. An anti-venom works <u>if</u> the person gets to a hospital fast enough. On a small animal, as a kitty, the stings or welts can be anywhere. Some ants can crawl in between the fur and sting a kitty. What is sad is that the many feral kitties that are in the Australian Outback are always in danger because of these ants (and other ants that are there, too). They will even sting around the face and eyes.

On the island of Tasmania (down from Australia), there are Bulldog Ants. Some, though fewer, are on the continent of Australia. Some of these ants are one-inch long. This means that they have a big stinger. Another ant-type is in East Africa—the Siafu Ant—and these must be avoided. Even animals stay away from them, if they can. These ants have jaws that cut. Actual pieces of flesh get cut, in other words. Some of the smaller ones then go in and break off pieces of cut-up flesh to carry away. Their colonies are huge. These Driver Ants (another name for them) can cut through a horse, down to the bone, in only a day. People who are asleep can easily be attacked by these ants. Babies can be very vulnerable because babies aren't mobile. A new litter of kittens, outside and sometimes even inside, can be killed off very quickly by these ants. They will attack living creatures if they are in their sight. The horde moves in for the kill. Another ant type, Army Ants, are mainly found in Costa Rica, Central America, but they've made their way up to the United States, especially the southern areas that are more humid. They're also carnivorous ants and they will prey on insects and small animals. They travel fast, in long lines.

In a dozen states in America, around southern grasslands, Fire Ants are multiplying. Mostly, they're in the South-East part of America, but now the State of California has them, too. (They came in from plants that were shipped into California areas, mainly into the Southern parts of the state.) These ants need water so they live around irrigation areas or water areas, in general. Garden watering contributes to their multiplying. These ants are brownish-red and some have a little black on them. They, too, have a venomous bite. Kitties will approach an area that has ants and will try to kill them with their paws. You can just guess what happens next. Sting. Sting. Sting. Sting. Sting. These Fire Ants keep increasing in numbers, and more mounds are around now so it's become an alarming issue.

In 1998, the State of Texas reported thousands of deaths of the trout that Park and Wildlife officials had put in the Guadalupe River, for anglers to fish. Close to twenty-five thousand were put in. Fire Ants are believed to have originally come in to America by ships carrying earth or dirt (with ants inside of it) and the ships (and dirt) came up from South America. The earth was used to stabilize loads. All it took was for a few such ants to come into the country and then multiply. Apparently, when these Fire Ants somehow landed on top of the Guadalupe River water, the trout gobbled them up. Someone may have dumped them in to feed them or the wind may have blown them over to the water. The Fire Ants perhaps stung them (inside of the trout) and the venom in the ants put in a poison that ended out killing the trout. The point to be made is that if kitties end out eating Fire Ants, they could perhaps suffer the same fate. Even very tiny ants inject a toxin when they sting, but very tiny ants don't generally cause harm. It's the larger ants that do, whenever enough of them sting a living creature. Kitties in any country, if they eat insects that carry venom, can become ill, suffer a paralysis, and/or die.

A kitty can get stung by an army of Fire Ants just by walking around an area where the ants happen to be. The kitty might just want a drink of water and suddenly, Fire Ants will descend on the kitty. Other types of ants (not in America) will shoot formic acid into a kitty's eyes, instead of stinging. Ants are a definite problem in a number of countries for any kitty that is outside. There are also very large black ants known as Carpenter Ants. Recently, I got stung by one and the welt seemed about four inches in diameter and the stinging feeling in the area stayed around for at least a half a day. It's one thing to be stung by just one ant. It's another thing to be stung by a number of ants at the same time. I fell into a red ant pile when I was a little girl, got stung many times, and I clearly remember that, even though it happened years ago. Kitties see ants and can start to play with them with their front paws, but, not for long. The fact that their paws are padded helps, but kitties can still be stung by ants, especially if there are many of them. Also, ants can get all over the food of kitties so kitties get stung around the mouth area if they try to eat the food (which is why you put a dish with food inside a pie pan with water in it if you feed outdoor kitties—the ants drown, trying to get to the food).

Tiny bedbugs are another problem. They're outside too, and not just in beds. Once they get inside, they're pests. They hide during the day and come out at night, in hopes of finding a meal. They're of the Cimicidae family, and they're found in tropical and temperate climates. They can live for months without feeding so they don't die quick without a host, like fleas do. Other insects are in the Cimicidae family and they feed on animals, too. They climb down into the fur and then crawl around on the skin. Outdoor kitties are vulnerable to these insects, needless to note. All these insects are outside. We can't always see them. We don't cross paths with them, but outdoor kitties do.

Leeches can be a problem for kitties, too. These are bloodsucking, somewhat thick worms. They're found in water—marine and fresh—and these ones aren't generally the problem for kitties. The problem leeches are the ones that live on land, in temperate and tropical areas. Europe has leeches. In fact, America's leeches, certain types, came in from Europe. Their salivary juices are used in the field of medicine. In the tropics, one leech type drops from trees and shrubs and lands on passing-by mammals, including people. The leech will quickly attach itself to the mammal and start sucking its blood. They can be as much as three inches long. Outdoor kitties can be menaced by them, and are. Certain areas of the world in particular have land leeches and these leeches can be around villages, towns, and cities. All leeches are rather ugly and they can cause animals to be in anguish. There are different types (and sizes) of leeches around the world. Some of them just drop off branches when an animal walks through an area and that is how they get on the animal.

Most areas in the world have mosquitoes and drawing in blood from a kitty is just fine with them because blood is blood. The female mosquito lives on blood. Mosquitoes live in tropical areas but they can be anywhere—in forests, on plains and prairies, and in deserts. Mosquitoes can pass diseases along to a host. They may pick up the disease from a previous animal that they drew blood from. Then, they pass the virus or bacterium along to their next host, which, of course, could be a kitty. The West Nile Virus, for example, is passed around by mosquitoes and, actually, kitties are one of the species that can get a strain of the West Nile Virus. Many kinds of mosquitoes carry this virus, too, in several parts of the world, including America. Some kitties can fight the virus with their immune system, but some cannot. Animals can die because of this virus. Seeing sick or dead animals is a sign that the virus may be around a particular area. Mosquitoes can also give cats heartworms, but this is much more common in dogs. Heartworms are rare in cats.

SARS (Severe Acute Respiratory Syndrome) is not caused by mosquitoes, but it could be a disease cats get if cats are forced to be outside (which is the case with a number of diseases). SARS has hit some areas of the world fairly hard. Bird Flu (Avian Flu) is out there, too. Outdoor cats play with, kill, and even eat birds (if they can ever get to any) and if Bird Flu kills birds, aren't we to assume that it can kill cats, or at least cause them some kind of internal problem(s)? Some diseases have not yet hit certain areas in full measure so there isn't much information out about those diseases (or strains of diseases) and therefore, they haven't been studied enough yet. The coronavirus or COVID-19 is a good example of this.) The USDA (U.S. Department of Agriculture) decides who will get funding for what research that relates to animals, particularly the animals that produce our food. They disperse funds on an 'as needed' basis. When something becomes a big issue or a threat, related research will be done very quickly. The government will even find scientists and researchers quickly and before such people even get a chance to approach the government on their own. The government zealously makes an effort to stay on top of diseases and potential diseases.

Some strains of mosquitoes have come in to areas by way of exported plants. For example, the Asian Tiger mosquito came in to California from Asian plants. These plants went in to several other areas of the world, as well. The mosquitoes laid eggs in the water that the plants had been watered with. Some of this water became standing water, where disease-spreading mosquitoes hatched. Infected mosquitoes bite whatever moves. The bites can cause fever and illness. What one mosquito carries can be passed on to the mosquito's young so these mosquitoes all require control. Areas where they're found have to be sprayed. Spraying has only partial success, however; and it doesn't take long for them to re-populate.

Anyone who wants to be as free of mosquitoes as possible, aside from spraying them, if they would remove all items where water collects, as, tires, birdbaths, pots, buckets, and similar items, and fill in dips in the roof and ground areas, their mosquito problem would significantly decrease. Use porous potting soil for your plants, too, so water will not collect in pots and planters. Both dogs and cats get bitten by mosquitoes. Mosquitoes can sometimes make them miserable, in addition to causing them certain medical problems.

With Global Warming, in some areas, mosquitoes are increasing. Erratic-weather and rains, sometimes associated with El Niño and La Niña, have also increased mosquito numbers. (La Niña only comes around every three to four years, however.) Some charity groups are getting mosquito nets out to areas that need them. Such nets reduce the cases of Malaria, considerably. If you live in an area where mosquitos are around, you have to open and shut doors very fast and have screens on your windows. Unfortunately, dogs and kitties don't usually get to be under mosquito nets.

In some parts of the world, the Deer Tick can bite animals. The Deer Tick causes Lyme Disease in humans and this disease has horrible effects, if not caught early. The disease was first reported in the town of Lyme, Connecticut. Ticks cause Rocky Mountain Spotted-Fever. (The disease was first reported in the area of the Rocky Mountains.) It is not good for domesticated animals to be loose in areas where ticks are found. Bites of ticks can affect them in ways that sometimes go undiagnosed. In other parts of the world, ticks can be a real problem, too. Ticks can be so bad in places that they cause an animal to bleed to death. Dogs get more ticks than cats do. Cats are more double-jointed, and can bite them off by twisting around to get to an area.

In Africa, the tsetse fly feeds off the blood of humans and animals and it can spread several diseases, one of which is Sleeping Sickness. This insect flies like a regular fly but it has a suction funnel or tube like a mosquito has and they use the funnel to draw in blood. There are worldwide pests of all types that outdoor kitties can encounter and are affected by, wherever they live. Again, kitties chase after insects and don't realize their harm until they are stung or bitten. When kitties try to eat these insects, bites or stings can be around the mouth. It can be very bad if an insect a pet swallows was carrying parasite eggs that can hatch inside the pet.

House flies are odd little creatures. You can swat at them and they'll soon re-land in the same area where you swatted them even though the swatting had just forced them away. You can be standing right there, with the flyswatter, and they'll still land. If you have kitties, you have to swat flies and remove their bodies or the kitties might see them and eat them. They follow flies around as they fly around and they will eventually kill them (and perhaps, then, eat them). You want to deter any kitty from doing this. Flies have germs both inside and outside of their body. Always clean up a swatted spot after killing a fly. Also, do not keep an outdoor garbage can right next to a door or window that is always being opened and closed or you will get flies galore inside your home.

You don't want a kitty eating cockroaches, either. Being sewer insects, they are germ carriers. Kittles love to chase after cockroaches and cockroaches get away by going under furniture (as do crickets but crickets aren't so dirty). Younger kitties are faster and they get cockroaches more easily than older kitties do. They kill them with their claws. Some, but not all kitties eat them. Generally, they just leave them dead. Roaches don't like the outdoors, though; they come in through plumbing piping. They like sewers, which is why they carry germs. Kitties do not like being near sewers or sewer outlets because the smell can be pungent.

Cats should not be contending with roaches, just like they really should not be contending with mice and rats. If they're around, the cats will contend with them. Kitties should be seen as companion animals, not as mousers or ratters…or roachers. Mousetraps get rid of mice. Rat traps get rid of rats. Use the Have-a-Heart types of traps for rats and relocate them. You can spare mice with similar traps, too, and mice can also be driven away with electronic 'noise' devices (that people cannot hear but mice can…and they don't like the sound). As for roaches, put out sturdy, curved and rounded glasses with sweet red wine half-way down and put such glasses of wine in strategic spots and the roaches will get caught in these glasses and drown and die. Since I've done that, I don't even see any cockroaches roaming around because they're all dead, in the wine. One spring/summer season, I'm sure I pulled out around fifty cockroaches, all total and maybe more, from just two wine glasses I'd put in areas where I thought they were most likely to be. My kitties never have to contend with them…and their germs.

Again, the subject of fleas is covered in-depth in CATegory 28 of *I Care for My Cats*. (Mites are covered in CATegory 29.) Outdoor kitties suffer grievously when flea season rolls around. It comes around in the spring when the nights warm up. Some flea seasons are quite long, too, if weather stays within a certain temperature range for a longer period of time than is usual. Flea season can even range from April to late October, in most southern areas. In a few areas of the world that are always warm, fleas can live through the whole year. If a kitty owner puts their kitty outside, the kitty can bring in fleas. Bringing in fleas would be avoided if the kitty was always kept inside. There are just so many reasons why kitties should be indoor-only.

There are also horned toads, Gila monsters, and similar critters outside. Some are quite dangerous. Some critters have teeth that can bite a paw or face. Some have some kind of toxin or poison that serves as defense. Horns (points) on a horned toad are their defense.

There are even Vampire Bats, which can attack and bite a kitty. Some bites of animals are so loaded with bacteria that it's the bacteria that slowly multiplies and kills the bitten animal. Such a death is awful, and this does happen to kitties. Vampire Bats get Rabies, too. If a kitty eats an animal that had Rabies, even one that it did not kill itself, the kitty will get Rabies. If a rabid animal came by and ate from a non-rabid animal carcass, it could leave the Rabies virus in or on that carcass so that any animal coming around later on could pick up the Rabies virus. A kitty can get Rabies in more than one way, in other words. Bats can carry the coronavirus, which kittles can get from other animals, too (besides bats). There are different strains of the coronavirus that animals can get so not all coronaviruses are COVID-19.

Any animal that has been used to being cared for has difficulty surviving when they've been dumped. They haven't learned how to fend for themselves or how to obtain food. Most dumped animals die fairly fast, for this reason.

When a baby penguin was stolen from the London Zoo in December of 2005 and was dumped in the ocean soon afterwards, most people believed it died quickly because its mother was not around anymore to protect the baby and to see that it got food. People were upset about the whole scenario. This story relates to young kittens being dumped, too, or any kitty that has never learned to survive out of doors. With regards to dumped kitties that had been pets, usually the owner had obtained the kitty when the kitty was very young and so the kitty had not learned anything that it needed to learn when it came to surviving in an outdoor setting. It is cruel to put kitties that are not familiar with the outdoors, outdoors permanently. It is thoughtless. They are happy to be with humans all the time, inside of a relatively well-organized home, where they can be safe.

7

Unsafe Areas/Cars/Poisons and Chemicals

Sheds can be a problem for outdoor kitties. Some people have unknowingly shut a kitty in their shed or in an infrequently-used building, and they then left the area indefinitely, which could mean a day, a week, a months, etc., so, of course, such a shut-in kitty can die fairly quickly. Sometimes, kitties sneak in while the door is open, and hide behind boxes or large items that are in a shed or building, while it is being used. Because they aren't seen, the door gets closed. If the shed is infrequently used, that's the end of the kitty. If the kitty is left for a while in a garage (and kitties shouldn't be in garages because they can get run over), people come and go in and out of garages fairly often so a kitty will likely be seen, but with sheds (and other kinds of enclosed constructs), they are generally entered infrequently and randomly. If accidentally shut-in, the kitty cannot get to food and water. We all know that a kitty will die without food and water. Kitties may or may not meow. Even if they do, they might not be heard.

Sheds are thinly made. If a kitty is inside of a shed, the kitty could freeze if the kitty gets real cold, or the kitty could die from the over-heating if it is hot outside and the shed that kitty gets stuck in gets really hot inside. With no air flow present, kitty will bake. Kitties cannot open shed doors with their paws. If your outdoor kitty is ever missing, look <u>all over</u> inside of your shed, right away, or look in any similar places, for that matter. Look in any hiding places in those places. The kitty may be skittish and be hiding.

A kitty can be stuck somewhere in a garage that has been closed. Some garages aren't used much and some are used for storage. If your kitty is ever missing, ask your neighbors to look inside their shed and/or garage, just in case your kitty is stuck in their shed or garage. Again, kitties starve to death or die of thirst in such places, or they die from heat or cold. If you don't take the time to look for your kitty right away, by the time you get around to doing it, your kitty will likely be dead. Kitties die from lack of thirst really fast—faster than most people realize.

Actually, barns aren't all that safe for kitties, either. They get very cold at night and hot and stuffy when the weather is warm or hot. There's often no ventilation. Animal dung collects and kitties are forced to walk on it, and to breathe in dung dust. Wild animals that kill kitties can get in some barns without anyone knowing about it. The kitties can get killed and eaten. Kitties often kill small animals in barns and the kitties end out getting their parasites. If water collects somewhere because of a leaky roof, which barns often have, areas around the barn can become unsanitary real fast, especially if dung and urine from barn animals is all around. If kitties drink water that will collect in certain places around the barn, they will get very sick. An occasional kitty eats straw or hay that is in a barn, too, and the pieces can catch down in the kitty's throat and clog their food intake. Kitties can get killed by the stomping and kicking of barn animals, too. Even at Alpaca farms or stations, kitties can get stomped on because Alpacas will sometimes try to kill whatever comes in to their area. Many a fox has been killed this way, and so have kitties and dogs.

People who think that kitties are safe in barns or similarly-used structures are deluded. Some of the farmers or ranches have to know this. They just hope for the best. They may be using kitties as barn mousers. Often, though, the worst happens and it's 'so long' kitty(ies). Kittens are particularly vulnerable in barns, to make note of the rather obvious.

Some backyards have swimming pools, and certain kitties will be unable to swim in a large, deep-water pool. Even the shallow end of a pool is too deep for a kitty. If kitty somehow ends out in a pool, kitty won't know what do to. Kitty will panic, and possibly drown. Most kitties don't like to get wet, but a kitty can end out in a pool, accidentally. Even a big gust of wind can blow a kitty in, or kitty could be trying to get away from a predator and end out in the water. Sometimes, mean children throw cats in a swimming pool and then don't help them out. If the cat does not know how to swim, it will be very frightened. They may or may not make it out of the pool, on their own. If a kitty just falls in, at an edge, it might be able to get out fairly fast, by using the edge for leverage, but it may have trouble doing this, because of the angle of the ledge.

Cats can be trained to learn to swim. They have to be held up, in the mid area initially, then you let them paddle as you move them along so they'll get the idea that they're moving. Eventually, you release them and let them swim on their own. They'll go over to the edge of the pool and most cats will try to pull themselves up over the edge. They can probably be taught to do this, too. This teaching to swim is done in a gentle, step-by-step way, but if a kitty falls in a pool without any pre-teaching, the kitty may drown unless they have some help. Certainly, they'll be traumatized.

Cats can get stuck inside of vehicle engines. This has happened, many times. They go in them to sleep because the engine may be warm, after the car had been driven. The kitties think they are safe, in that they are hidden and off the ground. If the driver of the vehicle starts up the vehicle and drives it, the cat may not be able to get out. It will get burns because the engine heats up. It can also get hurt by moving parts. The kitty can get transported to another area without anyone knowing about it (when it eventually gets out), and this relocation can end out killing the kitty because it may not be able to find food or water. It may also be exposed to new perils, in the new area. The kitty may not know how to avoid or overcome the new perils in the new environment. Different areas have different perils and sometimes the same perils.

There are several other car-situation perils for a kitty. Getting run over is but one car peril for kitties. If a kitty gets into a garage and likes to sleep in a vehicle's engine because it may be warm or because it seems like a safe, quiet place, again, the kitty could have a rude awakening and experience sudden harm or death if the vehicle is quickly started. This can happen if a car is in a carport too, or even if a vehicle is parked in a driveway or on a road. Some kitties have been killed by sudden vehicle-belt movement that can totally catch a sleeping or resting kitty off-guard. Under-the-hood moving parts are in certain spots, depending on the vehicle.

If you have a kitty that you suspect sleeps in your vehicle's engine, bang a couple of times on the hood of your car to wake the kitty up and to cause the kitty to leave that area before you start your car. Do this every time, too.

You might want to honk the horn, as well. Do both, to be safe. If you ever see little paw prints in the dust that has collected on your vehicle, bang on the car hood and honk your horn before you start your car, just in case a stray kitty is up in the engine area, underneath the hood.

One kitty I heard about was under someone's hood and it ended out travelling with the owner for several miles until the owner stopped and got out of the car. About the same time that she stopped her car, her kitty got out from somewhere under the hood of the car and someone else saw that the kitty was limping and bleeding and that person started talking to the kitty, which caused the kitty's owner to turn around and look over to see her own kitty this far from home. Several people tried to catch the frightened, wounded kitty and finally the owner was able to catch her kitty. The kitty had lost one claw and claw area, which had been permanently severed so the kitty was immediately taken to the vet. It's possible that the kitty tried to move when the car was first starting and the kitty put one paw next to a moving fan belt and got it cut off. The kitty then stayed still until the car stopped. Whatever happened, somehow, the kitty's life was spared and somehow, the owner got her kitty back. The owner was very fortunate to end out with her travelling kitty.

Also, carbon monoxide from a car can quickly kill a kitty if the kitty is near the rear of a car when it is started. It doesn't always matter if the car is somewhat enclosed in an area, either. It doesn't take very much carbon monoxide to kill a kitty, even a large one.

Another vehicle danger occurs right by the wheel and tire of vehicles. Even just slow car movement when someone is leaving an area could result in someone running over a kitty. A kitty could be sleeping right behind a wheel or tire or just be resting there, wide awake. Either way, the kitty could get run over. The kitty could be right behind a wheel and tire and the driver would not be able to see the kitty or hear the kitty cry, assuming the kitty was even able to let out a cry in time. Such an accident can happen if someone is pulling out or backing up after a vehicle has been in a parked position. This kind of accident has happened many times—to cats, dogs, and small children. It can all happen so fast. Kitties get behind a wheel and tire because they sometimes think it is a good place to hide, for whatever the reason, and, also, just because they are resting in the shade. The accident occurs more in front areas of vehicles with dogs and cats and in back areas with small children.

Because of carbon monoxide danger and because of car-movement danger, it is wise to check underneath your vehicle before you get in. Again, bang on the car hood and honk your horn, before you even start the car. Drive out real slow, too, so if a kitty is there it will, more likely, be able to escape the danger. If you make some initial noise, at least try to remember to drive out really slowly. It is a good habit to get into.

Antifreeze is a vehicle-related hazard. It kills kitties (and dogs). Many people do not realize how dangerous antifreeze is. It's definitely another one to add to the list and it has killed many kitties (for many years). It is believed that approximately ten thousand cats and dogs around the world died each year from licking up and drinking antifreeze (but these stats have been reduced). The trouble is, though, it's hard to know if a cat or dog has died from antifreeze poisoning because a toxicology test is rarely done, after the fact. They can be done if someone gets the animal to the vet clinic on time, which does not always happen. Consequently, statistics about antifreeze deaths are guesses. Still, the fact that <u>any</u> cat or dog dies from antifreeze poisoning is alarming enough.

Antifreeze constituency has been modified now to make it less lethal but this is because some children have accidently drunk antifreeze and died. (Antifreeze has also been used to poison people, and even to commit suicide.) It wasn't modified because of cats and dogs, per se, even though so many of them died from antifreeze spills and leaks. Some antifreeze can still be more lethal, in some countries, and also, there are still some older, more lethal antifreeze jugs around. It hasn't all been used up. It is the Ethylene Glycol in the antifreeze that is bad. There is now less of this in USA antifreeze. Some cleaning solvents have Ethylene glycol in them too, so family members have to be careful about these, as well as the antifreeze. Antifreeze spills and leaks under a vehicle or left out in open receptacles have been lethal to kitties. If the cap is left off the antifreeze jug, the container could accidentally get knocked over and spilled and a kitty could mistake the antifreeze for water.

Antifreeze has a green color to it so people can easily recognize it. Most antifreeze has a slightly sweet taste to it so cats (and dogs) like the taste. It has a sweet smell, too, so animals are attracted to it. If a kitty drinks or laps up antifreeze from the ground (or from anywhere), it is possible that if you do not get the kitty to a vet right away, the kitty could experience organ failure and die from the toxin (and do so fairly quickly). Antifreeze is almost always green because color is added to it, in an effort to prevent accidental ingestion. But, of course, kitties don't differentiate color when it comes to drinking anything liquid. (Children don't, either, and that was the problem.)

Ingested antifreeze harms the kidneys and the brain. It will cause a slow or sudden death, depending on how much was ingested and how large the animal is. It causes crystals to form that are razor sharp and these crystals cause awful pain. An animal will not be able to think right, either, if it ingests antifreeze. It will act out of sorts before it dies. Again, any pet must quickly be taken to see a vet.

Always clean up antifreeze spills right away, whether you spill them or someone else has spilled them. <u>Each time you put antifreeze in your car, get in the habit of looking under your car for any spillage.</u> Hose the area off, completely, but before you turn on the hose, <u>blot up the excess antifreeze liquid with paper towels and toss them in the trash. Then hose the area off.</u> By blotting off the excess liquid, you are removing most of the poison. If a kitty comes by and drinks the water of the hosed-off area, the remaining antifreeze will be so diluted that it cannot be harmful or too very harmful. At the very least (if you don't have a hose), get a gallon pitcher of water and dump it on top of the antifreeze that is on the ground. Maybe do this more than once so the antifreeze is more diluted but again, blot the spilled antifreeze up, first. It only takes a little antifreeze to kill a kitty or a dog. It's best to do a little extra, than not enough.

Kitties cannot tell that antifreeze is lethal when they smell it because it is almost odorless but it has a slightly detectable and appealing smell and a kitty can be drawn to it. Kitties have a very good sense of smell. A kitty will innocently drink it and then die a horrible death. You may never even see the kitty drink the antifreeze and you may never come to know what the kitty died from. Again, the death could be a slow one. Ethylene glycol in the antifreeze will crystallize in the kidneys and the brain and, as it does, oxalic acid is formed. Immediate treatment with ethanol may circumvent some or all of the damage but who keeps ethanol at their home? Who even knows what it

The Outdoor Perils of Cats

is? The closer a vet's office is, the better. If lots of antifreeze was ingested, the situation will be much worse; you can't always know how much was licked up and this is the problem. Again, it is imperative that you blot up and then hose down antifreeze spills as soon as they occur or that you see them. You cannot miss the green color of the liquid. Always keep antifreeze, and other products that are potentially lethal for kitties, <u>well</u> capped. Set them in such a way that they aren't apt to be tipped over.

Cruel people have been known to throw antifreeze-laced food out into yards where cats and dogs tend to be. They've also put out antifreeze-laced food in dishes, even outside their own doors so that when a roaming kitty comes around and eats the food, they will be on their way to dying when they head for home, if they have a home. People who would do this to an innocent, helpless animal have a short circuit in their brain and they are mentally and morally deficient. There would be jail and/or prison for a person caught doing this, and not just a fine. To emphasize, we are on Earth to help and protect our domesticated animals, not hurt them. Mercy and best care should go out to all animals.

<u>A few people do this in an effort to get rid of stray cats, which is so derelict.</u> What real harm are the kitties doing to anybody? All you have to do is trap them and then take them in to a shelter. You can also fix them up, and either keep them or find a home for them. It's a cruel, painful, frightening way for a beautiful, helpless, defenseless creature to have to die. Some people don't stop to think about the eternal destiny of their own soul.

However, sometimes antifreeze deaths are caused by negligence, because antifreeze spills aren't blotted up or hosed off. Don't go blaming anyone else if it was you who left antifreeze on the concrete at your home. The

163

negligence would be on you. It could be on a neighbor if the neighbor spilled the antifreeze. If it wasn't your antifreeze spill, then the blame could be on some unknown person out in the neighborhood somewhere, because anybody could have left an antifreeze spill around that a kitty or dog licked up. Neighbors genuinely may not realize the dangers of antifreeze spills and leaks. Maybe you should go over and inform them? This would be up to you. Some neighbors might genuinely want to know.

Intention to kill and cause grievous pain to an innocent animal is both seen and on record with a Higher Power so if such a person gets away with such a despicable, cowardly act now, they cannot escape a God who cares about animals, and about their welfare. Assuming it was God who allowed domesticated pets to be brought about and that He helped people with the domestication so that humans would have pets to love, enjoy, and take care of, then it could be assumed that God is not happy with people who are cruel to animals. Some of these people may not care now, but one day they may well be forced to care. They're going to realize, full-force, what they did. There'll be a day of reckoning. Sometimes negligence, when someone knows better but doesn't take the time out to prevent something, when they could, is very close to being an intentional act, and a judge would have to call that one. To determine if a pet is suffering or has died from antifreeze poisoning, a vet can check a blood sample but to detect it will require a special test. A special toxicology test can be done and the Ethylene glycol can be detected and sometimes even measured, as to amount ingested.

Hardly is intentionally poisoning domestic pets loving them or taking care of them. This kind of cruelty is just the opposite of that. Doing such a mean thing to an animal is just the opposite of what God's intentions are because He wants to bless lives with wonderful, loving pets. People who do such horrible things are going to have to live with themselves until they die, which sometimes is a justice all in itself, or, at least, it is a portion of justice. More laws are being passed to protect animals, fortunately. And more people are developing a conscience about animals, too, which is an ongoing improvement in society and our world.

Even people who are negligent and leave antifreeze lying around on their property or lot could possibly be prosecuted if it can be proven that an animal became sick or died because of the negligence. Any of us can spill antifreeze on the ground accidentally, but we usually know it if we did. If you are the one who poured too much antifreeze into the radiator and you know it spilled over onto the ground and is under your vehicle, then you must be the one to clean it up, right then and there. Blot it up and then hose it off (and do not let it puddle up). Too often, people just leave it there, to dry up, but kitties are all over any neighborhood and even a stray kitty could come by soon after or at night and lick or lap up spilled antifreeze that might still be on the concrete. So, you can never leave it around and assume that it will dry up. Actually, antifreeze does not dry up that fast. It isn't at all like water, which does dry up quickly. It has different properties in it than water has.

The longer the antifreeze sits on the concrete, the more chance there is that a kitty will come along and drink it. Again, it doesn't take much antifreeze to kill a kitty—any kitty, anywhere—so even a tiny puddle of it underneath a vehicle can do a kitty in. Even more than one kitty can come by, too, and then drink this and die from it because more than one kitty could possibly drink from the same puddle. Roaming or local dogs can drink it or lick it up, too. They don't go under vehicles as much as kitties do but if the vehicle leaves that spot, the antifreeze spot will be out in the open. Also, the smaller dogs will often go under cars.

You can buy low-toxic antifreeze now and no one should be buying the toxic kind. The low-toxic type is about the same price as is the toxic type (it is ballpark, anyway), and it works just as well. Service stations and auto repair centers or businesses should start stocking just the low-toxic type. Hopefully, more will do this. More and more people should buy this product for their vehicles. The product has been out, for some time now. <u>This kind of antifreeze isn't entirely non-toxic, though, because it does have some ethylene glycol in it, but it would take a whole lot of it to harm a pet, as opposed to the toxic type, which only takes about a quarter to a half of an ounce to seriously harm or kill the average pet.</u>

Sometimes, bears get into antifreeze containers, and drink the contents. Any poor animal that takes in antifreeze is doomed because the liver is also affected. It also becomes internally crystallized and immobilized and since the liver dispels toxins out of the body, if the liver is no longer functioning, the animal dies, either slowly or quickly, depending on the size of the animal and how much antifreeze the animal drank. Again, kidneys (like the liver) will no longer be able to function. Once the poisoning reaches a certain point, animals have to be euthanized even if they have been taken in to a vet clinic or shelter. Euthanizing is merciful, under such circumstances. Remember to always cap antifreeze containers extra tightly so if ever a pet tips the container over, it won't spill out and be tempting for the pet to lick or lap up.

For some time, people have had the option of buying the toxic versus the low-toxic antifreeze, but one day, we'll be fortunate enough to have the highly toxic antifreeze banned by State legislation, and even by Federal legislation.

Again, children have died from drinking antifreeze. Way more pets have died from this peril than has been medically recorded. The outdoor kitties just go somewhere to die after drinking antifreeze, which is why statistics about these deaths are not possible to record. Sometimes, people are too embarrassed or worried to report it, too. They fear repercussion. <u>Low-toxic antifreeze can be purchased at auto-parts stores and at large marts</u>. For sure, if you don't clean up your antifreeze spills, you should buy low-toxic antifreeze, but it's always wise to clean up <u>any</u> antifreeze spills.

Contact a poison control center or a vet immediately if you suspect an animal has antifreeze in its system. Be prepared to rush the animal to the vet. If you saw the animal drinking the antifreeze, take the animal to the vet right away. If you ever suspect foul play relative to antifreeze poisoning, contact the sheriff or the police, immediately. If you think a pet was intentionally harmed by someone who fed a pet antifreeze, that person needs to be in the hands of the law.

Unfortunately, low-toxic antifreeze wasn't as sought after as one might think so now there is also an antifreeze that has a bad taste to it that kitties (and dogs) don't like because a bitterant has been added. It has taken hold only because a law has been passed to include the bitterant. Future antifreeze has to have this bitterant added. The antifreeze can still be harmful to pets and people, however. You do not want antifreeze spills or leaks under any vehicle. If pets walk over spills or leaks and then clean their paws, this will not be good. If other countries besides the United States would follow suit and sell only low-toxic antifreeze with added bitterant, then there would be less of a chance that animals would accidentally lick or lap up antifreeze or walk on top of it and be forced to lick their paws. Such antifreeze wouldn't harm children and if it was used as a poison, it would be easily detected because of the bitterant.

Sometimes, kitties wander into open garages and there can be dangers around these areas (including any spilled antifreeze). Lids are sometimes left off of bottles and jars in garages and there are poisons, chemicals, and the like, which kitties can get into. Home cleaning, auto care, and lawn and garden products can be perilous for kitties. Rat poison in corners, mice-traps, and items soaking in chemicals can draw in a kitty and become perilous. Rat poison is also mice poison. People buy rodenticide to kill either one type or both types. You don't want kitties to be around such poison.

There are rat infestations in many cities around the world. Rats get in and out of places easily. They'll even twist and turn through small holes and squeeze themselves through. They are flexible and can even do some climbing. They're wild but they like city life, which is where so many cats are. Cats only kill smaller rats. Bigger rats are too big for them. Kitties kill mice of any size. People living in cities with rats and mice hope the outdoor cats will get the outdoor rats and mice (and kitties do get them, sometimes.) Some people want indoor kitties so the kitties will shoo away any entering rats and mice, and even kill them. Rats are dangerous when infants and toddlers are around (especially the infants because they cannot be mobile). Rats go in and chew on the baby or young child. Kitties can, and they have protected babies or young children, but you cannot always assume that they will, certainly not like a dog might. A kitty might be frightened away by all the noise, once an attack starts to occur. The kitty could drive a rat away <u>before</u> it can attack, however, but the rat could return unless its way of entrance gets blocked or plugged.

A few people have had a rat as a pet. Usually, the cage they are in is too small so the rat owner feels sorry for them and lets them out—not real smart. It's cruel to keep animals in a small cage. You can take rats out to the country and release them. They may love garbage dumps, but they may end out getting buried there, one day. Inside of a home, cats should never be kept in a cage, even a large one. They need to jump and spring and walk around. Long hallways are great. So are stairs. Kitties will chase and pounce on rodents that get inside homes . . . if they are smaller ones.

It cannot be assumed that a kitty will actually protect an infant or a bed-ridden person who can't move well from an attack by one or more rats. A dog might be able to do that, after an attack starts, but a kitty likely can't. Also, kitties have, on occasion, been killed by rats. Kitties really should not be considered to be mousers and ratters anymore. They should only be looked at as being companion animals . . . and they're also very lovely to look at so we enjoy being around kitties for that reason, too. The males are handsome and the females range from pretty to gorgeous. Kitties are living, moving home ornaments. They don't belong outside. And why do we have to view them as being mousers and ratters?

One sign of suffering from rat poison ingesting is a lack of energy and being slightly lame. Then, the kitty will struggle with breathing. Any time a kitty suddenly has trouble breathing, the kitty must quickly be taken to see a vet, and preferably one that is close by. Labored breathing is an emergency situation. There is nothing on the market that kills rodents that isn't poisonous, unless you want to use traps or something like a really strong sticky paper to catch them. Rodent poison often has strychnine in it and if a kitty eats it, the poor kitty will die a very painful death and be horribly sick before it does. Insect poison gets put on floors, counters, and in corners. They shouldn't be put down in areas where kitties walk.

A blood test checks for poison and can sometimes pin a poison down. For example, the warfarin in rat poison causes anemia due to blood loss. The kitty would not be able to absorb Vitamin K, which is needed for blood to be able to coagulate. Vets usually know what symptoms point to what. Sometimes, it's hit-and-miss and/or process of elimination, however (i.e. it involves troubleshooting). Time is always of the essence when treating poisons. Getting blood test results in quickly may save the kitty's life. Knowing what the poison is will speed up treatment and could be what saves the kitty's life.

Sprayed poisons and chemicals get on kitties' paws, but so do powdered poisons and chemicals. What is powdered gets on a kitty's paws and they lick it off and ingest it. Pellet poisons can be eaten whole or played with so that some of that poison can get on paws. Liquid poisons can be licked up. Kitties can step on it and get it on their paws and then lick it off their paws, and the poison can begin to do damage—be it minor or major. Think twice about keeping poison around for anything. You, of course, can't stop any of your neighbors if they are putting poisons out. What can you do? Just don't let your pet or pets ever be anywhere where poisons could be.

One slug poison in the form of pellets is another danger. Metaldehyde is used in that kind of poison, but it is also used in others. If this ever gets ingested, the kitty will be unco-ordinated and the muscles will be so weak that the kitty will collapse. Respiratory problems will occur, as well. Safer products are now made and if you see 'Metaldehyde' on a label, perhaps consider not buying the product and then look for a safer one.

You have to be aware of poison being placed in outdoor gardens if you let your kitty go outside. Garden-related poisons can kill a kitty. Sometimes, poison handicaps a kitty but doesn't kill the kitty. This is still bad. A kitty's lifespan can be shortened. Poison can affect the nervous system and the brain. Also, realize that there are certain plants outside that are poisonous to kitties, too. This subject is covered in CATegory 5 of *I Care for My Cats (and Other Animals)*, but there, it mainly deals with indoor plants (of which some are also outdoors). You have no control over what your neighbors chose to plant and grow.

People put insect poison out in their yard all the time and again, kitties are vulnerable to insecticides. A kitty could eat poison dry, or if it rains or you water the poison area, the poison will be in pools of water that a kitty might come along and drink. A spraying poison has an effect, too. Poison is poison. Ground-area pools of water, in general, can be very bad for a kitty anyway because small micro-organisms can multiply and if kitty drinks that water, wherever it is, the kitty could get giardiasis, an intestinal infection by a parasitic protozoan that is found in water. Absolutely, antibiotics will be needed with this ailment. It won't go away on its own.

Other insects are found outside and kitties can come in contact with many of them. They will externally and/or internally affect kitties. People who like to garden don't usually bother getting rid of some insects, but those insects are around, like mites, fleas, ticks, and many worm types. The sprays and poisons are usually for insects that affect what they are growing on a lot and the gardener isn't thinking about any roaming animals when they put out poison. There is more about insects and parasites that menace and harm kitties in Chapter 3.

It is horribly tormenting when outdoor kitties become prey to parasites. If there are no flea or lice treatments for them, areas on their body will itch all the time when certain parasites are on their skin and live on their blood. Fleas can be so plenteous on a kitty that the kitty can't sleep very well (or at all). Even just a few fleas can have this effect on a pet. All of the flea biting disturbs their sleep or keeps them awake. Even the movement of these tiny insects can have that affect. It's hard for kitties to sleep well outside anyway—to find a safe, quiet, comfortable place, all the time, so that their sleep is at least all right—but, when fleas and other parasites are always biting them, sleeping becomes difficult and sometimes impossible. If kitties don't sleep well, they can easily get sick, whether it's warm or cold outside. Their resistance is going to be down.

They can also get ear-mites. Tiny ear-mites get down in their ears and a kitty can do nothing about their eating the inside areas of the kitty's ears. It can become tormenting. So can lice, fleas, and ticks be torment. A kitty can have more than one parasite on their body at any one time.

Internal parasites can become bothersome and tormenting, too, and cause a number of medical problems. People cannot see these like they can the parasites that are on their head and body. Food digestion can be a problem, for one thing. Outdoor kitties suffer from these awful internal pests. Roundworms and tapeworms are common ones. A kitty can have more than one type of worm in its Gastro-Intestinal Tract. If a kitty was always indoors, their chances of getting these parasites would almost be nil and in most cases, would be nil.

Kitties can also get screwworms. These worms are the larvae of the blowfly. These worms are found as far north as Pennsylvania. They cluster in areas on kitties and have to be removed by a vet. The area must be cleaned out and treated. Then there is the botfly larvae. There are twenty-five species of botflies in the United States and Canada. These ugly, large larvae, which can get to be about an inch long, look like huge oval, light-colored vitamin pills that are implanted on the kitty. The larvae are buried in the skin and a vet has to remove the larvae and clean the area out. This ordeal leaves lesions and scars, after they are all removed. Kitties living where these insects live should always be inside four safe walls. Kitties should not be walking around on the ground or be in brush or vegetation.

The botfly is a very large, stout-bodied fly. Again, the larvae (bots) can live under the skin of mammals. They get quite large and cause horrible pain as flesh gets torn up when and as they burrow. The larvae are too far under the skin for a caretaker to be able to get at them. The bots can end out actually causing death. A vet has to remove them under anesthesia. There are different kinds of botflies and they're problems for mammals in a number of ways. The ones that can be in humans are whitish and about an inch long and they're very thick. They have tiny barbs on them, which help them to burrow. Any animal that gets larvae bots inside them will always need human intervention and medical care as soon as possible.

Outdoor kitties are vulnerable to various tiny and small pests and they can be very problematic. Some will cause prolonged pain and diarrhea that only antibiotics can cure (like the giardiasis bacteria). Kitties don't get very much water outside and they'll sometimes drink whatever water they can find. If water is outside, it gets dirty—hence, the intestinal problems can occur. Kitties can die faster with no water than they can with no food so a lack of water, which is often the situation for the outdoor kitties, can be lethal. Many outdoor kitties have died of thirst and it can be impossible to know what they died from.

Most people know very little about entomology (i.e. the subject of insects). Many are oblivious to which insects are found are in their own area, and to what the scope is relative to the effects of the different insects. Few people around the world even study the insect populations and numbers, cycles, and seasons. All animals are affected by several kinds of insects when they are outside. Many people subconsciously think, 'oh, insects are so tiny, they can't hurt or bother my dog, or my kitty' but that is false thinking. Insects can drive animals crazy and can even kill them. Insects can torment animals. It is negligent to not keep control over any insects that are plaguing the pets that are in someone's charge.

Outdoor kitties have no litter box available to them and so they are forced to find places outside to 'do their business' (or to urinate and defecate). They'll use leaves, dirt, sand, rocks, wood chips, and whatever they can, as a substitute for litter. They can pick up germs and parasites as they are digging around. They'll go under buildings, houses, and mobile homes. Some areas where they go can become unsanitary so they will go elsewhere. It isn't that easy for them to find suitable outdoor areas, especially because they have such a need to bury or cover 'their business' once they're done with urinating or defecating. If outdoor kitties are brought inside, they will have litter in a litter box, which makes things much easier for them. If a caretaker regularly de-clumps, the litter will always be ready for their kitty (or kitties), to use until it is time to change it for their kitty (or kitties) to use, subsequently.

An outdoor kitty will often select a garden area as a litter box equivalent. The insecticides a kitty may come in contact with, from pawing and digging and from rubbing up against bushes and the like, can be harmful to the kitty. If a kitty chews on any leaves, there is the insecticide problem affecting the kitty, in a different way. Kitty might even eat insects from a garden and some of those insects might have been exposed to an insecticide. (This can also relate to their eating mice and other rodents, and the rodenticides the rodents ingest.) A kitty can get sick from such ingesting, or even die.

Kitty could come down with a medical problem, or two, or three, after having been exposed to even just one insecticide or rodenticide, let alone, to several. Some people put rodent poison around their gardens or in their garages. Kitties can come in to direct contact with any poison at all, eat it, and die. Many outdoor kitties have had to die awful deaths from poisoning. Dying this kind of death is hard on the rodents, too. They're also mammals and have a similar make-up to the cat. There can be internal bleeding, shock, a fast heartbeat, shallow breathing, etc., just for starters.

You can buy pesticides now that are supposedly chemical-free, but you have to look around for them. Outdoor kitties can eat plant food, petals, leaves, and even berries, so a more natural insect repellent is better if there are kitties outside. Even inhaling or touching certain of the toxic pesticides can be harmful to kitties so if you can learn about and buy the non-toxic or low-toxic pesticides, it will be safer for any kitties that might happen to come around. There is even snail and slug bait you can get that is non-toxic. All you have to do, is do a search. Walk the aisles. Call around. Check the Internet. Do everything you can to go the non-harmful route.

Particularly when toxic pesticide is first sprayed and is wet is when it is maximally toxic for animals that get exposed to it. It's not so bad when it dries, unless it rains and gets wet again. Even then, it won't be 'as' toxic as it had been. If a kitty walks over or eats something that is wet that second time (by rain or hose watering) and it is an insecticide, it may or may not do damage to the kitty. It all depends on a number of factors as to whether or not it will harm the kitty and to what extent it would harm the kitty. If you know there are outdoor and stray cats about, think twice about using the stronger chemicals and poisons on and around your lawn and garden. Use only what is less toxic or non-toxic. Find the products and try them out.

Also think twice about using such substances in your outdoor potted plants. Water on the bottom of planter dishes collects after watering outdoor plants and it can be toxic just because of what is in the potting soil but especially because of what is in insecticides and growth-enhancing agents, like fertilizer or something similar. If you water trees and plants and water collects around the indented base of them, the same catastrophe can occur if a kitty drinks from the water and the water has mixed in with chemicals and poisons. On the subject of landscape and garden, again, there are certain tree, shrub, and plant leaves that are dangerous for a kitty to eat. Some flowers are, as well, and certain berries are, too (not the berries humans generally eat). Learn what these are and avoid having them on your lot if your kitty ever goes outside.

Fertilizer is not good for a kitty to be around and it is found in many yards, gardens, and fields. It is a topical layer composed of nitrites that emit methane gas. Occasionally, kitties claw in fertilized areas, using it for their litter areas. This is not good. There are chemicals in fertilizers that are not good for a kitty to be exposed to. Then, too, a kitty may even eat fertilizer, particularly if any of it gets stuck on or in-between their claw areas so that the kitty must lick it off to get rid of it. <u>You can now purchase all-natural fertilizer</u>. If you do, you won't have to worry so much about any of the outdoor kitties.

Areas where fungus grows are not good areas for kitties to be around, either. Any area where there is fungus, or bacterial build-up, is bad for a kitty to walk over or breathe in, in some cases. Sometimes, algae grow in areas. It's not usually a big problem for outdoor kitties but it can be if it gets to be real scummy and full of bacteria.

Whenever someone works in their garden or with their landscaping, gardening gloves are an item that should be worn, in many cases, especially when working in dirt. You never know what you are going to pick up in your hands or under your fingernails. If you weren't wearing gloves, especially don't pat your pets after you've been working around dirt and when your hands are dirty, after you've been gardening. Whenever I work in my yard, and I come inside, I wash my hands. If I wasn't using gloves, I try to remove whatever may be under my fingernails, too, before I pat or touch my kitties. Over the years, I've learned to be real careful about many things like that.

To relay the obvious, never use any part of used kitty litter as mulch or fertilizer for any gardening or planting. Never mix any of it in with dirt or potting soil. The reason for this is because of the danger of getting Toxoplasmosis, a 'negative' protozoa (Toxoplasma gonadii) that can be transferred to humans and even from a pregnant human mother to the fetus (that can result in birth defects or miscarriage.) Kitties can sometimes carry these protozoa, but they can build up an immunity to them even though they still carry them. Consider using gloves when gardening and try not to ever breathe in any dirt or dust particles as you are working.

Kitties can get Valley Fever, a fungus, from digging around in dirt, whether they did so in a garden or elsewhere. Spores carrying the fungus can get breathed in. Of course, humans can get Valley Fever, too. Dogs are more affected by Valley Fever and if a dog comes down with general flu-type symptoms, take the dog to a vet clinic. If the dog has trouble walking, take the dog in that very day and get them the needed treatment. They could have Valley Fever. Keep a watch over any kitties in your charge anyway, because on occasion, a kitty will get this fungus-related illness.

Some people are owners of dogs and cats. The cats may stay inside but the dogs go outside when they need to since, to date, there is no such product as in-home dog litter. Dogs can bring viruses, bacteria, and parasites into the home, where the cats are. People who own a dog and a cat have to be really careful about that. It is not good for dogs to be outside too, very long. It is one thing for them to periodically go outside to do their business and then come right back inside as fast as possible. It's another thing for a dog to be outside quite often and come inside periodically, to where the kitty is (or kitties are). The dog can then end out causing the kitty (or kitties) medical problems.

If you're worried about kitties coming around your garden and do not want them there, you can buy a sonic repellent. It's environmentally safe—no toxins. Sonic pulses are sent out by this apparatus every fifteen seconds or so. The device is small, and it sticks in the ground or into potted dirt. The pulses irritate small animals and so they leave. There are different brands of these. Not all of them are quite alike. Then, too, there's a dish-like item that sticks in the ground and holds a liquid substance that is so offensive to marauding mammals (which, of course, includes kitties) that they will leave the site. It's a sniffer repellant. You can also hang the item up somewhere.

It has a lid. You could get a couple of them. They're plain looking and you don't notice them. More filler can be bought whenever it is needed. Animals come around, smell it, don't like it, so they decide the area isn't very inviting and will then go somewhere else.

Again, it's good to buy the natural products for your garden, for obvious reasons. Such products are safe for humans so they're becoming more popular. Some people buy these products to keep all animals safe. They care about their welfare. These low-frequency audio repellants work and keep animals away from an area. You can get a motion-activated repellant whereby a motion in the unit triggers a really high-pitched sound that's unbearable for animals, including cats and dogs. Humans cannot hear it. These repellants work for cats and dogs, and probably for birds and any creature that can hear sounds. These devices take batteries.

8

Home and Lot Dangers/Hiding Places/Dumping Kitties

Some people have mentioned to me that they let their kitty out on their patio and they act like they're convinced that the kitty is safe when they are saying this. But, kitties are curious creatures. They like to explore their immediate surroundings. Once they've checked out their immediate surroundings, they'll venture out further. Eventually, and sooner or later, they'll run into trouble because trouble is out there. You can't watch a kitty on a patio all the time. People are up and about doing things in their home and they can't watch to see if their kitty leaves the patio area. And kitties that are left on patios almost always leave, for varying lengths of time. People who tell me that they just let their kitty out on their patio are avoiding reality and avoiding the serious issue of outdoor perils, in general. God bless them, but they need to look at the bigger picture, for their own sake and for their kitty's sake.

People who live on a floor higher than a ground floor have to be careful about kitties falling off their patio or balcony. Some put up boards if there are open areas in the patio or balcony guard or railing that goes around the whole area. I've seen clear plastic set up against guard or the railing, too. It's hard plastic and somehow, the pet owner attaches it to the guard or railing.

It's better that a kitty doesn't even go out on the patio or balcony, though, because they can still jump up to the top of the railing and try to jump down. They can even fall down. The safest choice would be to not let your kitty go outside, ever. Mine don't. They're happy.

An occasional kitty even falls out of a window. They get out on the windowsill or ledge and then somehow fall. Occasionally, a kitty is even pushed or thrown out of a window because of a deranged person or a cruel, misguided child. Strange as it may seem, such falling kitties get fewer fractures if they are higher up, compared to if they are somewhat lower down, and then fall. Some kitties have taken falls from many stories up. They immediately try to turn in mid-air, which involves some body twisting or swiveling, and they have to adjust their body and position it so their four legs are positioned to brace their fall. If they don't have enough time to completely position themselves when falling, which sometimes happens with the shorter distances that are lower down, they aren't, then, so prepared to reposition themselves and cushion the fall and one or more of their limbs could break. So could their spine. Be very careful about kitties being around a window. Pick them up or scoot them away from the window. Get a screen for all the windows in the home.

Any kitty that falls from a height must be taken to see a vet immediately and then <u>well</u> examined. Some x-rays may be needed. Screens should always be on high-up windows, or, windows should only be cracked and not open too very much if one or more kitties live in the home. High-rise apartments are <u>very</u> dangerous for kitties when people aren't careful and safeguard such danger areas.

Taking a kitty outside with you while you read, garden, or lay in the sun, etc. can become problematic. You cannot really pay attention to the kitty, for one thing. Plus, the kitty has too much freedom. One situation I heard about involved a young woman who went out with her kitten and let her kitten play on and around the grass. She did this a few times, each time letting the kitten go a little further away from her while the kitten was exploring and playing. She was keeping her eye on the kitten, but that wasn't enough because suddenly the kitten ran off and couldn't be caught. The kitten never returned to the area, and the young woman was out a kitten. God only knows what happened to the kitten. It could have become prey or victim to one of the many outdoor perils, or, some nice person could have taken in the kitten, which would have been the best-case scenario but who is to know what happened to the kitten? The kitten could have starved to death, or have even been run over. For the kitten's previous caretaker, my guess is that ignorance about what could have happened to the kitten was not bliss. The not knowing can make for a lack of peace, for sure.

Quite often, kitties will live under houses or mobile homes. Sometimes, they'll find an opening and go in and out and live under a home or in a crawl space. Mobile homes are extremely easy for them to live under. This is not always good. Kittens can be born underneath these places when they should be born, safe, inside a home. Often, kitties will live around insulation under a home and if it is made of fiberglass, this is not good for the kittens because they can breathe in the tiny particles when they play with it. Kittens may pull it down and pull it apart. They can harm wiring under a home, too, which would include a mobile home. Kittens or very young cats will especially do this. They pull it down, and can even chew on it. You want to make sure all wires are tacked or tied down up high and that insulation is well taped. You'll want to do these two tasks no matter what. That way, no kitty will want to play with it if they get under your home.

Boarding up any spaces that kitties can use to get in under a home is what has to be done (when it is not close to kitten season and kittens may already be under there). Even buying large concrete blocks to cover up an open space, and then placing them in position, would be better than doing nothing. Before you cover or block such an opening, though, positively go in under the home first, if you can, to make sure no kitties of any age are already underneath. Double-check for kittens. They're smaller and harder to see. Check for any kitties and then, re-check. Try using a really good power light and shine it under the area, but you may not be able to see the whole area, underneath. If you have to and can't look underneath, wait until any and all come out. Just don't block any kitties in or the space underneath will become their death tomb.

If you ever see a cat go underneath a house or mobile home, do not plug up that entrance area unless you are absolutely positive there are no cats or kittens underneath and you know they are gone and not there. The cat you saw may have a litter of kittens she is tending to and she may still need to get in to feed them so if a cat comes out and you see it, then that could be a mom cat that has kittens under the home. If there are, and you block her entrance, you will be causing the kittens to die a slow death. The mother will be stressed. It would be like leaving cats in a cage to die, with no food or water. The area below the home would become 'as a cage', if there was no way out. You may not even know if the cat has kittens underneath the home. Some people will even go in and crawl under the space and check <u>all</u> over and then block the entrance. You could hire an expert to do this. Some pest-rid companies might do this, for pay. They'd be looking for cats, not spiders or termites. They'd have to look very carefully for cats or kittens. Maybe they could treat for an insect problem afterwards, since some insects are probably there (but kitties aren't).

So often, cats do have kittens under homes, and with Global Warming now and the related warmer temperatures, a cat can have two litters of kittens during the warmer months, which can go from March to October. Mating may start in March and can go as late as October, in warmer areas. There is time to have two litters in some areas, now. Kittens can even be born after October now and during the colder months, and they can, then, die from the cold because they're small and vulnerable. If that were the case, you should, for sure, consider getting the kittens out and putting them, and the mother, somewhere warm. Again, you just can't know if kittens are under a home and you just can't plug up the entranceway without knowing. You have to look. Even if a cat has come out from underneath, it doesn't mean there aren't more in there. It is rare that there are two litters of kittens underneath a home, but this has happened. In other words, there could be two mother cats that are coming and going and needing to get to their kittens.

You have to get in underneath with a superior-working light and <u>completely</u> check the <u>whole</u> area. If you see no kitties, <u>then</u> you plug the entranceway right then and there. Make sure there is only one entranceway into the area. You don't wait for <u>any</u> length of time to plug the area up because, in the meantime, a kitty could go in underneath. You might not see that happen and it will be death for that kitty if you, then, plug up the area. If you see kittens and they are very small, you might want to leave them and the entranceway alone—at least for a time. When the kittens are old enough, the mother cat will bring them out and you can get them then. Count them, though. Or, if you do remove the kittens and you have a <u>safe</u> place for them and you know the mother will find them (wherever it is that you put them), that might be okay to do, too.

After you've transplanted them all, you will need to quickly block the entrance area. You can put the kittens in what you think is a safe place, outside, but the mother has to think it is a safe place. The mother may end out moving them to a place of her own choosing but, at least the area under your home will have been blocked. So, this is but another outdoor peril—that kitties are underneath houses and mobile homes that get plugged up, covered over, or sealed. Many kitties have died because of this too-soon blocking of an entranceway. It will be negligence on the part of a resident to not first look underneath.

The mother cat must get out from wherever her kittens are from time to time and find food so her milk supply can be replenished to allow her to keep nursing her kittens. She is not a cruse of milk. She has to eat so milk will keep coming in. If she gets little to no food, she will have little to no milk. The specific outdoor peril is that people inadvertently kill kitties when they close up entranceways. An entranceway for kitties can even be very small and a resident might think a cat can't use it, but you might be surprised to know that even larger cats can squeeze into very small openings. In fact, mother cats like small openings and because she assumes her kittens will be safer, she squeezes herself through such a small opening. The entrance area would have to be large enough for her to get through, pregnant, but that is not going to be too big of an opening. Houses sometimes have crawl spaces under them.

Mobile homes have a big area underneath them and they are enclosed at the bottom by skirting. Kitties love such areas.

If an area is quiet, undisturbed, and seems safe, the mother will settle in. She doesn't care if the area is dark, or even dirty (but having kittens on the ground is not ideal). Mom cats usually don't mind the smaller spiders that are in a crawl space or under a home. She may try to kill some of them. Some dangerous spiders live under homes—the Black Widow for one. The Black Widow is not that large. The female has a red spot on her abdomen. There can be several Black Widows in a dark, dank area. They seem to like areas that drip water, and that are moist. A Black Widow could sting a kitten or a mom cat, if a litter of kittens were to be born near where the spider had spun a web. In South-West areas, there can be some scorpions under homes. Tarantulas are rarely seen in most South-West areas. Kittens might see them as playthings, though, if they encounter them.

Quite a few kitties die under houses and mobile homes. It's dark and private and if they're sick or hurt, they'll go under houses or mobile homes to die. Kitties will always hide when they're about to die. They know they need to be unbothered, and alone. They want to be alone. They are weakening and don't want to be disturbed.

Kittens die under homes because of cold or because mom cat was not able to return to them for some reason or other, and so they starve or got too cold. On occasion, they do get sealed or blocked in and can't get out, so they have to die a slow death. The mother may have been out, looking for food and then something happened to her. She could have been run over by a vehicle, killed by a dog, or caught in a trap. (If anyone ever catches a kitty in a trap and it appears she is lactating and has large teats that have been pulled on recently, from suckling, <u>quickly</u> let that kitty go so she can <u>quickly</u> get back to her babies. If the kitty is in a wire-type trap, lift it up high and you can look and see what her teats look like, immediately. You don't have to take the cat out of the trap to inspect the cat's teats—just lift the cage up and carefully look.

If you ever even suspect you have caught a mother cat, let her go. Always double-check the condition of a kitty's teats during the kittening season, which tends to be May through late October, but you should, really, always routinely check a kitty's underside. If a mom cat has kittens, you do not want to catch her and take her away from her kittens. Again, if kittens are living under a home, someone needs to find a home for them when they are old enough, or bring them in to their own home. Keep mom cat with her kittens until they are older, any way you can.

An outdoor kitty of any type can live under a home. Boarding up or blocking an opening that allows kitties to go in and out under a home forces outdoor cats to be out in the open. (You may want to think twice about blocking up the area.) Again, just make <u>positive</u> sure there are no kitties in there before an opening gets blocked up. Having the outdoor kitties be more out in the open can be good if there are people around who want to catch the strays and bring them inside or take them to a shelter. If these outdoor kitties are fed, they'll stay around, and, eventually, they can be caught, taken to see a vet, fixed up, and brought inside to live. Sometimes, a housing complex management catches loose kitties around the complex if the kitties aren't wearing collars, and they take them to the local pound or to a shelter. Many of these kitties end out being euthanized and that is a fact. Most outdoor kitties are hard to place. Sometimes, neighbors will do this, too, and they can even capture your own kitty, if you put your kitty outdoors. Your kitty will be missing, and they may or may not tell you what happened. They may not even know it was your kitty that they captured and took to the pound or shelter. You may not even know those neighbors.

These kitty capturers will sometimes use, as an excuse, that the kitties mess up their garden, but really, it's so easy to clean up a fecal-laden garden. You just use an old pair of kitchen tongs. I use old tongs and it all goes real fast. And, it isn't that hard to put a litter box with litter in it out on a porch or patio, either. Potential kitty capturers <u>could</u> decide to do both these things, instead of taking kitties to a pound or shelter. When outdoor kitties that are considered stray or feral are taken in to pounds or shelters, they're often put to sleep. The ones that make it through to adoption are more apt to be the abandoned pets or the kittens.

I get upset with short-sighted people who keep kitties around a property area that is fairly large (with acreage), for the express purpose of using the kitties to kill the mice or certain small animals that are in the vicinity. I call these kitties Acreage Kitties or Cats. Usually, it is men who are behind this decision. Kitties are put outside and some of them aren't even spayed or neutered. Some are, though, but usually, the owners don't really care about the kitties all that much. All the kitties are to them is 'background' and they hardly give the kitties any thought. They just want to get rid of the mice or certain of the small animals that they see as problematic for them, for some reason or another. Some of these people don't even feed these kitties, or they feed them very little.

I encountered a man who put some cats outside of his rather large place (where auction goods were brought in and then sold) and he said to me (not knowing I was writing this book), "well, if the coyotes get them (i.e.

his mouser cats), that's life. That's just the way it goes. I figure, it's nature." Some coyotes had even recently killed some of the cats there and he was quite uncaring about it. He had another, second home elsewhere, and he put some cats outside there, too. The areas where his two places were, were both 'country-ish'. I tried to tell him about some of the perils but he wasn't open to listening to the points I made or hearing what I was saying because he wanted to keep the 'utilitarian' cats outside. Period. And that was that, with him. He wasn't all that busy to not have the time to think about these issues, either, so he knew what was going on and that cats were being eaten by coyotes. He did not want to take time out to care. If only he'd wanted to. I suspect he only kept the cats around to impress the women buyers, too, so they'd think he was a good person who liked cats and so they would keep coming back, to buy items there. The real truth is that he couldn't have liked cats very much or very sincerely because his overall view about cats was so deficient and limited and he knew cats were getting picked off by coyotes.

There are a lot of people out there who are like that man is. If an outdoor cat gets killed, so be it. They don't care. It's nature, so they erroneously think. It isn't nature at all because the odds are well stacked against the kitties when they are forced to be outside in a dangerous environment. It isn't nature because kitties are <u>not</u> wild animals. A wild animal is a skunk, a raccoon, a porcupine, et al. Kitties are tame now and were bred down to be loving and faithful friends and companion animals. But what can you tell someone who will not listen? Nothing, is the answer to that question. Whatever you say doesn't ever register with some people. They've set their mind against listening, and against receiving what you have to say. It's really a waste of words but you have to <u>try</u> to reach people and just hope that something you say will eventually get through to them.

One thing for sure, people have to want to change. These resistant, closed-minded types usually take no blame, when really some things are their fault. In this case, it was his fault that a number of the kitties got killed and continued to be killed. Many people harden their hearts about many things. It's too bad this happens when it brings harm to innocent animals. On the other hand, there have been many men who would only keep kitties inside and they are all for kitties. They do not want kitties to have to die young, or die at any age, outside. There are the two extremes but more people are going in the direction of the cat protector.

People who own farms, ranches, auto salvage yards, and big land areas for some kind of business often put cats out and they have this 'que sera, sera' or 'so what' attitude about the cats. They could have learned to be this way from their own parents. Kitties have suffered so much over the years because of lack of caring. I hope that information about outdoor perils goes out to as many of these kinds of people as possible so they can see into the situation more inclusively. Some will listen and change and some won't. I don't want kitties to be hurt. Some pet stores and animal shelters won't now sell or adopt out a kitty if they know the kitty is going to be used for catching mice and small animals. Getting kitties to catch mice, etc., just isn't a very loving reason for adopting a kitty. In some cases, it's an ignorant reason because some people do not realize so many perils are outside. Again, the mice and small animals the kitties catch and get rid of can even be carriers of parasites and/or diseases that the kitties can easily pick up.

In past years, kitties killed mice and even rats, but just because kitties were used as mousers and ratters in the past doesn't make it right for them to be used as mousers and ratters in the present. We have progressed, as people. Again, some rats have killed kitties so don't expect kitties to kill or get rid of some of the rats that are around. Some rats are extremely large. Find a way to kill or get rid of the rats yourself and don't even use cats. Use a rat poison (put in a very safe place), or better still, be humane and catch the rats in humane traps. Rats can actually be euthanized, or they can be taken elsewhere and dumped...maybe? If they're dumped somewhere, the area has to be a humane area for them so they can go on living (in a habitat conducive to them). It shouldn't be near any human populations, either.

Some people just dump their kitties outside and use as an 'excuse' that they're mousers, etc. There may be no mice around, or but a rare one around, but they have to come up with some kind of an excuse for putting the kitty outside because they don't want to take care of an indoor cat. Some people have several cats, and they're all mousers. Their kitties could be indoor kitties, especially in this day and age, but the owners of the kitties don't want the extra trouble. Some rural dwellers, be they farmers or not, don't even bother to have their kitties altered. You'd think they'd at least do that, and go that humane route, but some don't. And again, do they even really need to have kitties as mousers or ratters? Probably not. There are other ways, these days, to get rid of mice and rats.

When a trusting or almost-trusting kitty is dumped outside, their behavior usually changes. They become skittish around humans. If the caretaker brings them in from time to time, they may be okay around the caretaker (at least, initially), but if the caretaker doesn't do that, the kitty will likely want to stay away from humans. There are some exceptions to this, but not many. A few kitties may remain as they were, but they're the exception rather than the rule. Kitties change after they've been outside for a long enough period of time. They learn bad and undesired behaviors. They learn to fear and become fearful. Kitties just aren't safe outside, ever—that's the point. Whether they're friendly, partly friendly, or fearful, they are not safe outside.

Granted, some kitties are not dumped outside, per se, they're put outside most or all of the time, and given food. Their owner does not have much of a bond with them. The owner will consider the cat to be his or hers because they feed the kitty, but that's really all they do. Some microchipped kitties are put outside, but a kitty can get lost and even die. No one can check a microchip if the outdoor kitty is not taken in to a vet clinic or a shelter. One cat named Dopey was lost for six years. Someone who lived forty miles from Dopey's home found him and took him in, had him for six years, died, and then Dopey was taken in to a shelter, whereupon Dopey's first owner was found because of a microchip and Dopey was returned to his first home. This made the News early July of 2009.

Kitties need to be inside where they'll be safe and receive day-to-day love and attention. To say, "well if something gets them, then it does" is way too passive and uncaring. It's really animal neglect bordering on abuse. It's way too 'ho hum'. Some people just shouldn't be allowed to have kitties. They are cold or lukewarm only, in their attitude about pet care and pet protection. They can change, though, and thankfully, many do.

Kitties that live in other countries besides America are vulnerable to many of the same perils that exist in America. But every area around the world has different perils, too. There are some areas around the world that are just too dangerous for domestic kitties and there are few, if any, kitties in those areas. (They all die or get killed. Some of them are eaten.) I wouldn't want to encourage people in certain areas of certain countries to ever have domestic kitties, especially if they plan to let them go outside. Many put/ keep their kitties outside, and may rarely even feed them. When the kitties are forced to roam around for food, they encounter a peril that will often take their life. Where there are lots of poisonous spiders and snakes, crocodiles, alligators, and dangerous, wild animals, kitties should not be. Where there are dangerous people, kitties should not be.

Countries where there is war going on should get their dogs and cats over to a safer area, possibly a border country that is not at war. (They should (and do) get themselves there, too.) Some cannot do this. A war is awful as far as pets are concerned. Guns and other weapons, bombs, land mines, grenades, tanks, etc. are not good for kitties to have to be around. Kitties in these upheaval and dangerous areas should be kept inside, but the trouble is, they aren't, and sometimes can't be. They're put outside, or are abandoned to the out-of-doors. Many of these kitties starve to death. Few are even fed. Most are fed very little, if anything at all. Again, many of them get eaten. Many war-torn or highly factious countries usually have no humane-type of organizations around, either. There might be some help but there wouldn't be enough help for the country's kitties.

What is a sad plight for dumped kitties is that outdoor kitties become solo kitties. Most outdoor cats don't hang out together all that much, if there is a fight for food. Sometimes, you'll see them together, at a place where food might be put out because they are waiting for the food and they know there is enough food for all of them, but after they eat, and they will sometimes take turns eating, they will split up and go a separate way. If there is enough food for all the cats at a feeding area, there won't be any fighting, usually (with an occasional exception). Cats that are siblings may stay in the same area together, as may a mother cat with kitties she birthed and raised. Otherwise, kitties have an independence and go their separate way. There is more apt to be acceptance of other kitties when the cats can all depend on getting enough food. If there are issues because there isn't enough food for all the cats that frequent a feeding area, there could be some actual fighting, which is when outsiders can misperceive that the kitties are wild and feral. <u>Feral, in my view is a misnomer—it is a wrong word application for describing cats.</u> <u>The word gets misapplied.</u> (I cover feral cats more in Chapter 9, near the end of this book.) I feel this way because I know that <u>all feral cats can be rescued and tamed, by degrees.</u>

Outdoor kitties of any kind tend to live solo and be solo but they do group together at feeding sites. There are some exceptions, but not that many. Kitties may have blood relatives in the neighborhood and they tend to be closer. I've been feeding outdoor strays for a long time (thirty plus years) and when there are a lot of them, they come in close to the feeding area one or two at a time while the others wait their turn. Occasionally, I hear cat fights or screeching outside by the feeding area because one kitty came in too close while another one was intending to eat or was eating. Only one or two kitties get that bossy, but even so, flare-ups are rare if they always get food.

<u>Outdoor kitties are lonely kitties.</u> Most are isolated, and they can't be all that happy. They're under constant stress, about this and that. They're happy when they are in a stable and secure environment, indoors, being cared for by a human caretaker. It's always good if there are two kitties, too. Then

they'll always feel like company is around. Kitties get into a routine. They come to depend on a general routine. They surely don't need to live outside to be happy, which is what some people erroneously believe. They're happy inside because their needs are always met and they don't have to be afraid all the time. They know they're safe inside, and they know they'll always have decent food and water, inside. When two or more kitties are always inside, and there is always food and water, there usually are no fights, for the most part. Outside, though, it is a different world. Male cats will fight over mating rights if a female is in heat, too.

<u>What I find very, very sad about kitties being outdoors is that they are kept from giving and receiving love</u> (to a human and from a human). As previously noted, kitties will gradually become more and more skittish and fearful around humans the longer they've been forced to be outside. They become this way because they instinctively want to live and survive and they do not know for sure, anymore, if a particular human is a friend or foe. So, they develop an approach-avoidance conflict, as well they should because some humans are very definitely a foe. Outdoor kitties have very little actual contact with humans and some have no contact at all. Such a kitty will rarely (or never) encounter human love, unless the kitty is an indoor/outdoor kitty that has a part-time home. I write more about the indoor /outdoor kitty problems in several CATegories of my *I Care for My Cats* book. For the most part, the problems for indoor/outdoor kitties parallel the problems that stray and feral kitties encounter.

If your own kitty is outside a lot, what will happen is that, whereas once your kitty was not afraid of you and always let you pick him or her up, your kitty can become alienated from you, may not let you pick him or her up, and may even run away from you and not let you catch him or her. What is the point of having a pet if you aren't continually bonded with the pet and don't continually see the pet and enjoy the pet? Keeping your kitty indoors prevents this gradual alienation from happening. Most people want to share their home with their kitty. They move heaven and earth so their kitty will be as a family member inside the home.

There are people out there who let their kitty go outside when they could easily keep the kitty inside. Some kitties may act like they want to go outside but don't play into that and don't ever let them. They'll get the idea. And they'll settle down and accept being closed in. As long as you're around, taking care of them, they'll be secure inside the home. All a caretaker has to do is keep saying no to a kitty if a kitty wants to go outside, and, of course, make the inside environment for the kitty a pleasant one because that will also cause a kitty to want to stay inside. The kitty must be altered, too. That is essential. Absolutely.

Quite a few of the people who put their kitty outside—perhaps all of them—secretly don't want to a) buy any litter, b) buy very much litter, c) change any litter and d) change litter all that often. If you get a kitty, it should stay inside and you will need to get litter, consistently, and you will have to change it, consistently. Everyone else does. I've never met anyone who complains about any of that. None of it is that hard to carry out and the clay litter is inexpensive and you can de-clump it so it will last longer. Clearly, there are way too many perils outside. You'll have way more vet bills if your kitty is put outside, and furthermore, statistics reveal that the kitty won't live near as long as it would have, had it always been inside.

Any kitty that goes outside, even for a sun rest, should be supervised by the caretaker who should also be outside with the kitty at the same time but even doing that can be perilous and a danger. The kitty may not stay around. (Kitties really don't need to be out in the sun. Let them rest next to a sunny window.) Any cat, outside, even with their caretaker there, can run away if it is not on a leash with a halter. Or, something in the immediate environment can be a peril—like poison, dangerous-to-eat plants, snakes, poisonous insects, et al. A dangerous dog could come by if a kitty isn't in a fenced area and could chase the kitty away or hurt the kitty. To be clear, even fences aren't enough to contain a kitty. Kitties can spring-jump very high (whereas dogs cannot do that). If someone says they have a fenced yard and they let the kitty go outside because they think the kitty is safe, they are deluding themselves. They have to know the kitty goes roaming. Deep down, they know they are putting their kitty at risk. They really do know that.

When kitties are forced to live outside, especially if they aren't given any food, they essentially have to live like wild animals do, yet they're very small and are domesticated animals and they really don't do well outside. They're small prey to bigger animals in the wild and if they live around people, they are more often killed by dogs than people realize. Quite a few people have dogs. Dogs will drive kitties away from food, too, because dogs will eat food put out for kitties and will drink their water—fast and sometimes down to the bottom of the water dish. They'll sometimes leave their water very dirty, too. Unless someone is always putting water out, there are usually very few clean water sources for outdoor kitties. Sometimes, there's none. Always keep their water clean.

Kitties don't realize all the dangers outside. If they've never been outside, they don't know what is out there. Kitties that have been outside may try to scoot out when they are inside. A scooting-out problem can become very irritating for a caretaker. I once had a scooter, and I had to gradually train the kitty to not scoot out. It's stress when a kitty scoots out when you open the door, especially when it gets outside. You have to go out and get the kitty, every time. You have to be careful around the front or back door until the kitty finally gets it.

When any doors are open, watch the floor area for the kitty wanting to go outside. Do not leave a door open for very long, especially if your eyes are turned away from the area. Some people leave the door open when they get things out of their car, as the groceries. I never do. I put my grocery sacks by the door, and then I quickly put them inside on the floor while I look around for that one kitty. If I have lots of grocery sacks, I do this several times. The door is closed until I put several of them in, i.e., put the ones in that I already placed by the door.

If an indoor/outdoor kitty is outside some or all of the time, what will happen if the kitty needs vet care? If a kitty is hurt, they may go off somewhere, to die. This is what kitties do, if they're really hurt or ill. I ran into one woman recently who kept her several cats outside and I could tell by talking with her that she had no intention of providing the cats with vet care. Also, by keeping her cats outside, she was causing the cats to need extra, additional vet care because to maintain outdoor kitties, vet care costs, all cum, are much higher. She was also increasing the cat's chances of suffering or dying because of all the outdoor perils. In essence, the cats weren't really 'her' cats in the fullest sense of the word. They were hers on the surface but they weren't getting full and adequate care. She put food out for them (which is a good thing), but to feed them was only partial and minimal care. The young woman acted so smug and proud of herself, too, because she was feeding some kitties that she claimed were her kitties, and I thought, "my, how can I reach this person without alienating her". She was only being responsible for the kitties, in part.

When kitties are outside, you can monitor their health, assuming you see them when you feed them. If anything is wrong with them, you can take them to see a vet, assuming you can pick them up. If you put food out at random times, you may not see them. If you put food out at specific times, they may be there waiting for you so you will see them then, and can look them over for obvious medical problems and even for some not-so-obvious ones. Kitties should have occasional general check-ups by a vet, though, and strays and feral cats never get this. Even some indoor/outdoor kitties don't get this. Some do, though.

I've heard of people putting a sick kitty outside because they didn't want to care for the cat and pay for vet care. This kind of thing is actually a criminal offense. If the kitty has something infectious, other kitties that are outside will be exposed. Also, the kitty will be too weak to defend itself from certain perils. Being ill, the kitty will suffer and likely die so it is animal abuse to put a sick cat outside. If you have absolutely no other choice, take the kitty to a pound or an animal shelter. However, the kitty may end out being euthanized, but it will depend on what the medical problem is. Some medical problems aren't too hard to fix. Others are. The kitty will, at least, be diagnosed by a vet when they enter the pound or animal shelter. Some people don't have much money to pay for vet care (or they don't think they do, even though they might—but keep in mind that vet-related costs have gone up). Ideally, and what would be best, is that you should try to get vet care for the suffering kitty. All sick animals suffer. It's just like us—we suffer when we are sick. And, we're worried and sad when we know we are sick and especially if we know we are dying. (Does this make you think of the coronavirus deaths? So many people had to die in isolation—very sad.

All kitties deserve to live indoors, all the time, with loving, caring, responsible, caretakers. <u>It is kind to take more complete care of outdoor kitties, in as much as is possible. It is kind to adopt kitties from rescues or shelters. It is kind to bring in and keep kitties inside, or to bring them in and find homes for them, where they'll be kept indoors. There is 'kind' and there is 'kinder'. There is partial kind and there is more complete kind.</u> It is kind to feed outdoor cats and to take sick or hurt ones to a pound or shelter but it is kinder to oversee their vet needs yourself and to bring outdoor kitties into your own home or find a good home for any that you can.

Ever since kitty litter was first manufactured in America in the middle 1940s, more and more people have been keeping their kitties indoors. Since kitties are now domesticated and are so small, they aren't able to adapt to the rigors of the outdoors, very well. <u>If kitties had stayed as bigger cats living in the wild (the wilderness cats), they would have been able to adapt to outdoor rigors but we made them smaller, weaker, and gentler, over a period of time. In short, we domesticated them and so they should not be left outside. As with domesticated dogs, they are not wild animals. It is our responsibility to take care of them.</u>

They live about two-thirds less long, on average, when they are forced to live outside. It could be even less than that. It depends on the country, and the neighborhood.

9

Lack of Available Food/The Need for Homes

<u>Kitties cannot take care of themselves, on their own, outside—not well enough, and not for very long.</u> For one thing, <u>food is not very plentiful outside for domestic kitties.</u> <u>People think it is, but it isn't.</u> A scarcity of mice is one example of this, and the few mice that are around are hard for kitties to find, in most areas. Birds are not that easy for kitties to catch, which is contrary to the general opinion circulating about the subject. Birds fly away very fast. Sometimes, kitties can catch wounded or baby birds, but it isn't that easy to get the older birds that are able to fly. Most kitties that are stuck outside never get enough food on their own. God help them if they have kittens and no one has been or is feeding the mother.

Kitties will climb trees to get birds, but they don't like climbing trees. I've heard of them even climbing up telephone poles to get a bird. Then, the bird flies away and the kitty gets stuck and they aren't able to climb down the rather tall pole. (Call the firemen.) But some kitties don't ever venture up trees to get birds. They're smart enough to avoid what could be a problem for them. It does, somewhat, depend on the tree. Not all trees are that approachable for kitties. Some kitties can't always get down trees very well (or at all) so they don't climb trees to get birds. Some bird's nests are very high or in types of trees that kitties cannot climb or do not dare climb. Birds that live in cactus in the South-West are protected from outdoor kitties (unless young birds fall out on the ground). But, there are birds in conifers and deciduous trees in desert areas so desert kitties might try to go after those birds. They may not be successful, though. Also, some desert trees are thorny.

Any birds a kitty might get are usually very small, anyway, and, of course, they're loaded with feathers. Kitties do not like to eat feathers and they may just leave the bird without eating it. If they eat the part of the bird that has shorter feathers, when you subtract the bird meat from the bird bones, that isn't much of a meal for a kitty. As noted before, birds carry disease (inside of them), too. If they've eaten certain insects that carry disease, then all that goes into the cat when the cat eats any part of the bird.

Birds can make kitties be prey, too, and bigger ones do. Birds, if they see kitties, will swoop down and get them in their talons and carry them off. They'll become their food, and food for their babies in a nest somewhere, if they have babies. Kittens are definitely easy prey. Some birds will attack kittens that are right on the ground, especially if the mother has temporarily left. One bird, found in the South-Western United States—the Roadrunner— finds its food on the ground. It eats meat rather often. Many a kitten, born outside, has been food for a Roadrunner, which is a fairly good-sized bird when it is full grown. Kitties won't necessarily find that this bird will be their prey. Its beak is its protection. Many birds peck their prey to death, in fact, which is an awful way to die. They go for the head.

Again, kitties shouldn't really be eating birds. There can be insects on a bird that can bring harm to a kitty. Even just one insect can bring harm to a kitty if it is ingested. When a kitty comes upon a larger insect, directly, sometimes only parts of the insect get eaten by the kitty because often the kitty just wants to kill the insect. Sometimes, they just break the insect up into pieces. Kitties may or may not eat the insect. But, oftentimes, they do eat the insect, and again, insects can be carriers of germs, parasites, and even viruses. Also, insects surely don't offer a kitty much substance and doesn't fill their empty stomach. A number of insect types sting or bite and can put in poison, too, so kitty could be greatly harmed and be incapable of preying on anything for a while, or even forever, if it dies.

Kitties are not good at catching animals much larger than mice, and how many of those-sized animals are out there for them. Not that many. They can't kill foxes or raccoons or skunks or small armadillos, though dogs can, but there aren't too many feral dogs, only the more domesticated dogs. Dogs can't survive out in the wild, or outdoors—not for long. Nor can kitties. Animals in the wild will hurt them, with their bites, claws, and hooves, although, no kitty will try to tackle an animal with hooves.

So, <u>there is little food for outdoor kitties unless kind-hearted people feed them.</u> Food is scarce outside for kitties, it truly is. Large cats in the wild are big enough to hunt larger, meatier animals, but, to emphasize, <u>our domestic kitties have been domesticated down to be so small that they are more limited in their finding food that is outside and finding it on their own.</u> Kitties can catch and eat certain insects but again, insects are not very substantive and they hardly fill a kitty's hunger needs. If there is a river or lake, kitties don't like water and so fish are out. Kitties don't generally eat frogs (or toads), but they'll practice their hunting skills and will catch them. Their hunting skills do kitties little good, in the main. They'll do the same with turtles, and they will play with them and turn them over and over, but they won't eat them.

So, there's no food there, either. <u>The little food kitties can get on their own must taste pretty bad, too, and again, it can be very hard for them to get to.</u>

Rodents, lizards, salamanders, crawdads, snails and slugs, small non-poisonous snakes (and again, kitties can't tell which ones are poisonous and which aren't), are, in some cases, hard to catch, and they generally aren't that easy to eat or that tasty to eat. They can't get to turtles, and frogs certainly aren't preferred as food and insects are not ample as food. We know that cat food tastes good to kitties, but stray and feral kitties do not ordinarily get any commercially-manufactured cat food. Commercial cat food is sanitary to eat, too. Usually, these small animals that outdoor cats eat are not sanitary, including the waste matter that is still in their bodies, which is something that is not allowed in commercial cat food.

If stray or feral kitties that are outside ever do get to commercial cat food that someone has put out for their own outdoor cat, that food loses its freshness really fast if it sits around too long. Warm or hot air dries it out. Moisture from rainy weather or humidity can moisten dry cat food and cause bacteria to quickly grow in it if it is out too long. Usually, though, it gets eaten up fast. For anyone who feeds their outdoor kitty by putting food outside for the kitty, realize that other kitties may come around and eat from the dish of food (or drink from the dish of water). Then, what is the owner's kitty to eat? Frankly, some outdoor kitties nearly starve and will get real thin because food is not available for them. In some areas, kitties slowly starve to death. Some kitties actually die of starvation and nobody even realizes it. Also, when they get weak, a predator can get them so the fact that they were starving gets masked. Many kitties that are outside come to this end.

Yes, the food can lose its freshness and yes, other kitties can come by and eat the food but I'm not indicating that food should <u>not</u> be left out for kitties—not even close. In fact, if food is put out, a container or bowl of it should go out in the morning—a container or bowl inside of a flat pan that has water below the level of the container or bowl of food so no ants can get to the food. Then, at night, a container or bowl of food should be put out. If you are feeding quite a few stray and feral cats, you may want to put food out around early sundown, and then some more right before you retire for the evening. If, in the morning, the food is always gone, then you will want to put out more food at night, from then on. You will always want to come out and see at least a little food left in the container or bowl so you'll know that the outdoor kitties in your vicinity were able to eat their fill.

Anything moist, don't put out during real warm days because flies are going to be all over it. Flies especially like wet food. Even dry food during the day will draw some flies. You can put the food under a stairway or a piece of patio furniture and the flies won't see it but the kitties will find it. Flies, and ants, when the weather is warmer, can't be totally avoided (but again, if you can set the container or bowl of food underneath something (and in a pie tin with water), there will be few to no flies landing on the dry food because the flies cannot see the food, and there will be no ants on the food.)

For quite a few months, flies can be problem for the outdoor kitties. This is why you have to be careful where you set the dish and why you only want to put out commercial <u>dry</u> food. Flies can deposit eggs in the food, particularly in the moist or wet food, and the kitty can ingest those eggs. Monitor the amount of food you put out during the day if you are home, but, again, only put dry food out during the day—never wet food. (Keep in mind that flies do not come around at night, but the ants might.) Only dry food is ever needed for kitties, really—day and night. It fills kitties up fast and has good nutrients, etc.. It has everything in it that kitties need, whereas human food does not.

At night, especially, but also during the day, outdoor kitties will roam and they go around looking for any and all food sites (and for the best food sites, when they can). They roam because they want to know where all the food sites are, just in case they ever need to eat at one of the sites. If food gets eaten at one site (by other kitties), then they'll know to go to another site for a feeding. It's first come, first served, at these feeding sites and there aren't usually that many of these sites around. Even if they eat at one site, they may still roam around until they find other sites. They want to learn where they all are. If a contesting kitty is at one site (and there can be occasional cat fights at these sites), one kitty may be chased away and even attacked. Some outdoor kitties will even hang around a food site; they may or may not want to share the food. If food has been scarce, there can be occasional tooth and claw fights or at least, a chasing away (both during the night and during the day). This is why knowing about more than one feeding site is important to outdoor kitties. Kitties that were chased away will likely return to a feeding site a little later, hoping there will still be some food and that the chaser cat is gone.

Kitties roam around at night because it is quieter at night (and so they can hear danger noises). It is also cooler and they don't have to get over-heated (assuming the days are hot). Depending on their locality or environment, night-time for kitties might be safer, at least regarding some perils (but certainly not all of them).

Most perils for cats are around day and night. Certain ones are around day and night, certain ones are around either during the day or during the night (but not both), and certain ones are around at random times. There might be quite a few around in one area but quite a few in another area. This can shift, though, and go either way. The bottom line is that there will always be outdoor perils out there and kitties are never really safe and will always need human protection. Will more people help them?

Putting food out for kitties will help to protect them (but not entirely). Obviously, if you put food out for stray and feral cats, you should put water out for them, too. Strays and outdoor kitties have trouble finding decent water and they have more trouble finding water when it's hot outside. The water level goes down faster when it is hot and dry. It will completely evaporate. Any water receptacles have to be filled more often. I always have three good-sized containers out for the stray and feral cats. They are forty ounce ex-ice cream tubs. They work quite well. Sometimes, one of them gets knocked over, so it's good if there are extra ones. Windy conditions can put blown particles into the water and they can all add up and water can get dirty and need changing. There is also apt to be food particles that build up in the water because kitties are drinking from the water container after they have eaten. Particles get in there because they are in the mouth or outside the mouth of the cats that eat the food and drink the water. Eventually, in other words, water gets dirty and bacteria can start to build up on the inside of the container and on top of the water. A scum can begin to develop around the inside of the container. The water <u>has</u> to periodically be changed. Scum can build up on the bottom and that needs to be washed out and not just rinsed out. It has to be wiped out with a soapy sponge or dishcloth.

All kitties love good water and they should drink fresh water, every day. Cats can survive without food longer than people realize, but this is not so, if they have no water. A ten percent water loss in a cat's body can be fatal. Some cats can live two to three weeks without food before problems set in (or so it's been said but I would say it takes less time than that); starvation wouldn't be all that far away, in other words. A cat can lose around forty percent of it body weight and still be alive. Lack of water can cause a number of problems. A cat that has little access to food will want to drink as much water as they can. The water will help to fill their stomach.

If you feed outdoor kitties, and neighbors on the side where you feed them complain about the cats in the neighborhood, you may need to consider putting the food and water over to the other side of the home from where those neighbors are. You should be going out, on occasion, and picking up any of their leavings or stools with an old pair of tongs (and then stapling them up in a bag) so the neighbors won't be so apt to complain.

Again, there are ways the food you put out can be shielded from sun, rain, wind, and most all flying pests. Use your ingenuity to figure out how to protect the food. Putting the food and water under a patio chair or table is but one way to protect it. If one of the kitties you feed is claimed as your own, I'm not sure that any neighborhood complaints about your putting food and water out can hold up. If one of the kitties you claim as your own ever does anything that causes legitimate (versus illegitimate) complaining, the local pound might be able to take the kitty away from you, unless you were to bring the kitty inside. Depending on what the kitty had done will determine whether or not the local pound can take the kitty away. In any event, you want to avoid neighborhood complaints. You want to try to work with the neighbors and get along with them. You hope they will join in on the cause to rescue outdoor kitties. Some of them will.

No kitty should ever be translocated and have to go to a strange area. They don't know a new area. No one in the area knows them (as being a neighborhood cat). There may be no food for them in the new area and this would be the biggest problem. Whereas there could have been food out for them at the previous area, the likelihood of them finding food in the new area may not be good. They could get run over, too, trying to find their old environment (so they can find food there and so they can become 'unlost'). Some people have been known to take a kitty from their area and dump it in another. They may even dump the kitty in a nicer neighborhood. This is not a good idea. Just take the kitty to the pound or shelter, instead, or leave the kitty be if you know it is getting food and water and you are not able to take the kitty in.

Again, if there are kitty leavings on your property or lot, go out and put them in a bag, promptly, so there will be no smells. This takes very little time to do, and old tongs work really well for this task. Neighbors are certainly at liberty to put a slam trap out, and capture any outdoor kitties and take them to a local pound or shelter. (Some will cruelly take them to a neighborhood fairly far away and dump them there, and again, this will cause the transplanted kitty to be under great stress and furthermore, the kitty may not be able to find any food or water in the new area so the deed done was a really bad one. It could be considered a cruel one. Some people have been known to dump a kitty out on the desert—that is really cruel. Anyone can take a stray kitty to a pound or shelter. You will never know if they will be euthanized, though. It's almost guaranteed that some will be euthanized. The best thing you can do when it comes to outdoor kitties you believe to be strays or feral cats is to trap them yourself, take them to a vet, and get them altered, and then release them back to the same exact area where they were captured, or, better still, keep them yourself and keep them indoors. All kitties should be indoor-only.

One couple I know had an extension built on to their home. It enclosed all the stray and feral kitties that came around. Therefore, the kitties stayed in one area. Litter boxes were put in the extension and the kitties got used to using them. One by one, the kitties were altered. This worked out because the wife was home all the time and wasn't working, but it could have worked out even if she had been working, full or part time. It is good that people trap and then return kitties to the area they came from, or set up a separate, enclosed area for strays and feral cats like these people did and then get them fixed up. It is very chancy to take such kitties to a do-kill shelter. In fact, it could be a danger for the kitties, like all the other perils are. They may be euthanized there. They may especially be if they are stray or feral and not owner-relinquished kitties.

When neighbors trap a kitty and take it to a do-kill shelter (sometimes no-kill shelters won't have room for them or may not want to take them), the kitty's life will very possibly be terminated, and terminated soon. Frankly, one reason the average age of outdoor stray and feral kitties is as low as it is because of this trapping and then taking them in to a do-kill shelter. The outdoor stray and feral kitties do not always pass entrance tests at pounds and shelters. Some of them do not pass the temperament test because they are skittish, and, at time, hostile. And, they can have too many medical issues, as well. The kitties are euthanized, and can even be put down that very day, depending on the situation.

Once, I made the mistake of taking two stray kitties to the local pound and felt so bad about it that I returned before they closed so I could get the two kitties back, but someone told me they had already euthanized them. Wow. You could have knocked me over with a feather. I was sad (and mad) for days. This occurred before I had learned certain key, essential bits of knowledge, but I will forever feel responsible, and badly. I had been told they always held kitties for at least two or three days, so I had somehow been duped. In truth, if certain places get too many kitties, they might euthanize some of them that very day, but, they do not let that information get out. They should, though, since it is true. They don't let a lot of their secrets out, but that is all right. They are actually running a business (of sorts), even though most shelters receive some government funding. The local pounds are supposed to be public service, like libraries are. If the pound decides that a kitty is sick, they may euthanize that same day, too, even if they have room for it. Some of the kitties get medical care but not all of them do.

Usually, if a kitty is a stray, they are supposed to hold the kitty for a few days in case the kitty had an owner and the owner shows up (but this time, they didn't do that, which I thought was quite odd). If you relinquish your own kitty, they may not wait so long to euthanize the kitty, either (particularly if they don't have much room), since no one needs to take time out to find the kitty. They do what they believe is best and what they believe they have to do as different situations come into being. There are quite a few things that the pound, and certain animal shelters do not want the public to know. (Some of the workers don't always know about some of the decisions.) It is possible, though, that the two kitties I brought in were not euthanized and that the employee was mistaken. Many kitties look like other kitties and it is easy for employees to get confused in their thinking. I hope that was the case.

The point here is this, do not always assume a kitty you leave at a pound or shelter is going to pass their entrance tests and end out being adopted. They may not be. They may not get through. The place may be overly filled up, too. They may be euthanized and be euthanized faster than you had expected. Also, shelters don't always do things the same way as other shelters do so don't assume that just because one shelter has certain policies that other shelters will, too. Some shelters can 'improvise' behind the scenes, too, so their policies may not <u>always</u> be what is adhered to. They may generally be adhered to, but not always (oftentimes because of what is necessary or what they believe to be necessary).

People think that if they put out one dish of food a day for their outdoor kitty that this is all they have to do, but that is not enough because other kitties come around and eat the food. Besides, kitties tend to eat small amounts of food throughout the day and the night. Because of this grazing pattern, if other kitties, or dogs, come by and eat their food, they will then be hungry for long periods of time if the dish is empty and if no food is out for them. This is not good and is another reason why kitties should be indoors, all the time. If a kitty is younger and smaller, and a larger kitty comes around the food area expecting food, the older kitty might chase the younger kitty away. They usually don't, but they could and so younger and smaller kitties get very skittish around feeding areas. They suspect they might be in danger, by just being there. They know to wait their turn. Usually, though, the older kitties leave the younger, smaller kitties alone, but the younger ones usually have to wait until the older ones leave.

Kitties outside get lots of exercise—sometimes too much exercise—and this is another reason why the food goes fast. Some kitties you put food out for may initially come in, starving. If you feed these unfortunates, you'll be saving their lives. You can occasionally put your human-food leftovers out for them, too—certain of it—but dry cat food is so very filling for them, and nutritional, in that it is formulated for kitties to eat. Putting out your leftovers should only be supplemental and they should be eating dry cat food, day and night. As noted before, always cut up any leftovers into small bits, too, and don't put out anything that has bones.

Wild animals can come by and eat the food that is put out, too, depending on the area. These animals can be small, medium, or large-sized animals. Marauder dogs can come by and gobble up the food very fast. Even birds will come by and eat dry cat food bits. I've seen this happen, myself. You may not even know if your own outdoor kitty is getting any food (if you put a kitty outside) because you won't see what happens to the food. You'll be inside. You'll just have to keep putting more food out to make sure your kitty gets to eat and that any kitties that come by are getting enough food.

If food is put out for pets, in areas where there are wild animals, you may have to let the pets eat their fill and then bring in the dish. Don't leave the dish outside—not for long. Keep dogs in a chain-linked fence, preferably one that's well built and high enough. Keep kitties inside—for sure—if dangerous wild animals come around. Try hard to bring in any stray or feral cats and find homes for them. Don't let pets roam free, either. Dangerous wild animals can get them. Best to well cover and insulate any garbage left outside. Wait until the morning of any garbage collection to put house garbage outside, if you can. Don't feed the wildlife, either, or they'll keep coming around. They can kill any outdoor pets. They can kill you. Don't approach the wildlife. It's all right to admire wildlife from a distance but best stay clear. A barking dog can incite some animals, and cause them to attack, particularly if the dog is smaller than they are.

Whether urban or rural, people often put the dry cat food outside at a time when they don't see their outdoor kitty in view, and God only knows how long it will be before the kitty comes around to eat. If it rains, dry food gets soggy, but outdoor kitties will still eat the food because they get hungry. If sun shines on the food, it loses its flavor real fast. Usually, cat food put outside is eventually eaten. Then, there is no more food. One dish of cat food may not be enough to feed all the outdoor kitties in a neighborhood that come around and your own outdoor kitty could end out starving. The solution to this problem is to bring your kitty inside, permanently. If you do not, enough food has to always be outside for the cat, despite the problems.

If you put leftover human food out for outdoor and stray kitties, make positive sure it is not spoiled or is bad food. People put leftovers out, sometimes because they've been in the refrigerator too long; they may suspect the food may be 'going bad'. Putting such food out is a very bad plan. If bacteria are in the food, kitties will get food poisoning. It's as simple as that. There are different kinds of bacteria that can form. Some make pets (and humans) sicker than others do. Food poisoning can, of course, happen with indoor-only kitties, as well. Never let kitties get to spoiled food, including in the trash. Some food poisonings can cause disorientation and so much pain around the stomach and chest area that walking and being upright is near impossible and even lying down doesn't relieve the pain and discomfort. Food poisoning takes a while to fight and sometimes death can occur because of it. If outdoor kitties get it, they must go off somewhere and grievously suffer. If their body fights it, they will be drained and fatigued (and weak) for at least twenty-four hours, thereafter. <u>A</u>lways <u>B</u>e <u>C</u>areful (ABC) about what you feed or put out for kitties. Some food poisonings only affect kitties in a minor way; other food poisonings can almost kill or can kill a kitty.

<u>If outdoor kitties ever get into your garbage cans or sacks of garbage, which you placed outside for garbage pick-up, do not become hostile towards the kitties for doing this.</u> <u>The kitties are merely trying to avoid starving to death, which is not a nice way to have to die.</u> If you feed these kitties, even just putting a dish of less costly kitty food outside for these forsaken and abandoned kitties will keep them out of the garbage. You can give them more costly food too, if you can afford it. Get a good-sized lidded garbage can, preferably with wheels if you can so animals, and flies, have to stay away from your garbage bin. Some cities supply jumbo garbage containers with wheels, for their residents. This keeps kitties out of the garbage, but outdoor kitties will still need food. Someone has to feed them or they'll starve.

When kitties get into garbage, they are often and almost always hungry. Kitties get into Dumpsters® hoping to find anything to eat. Kitties can get sick from eating outside garbage food. Some kitties get closed inside of Dumpsters®. Occasionally, a kitty will get dumped from a Dumpster® into a garbage truck, which, as you can imagine, is not good for a kitty. Garbage pick-up personnel try to keep their eyes open for kitties and will let the kitties jump out before they continue with their work, if they are able to see the kitty in time, which, sometimes, they don't. Sometimes, the weight and sudden tossing around of heavy garbage bags can be too much for a small kitty, inside of a garbage truck. Never let a kitty be or stay inside of a Dumpster® because the kitty could end out being killed as it is being dumped into the truck and while it is in the truck. Many Dumpsters® have metal or plastic, flap-type lids that open and shut but some businesses or apartment areas keep the lids open, all the time. Dumpsters® are magnets for outdoor kitties.

Some kitties live off of Dumpster® garbage and have no choice in the matter. Sometimes, legless fly larvae, or maggots, are in the garbage, and dirty ole flies are also buzzing all over the place. Outdoor kitties cannot get food when they need it and often go hungry if they can't get into garbage and Dumpsters®. Some get caught in these Dumpsters® on garbage pick-up day. But if people in the neighborhood would put food out for these kitties, they wouldn't be so hungry that they're forced to go in and around garbage places, anywhere.

Kitties even eat bad food that has been sitting in a Dumpster®. Germs multiply fast inside garbage food. Often, there are parasite eggs. Another problem is with regards to fish, chicken, and turkey bones. Outdoor kitties will sometimes get these bones and bone splinters get lodged between their teeth, and, sometimes, they will get lodged in the pharynx, the larynx, and the esophagus and no one can be there to help the kitty when things become so disruptive, bothersome, or painful.

An outdoor kitty can be sick for any number of reasons. On occasion, they get well by themselves and on their own but so often, they don't. If a kitty is sick, it will likely lose some or all of its appetite. It can, then, begin to die if there is no way for it to get well. It can't walk into the vet clinic by itself.

Occasionally, inhumane people put bad food out for kitties, intentionally, including poisonous food. They want to kill kitties. A kitty that eats poisonous food will crawl into a hiding area and die a painful death. Doing this is cruelty to animals. People who do cruel things to animals are marked by

God. God has a long memory. Life is getting hard for everybody. Thoughtless people take their frustrations out on innocent animals.

If a kitty is outside for very long, after a while, they will not let you catch them even if you want to rescue any Dumpster® kitties. They become fearful of everything that moves, including humans, even a human who might want to feed them or help them. If you see any outdoor kitties, put food out for them anyway so they don't have to starve, even if you cannot catch them. For the kitties that eat garbage and get sick, there is never anyone to take care of them. Try to have some compassion for these helpless creatures that 'we' have domesticated for indoor living. Principally, the 'we' refers to you and me. How do you even go about rescuing Dumpster® kitties? It will be a challenge.

Often, a Dumpster® kitty is a pregnant female. She may have no other source of food. Whatever happens to her when she eats from the Dumpster® will affect her kittens. When her kittens are born and become a certain size, they'll be taught to find food in Dumpsters®, too, and this can go on with any litter of kittens that comes after them. Eating out of Dumpsters® can become cyclical and generational. If ever you close a Dumpster® lid, look inside first to see if you notice any kitties.

Occasionally (not always), an outdoor kitty may mark a spot not far from a feeding area, by spraying. Spraying odor doesn't bother me one bit. The odor fades, and rain usually washes it away. Sometimes, I just spray hose water on it if it is ever around the outside of my home. If the spot is re-sprayed by the cat, it still doesn't bother me. I know it's just the way of some and certain cats. They discover food. They want to be the one eating the food. They mark what they want to be their territory and then they hope other cats won't come around for the food, too, but other cats always do. Spraying, for kitties, is like putting up a 'No Trespassing' sign. With humans, they can talk, and, by using their intelligence, they are able to get food. Cats can't talk. They have to spray to let other cats know that if they enter and stay around, they do so at their own risk. It is very easy to wash off the dried spray on the side of an area with hose water. I feed the outdoor kitties, anyway, come what may. I don't care if any of them spray. Whenever I can, I bring them in and fix them up and find them a good home. They do not spray if they have been altered, not usually, and if there is no need for them to be territorial. If they have continual food and water, a nice home and caretaker, they have no need to be territorial.

A kitty without a home is, to relay the obvious, a homeless one and such kitties are on a similar par with homeless humans. In some ways, the two can be related; in other ways, of course, they can't be related. Homelessness causes problems, though, all across the board. Humans need homes. And kitties need homes. It's actually disgraceful that so many kitties do not have homes. Disgraceful is a strong word but it's true. Collectively, we have missed the mark. It's time to rally for the kitty cause and double and triple all efforts.

10

Stress on Pregnant Cats and Kittens/Stray and Feral Cats

Sadly, too many young females forced to live outside are impregnated before they're a year old. Their first heat will be at around five to six months of age, and so around come the tom cats. Before the female's heat is over with, she may have mated up to eight times (and possibly more), which means she may have as many as eight kittens. Often, they'll have around five kittens. The female cat will not yet be fully grown and the kittens will take away from any vitamins and nutrients she may be getting so her own growth will be curtailed. She is likely to end out being a smaller cat, for life, because she had kittens before she was able to reach more maturity and get to be one year of age.

Kittens keep growing until they are a year old and that growth should not be interrupted. At age one year, they are a cat and full grown. We should all want larger, healthier kitties, quite frankly. It is best for the kitties to attain maximum size. No kittens should be born outside, either, but they are. To emphasize, responsible citizens around the world need to take the time/make the time to capture them and bring them in or have them altered, then return them to their previous locale unless they can keep them or find a good home for them, both of which would be the better alternatives. Some outdoor kitties you can find homes for but you may have to work with them first, and give them adequate adjustment and conformity time.

Female cats that are outside and pregnant can suffer miscarriages. This can especially happen if they have to run too fast, too hard, or too far, when they are pregnant. And, of course, they can fall from any height and have trouble landing because they cannot twist and turn as easily as they could, had they not been pregnant. Any kind of accident or trauma can be the reason why one or more of the kittens end out being stillborn, too, when she delivers. An outdoor female kitty may become particularly skittish more so than usual because she thinks that by being so, she is protecting her unborn kittens. If you know there are one or more pregnant females outside, or that there's a litter of kittens somewhere, you should put more food out for them than you usually do. For sure, put out some food so the kitties won't starve. Bring the female in before she has her kittens if you can. Give her a safe place to have her kittens.

Just having to experience stress from having to be outside is problematic for pregnant cats—and all cats, really. Stress brings on mental and physical problems, but, of course, indoor-only kitties can have stress, too. Their stress is just going to be much less. Even little kittens can experience stress and if they are forced to be outside, they may end out experiencing more stress than they should, for being such small and inexperienced creatures. One of my children's books, *Charlie and Mom Cat*, covers this very subject.

Kittens born in the wild quickly learn the ways of the wild. They are very hard to catch and they run about pell-mell after they reach a certain age. They become very frightened around humans. If, perchance, you catch any outdoor or stray kittens, bring them in, isolate them in a small room, even a bathroom, and give them two or three weeks, at least, before taking them in to a pound or a shelter. They will settle down and bond with you, since you are feeding them and because the room is small and they can't go anywhere. They will get to know you and to trust you. Frankly, many pounds and shelters will even euthanize kittens if they have too many of them and if there are medical issues, even slight ones, and if the kittens are not of a generally docile or non-fearful temperament, which could go against them were they to be placed for adoption.

If you go into a small room (where you keep the kittens), and begin handling them on a regular basis (when they are that young), they generally will not protest too much. Soon, every time you go in to the room (as a bathroom), they'll become pretty calm. You have to pick them up and handle them on a regular basis…and put lots of floor toys out for them. They can't be able to run and hide, though, and get under furniture (as a bed or couch), which is why a bathroom is perfect. Kittens just need to experience a more quieted and isolated life. They'll take to a litter box, too, when you keep one in the bathroom for them. Make sure it is a low-edged one if the kittens are real small.

In other words, settle the kittens down and give them new experiences before you take them in to a pound or shelter so they'll have a better chance of getting through the screening for temperament and adaptability. If you don't work with them for a while, they could end out being euthanized. The pounds and shelters do not like the public to know that they euthanize kittens, but most of them will if they feel they must. They also euthanize some of the ill kitties and the kitties that do not pass a temperament test. As noted before, if you are able to bring the mother cat in to your home, all the better, especially if the kittens are still suckling—all the time or some of the time. The mother cat will start to trust you, too, because you are feeding her and seem safe.

Never take feral kittens that are wild-ish in to a pound or animal shelter. All wild-ish kittens can settle down, I know, because I've seen it happen—many times. <u>Keep the kittens long enough for them to settle down and become trusting, and again, they have to be in a small room</u> so they cannot get away from you. It should be large enough for them to play with lots of floor toys, though. You have to regularly pick them up even when they seem to not like it. Then, always pat them very gently. In time, they'll stop trying to get away. The kittens <u>must</u> become socialized. They're easier to grab hold of and pat if the room is real small. They get used to the handling, and come to expect it and to even like it.

Few realize that kittens are euthanized at pounds and shelters. Foster care the kittens for a while, yourself, get them used to eating, using the litter box, being contained, and to accepting human handling so you can save their lives. Remember, though, that they shouldn't be under at least six weeks of age if you bring them inside without their mother because likely, they are still nursing their mother (or suckling). Eight weeks is all the better. Six weeks of age could work, but you may have to wet and mash their food and buy special kitten milk for them and put the kittens up to the dish until they figure out what they need to do. If you bring them in and they are younger, you may have to hand-feed the kittens and take special round-the-clock care of them. Some people are not very good at this. It can be tricky.

If you separate kittens from their mother when they are too young and too small, you will be risking the lives of those kittens. Never remove kittens from their den area when they are too young. The kittens will probably die. Children or young people have been known to do this, because the kittens are so cute, but teach them, early on, to never do this and admonish children if they ever do. Try to get the kittens back to their den, if possible. Make sure the mother comes back around, too, or the kittens will die.

Outside, when it comes to food, the bigger and stronger outdoor cats will chase the other cats away from the area so if a mom cat gets chased away, the kittens will have to leave. Usually, stronger cats will make all the other kitties wait their turn. They tend to be more tolerable around kittens but kittens will still have to wait their turn. The bigger, stronger cats may even hang around the food source all the time so that none of the other cats can come near the food (but some will come around and eat it anyways, and take a chance). Larger kitties can actually be particular about who they boss around. They usually do not hurt the smaller and younger cats. The smaller and younger cats are no threat to them . . . and this would also include most females but not all females. It is the cats near to their own size that they sometimes want to drive away from the food site, and from anywhere, really. They are intimidated by them and see them as a threat. The intimidation is generally felt between males that are close in size. It doesn't always relate to age. It mainly relates to size. Usually any actual fighting or chasing away relates to males.

A mom cat may first investigate a food area for her kittens and, if it seems safe, she'll beckon them over. But if other cats keep her away from a food area, her kittens can't eat. Some food sites have very little food, sadly, and it is not enough for all the neighborhood cats, many of which are stray or feral. A lost or dumped indoor/outdoor cat had an owner. Such a stray cat wandered away from their home or was dumped after having a home and an owner. A feral cat was born outside and never had an owner. Some think of a feral cat as being any kitty that is not or does not seem to be socialized or accepting of humans and is thereby anti-social. They also think of a feral cat as a cat that has lived outside long enough to become overly skittish and unfriendly and to even be hostile around humans. These descriptions generally fits some of the feral cats but some strays (lost or abandoned cats that once had a home) can become similarly inclined, too. To emphasize and clarify, a feral cat is <u>not</u> a stray cat and they should not be lumped in together…but they are. A feral cat (born outside) can even be somewhat genteel whereas conversely, a stray cat can be extremely feisty. Temperament factors in and I have a chapter on temperament in my already-noted large cat book or compendium.

After outdoor kittens are weaned, they 'must' eat whatever is around. If they can't get to food, their lives will be woeful. This happens a lot to outdoor kittens, especially in areas where no food is put out for them. Kittens have to eat way more times per day than grown cats do because they have so much constant growing to do and are so high energy. If you feed outdoor kitties, put food outside around both the front and the back-door areas, and do your best to make sure that there's always enough food out for <u>all</u> of them. If food is out, in two outside areas around a home, then likely all the outdoor kitties can eat because if some are afraid to eat at one side of the home, they may not be so fearful of eating at the other side. Make sure the dry cat food bits are small enough for kittens to chew and that it has taurine in it.

You might consider putting cheaper, less palatable food out for outdoor kitties first because if they are being fed elsewhere (with better-tasting food), they won't eat it and you can then, at least, suspect that they have a home. I don't like to do this, though. My belief is that the majority of outside kitties do not have homes. I have to think that way because I know enough of them don't and I want to make sure they all get decent food. Most outdoor kitties will eat practically anything you put out because they are so hungry and because they sense there may be no more food anywhere else or around for some time. I make sure the food is nutritious. Outdoor kitties suffer from the anxiety and torment of random eating. They aren't always certain there will even be any food. Many of them do not eat consistently. Even if you end out feeding a kitty that belongs to someone, any food they put out for that kitty could be being eaten by various other kitties so that the owned kitty has to eat your store-bought food. This kind of issue never bothers me. I only care that they all get enough food.

Outdoor kitties get hungrier, faster, compared with indoor-only kitties. They burn up calories faster, as a general rule. The outdoor cats have to walk a great deal—often great distances—in order to find food and water. They walk distances for other reasons, as well. They expend much more energy because they must often run to keep from being hurt or from being the prey of a predator. If you are able to feed outdoor kitties, don't be surprised if the food goes fairly fast. At first, it might not, until enough of them around the neighborhood, or even community, learn about the location, but after a time, it will be eaten up, faster, which is what you want to happen if you want to keep the outdoor kitties from starving. Some outdoor kitties may come around to your feed area and actually be starving. How much you put out will ebb and flow, too, but not usually too much. All kitties need to eat on a regular basis. When you feed a number of outdoor kitties, there are certain ones—perhaps all of them—that you are saving from death by starvation. If you leave food out, for a time, outdoor kitties will gradually and eventually come around. They very much need you to help them. You may want to claim them all as being your own, however, so you can start formally rescuing them.

If you've never fed outdoor kitties and you don't know if they're around, put a bowl of food out for them for a number of days and just see what happens. Give it a try because outdoor kitties are out there—owned ones, strays, and feral cats—and, again, they will come around, in time. You cannot be concerned if an owned kitty, ever, eats some of the food you put out. Mainly, be concerned about getting food out to the bona fide strays and feral cats that could be starving.

Be relieved that stray or feral cats are getting food, since no one else is likely feeding them. <u>You can never assume that someone else is feeding them.</u> You may think someone else might be, but how do you, ever, really know? You do not know <u>what</u> anyone might be putting out, either, or <u>how much</u> they might be putting out. They could be putting out what lacks nutrition, like their left-overs. No other commercial dry cat food may be out. You never know. And, you never know if food is being <u>consistently</u> put out, either.

Outdoor kitties aren't usually very affectionate with one another because of a fight for food and because of other competitive situations. They can be a little nervous around other kitties but not that many kitties actually fight with other kitties. There can be clashes, but one of the kitties runs away before there is a fight. There are some fights, though. In the main, their need to secure food causes them to be alienated from other outdoor kitties. Outdoor kitties learn unkindly and undesirable behaviors, in general, and much of this relates to food and mating issues. Tom cats will fight with other males so they will be the cat that mates. A female kitty will mate with any tom cat that comes around. She can mate with several males.

On occasion, an outdoor kitty has been known to mate with a bona fide cat in the wild, but obviously, the cat in the wild would be a smaller one. The kittens can end out being a little larger in size than most domestic kittens are, and they can end out being rather large in size. When they are full-grown, they can even weigh twenty pounds or very close to that weight. Coming from a mother that could have weighed around eight pounds, the weight of her offspring is a sure indicator that she has, mated with a rather large domestic cat and probably, with a smaller cat in the wild. A cat in the wild is sometimes called a wildcat. Such offspring can have a bit of a wild look to them, too, which is another indicator that the mother cat mated with a smaller cat in the wild.

The outdoor kitty is a very deprived one, all in all; it's a sad situation. There are bona fide feral kitties all over the world, too. Some of them only know the wild, and each other, and some of them do not live near humans. Their life spans are never very long, but they are long enough for some litters to be born so there continues to be a number of feral cats in certain areas. This cycle of feral births goes on in certain countries, especially, and in certain areas of those countries, particularly. We all know that cats are found all over the world.

Australia has areas where feral kitties live, but really, feral kitties live on every continent. In the mid-1900's, approximately eighteen hundred cats were brought in to kill rabbits in Australia because the rabbits were over-populating. This, really, was not a good move on the checkerboard and that checker cannot be crowned. What were they thinking? The kitties weren't altered. Now, feral kitties are a problem in Australia's Outback. The rabbits were killed but afterwards, the kitties could not be caught. (Some small rodent-type animals were also killed by the cats.) In most cases, the feral kitties couldn't even be found, to catch, because the area was so vast. Now, the kitties there do not get food from humans and there are few to no rabbits or rodents but somehow, some of the feral cats are still around so they are eating something, though God know what.

Quite a few of these kitties died from lack of food and water and also, from illness. If the Aussies were going to bring in eighteen hundred cats to kill rabbits, those cats should have all been spayed and neutered to begin with. Why couldn't Australians have just gone in and hunted some of the rabbits, themselves? And set rabbit traps? Why bring domesticated kitties in, to be forced to live out in the wild? Those kitties were already domesticated and were generally tame. Why dump them in the Outback, or wherever else they may have been dumped? These kitties needed to be inside homes, not out in the wild. Like all kitties, they needed continued human care and protection. They had none, and still have none.

Outdoor kitties of any type usually don't eat very well and so they don't grow and develop as well as indoor kitties do. Indoor ones do not miss any feedings or meals whenever they are hungry. Stray and feral kitties end out with a bonier, thinner structure than they would have had, had they been born and reared inside. An outdoor mother cat has to run all over the place trying to get food. Food helps her milk supply so she must get food continually. Many outdoor mom cats don't get enough food during pregnancy or their lactation period. They're unable to. Often, their kittens have to do without suckling from time to time or with much milk, when they suckle. There are many delayed suckling times, which will affect the kitten's growth and even its state of mind. It will become more fearful and insecure, and possibly be more hostile. Indoor kittens feed around the clock and on time, every time, so they end out with different dispositions than the outdoor kittens have.

Some outdoor kittens even lose their mother, which, of course, puts them in immediate peril. This kind of thing happens more often than most people realize. Sometimes, with strays and feral cats, the mother will just suddenly disappear. She won't return and the kittens experience a horrible sense of dread. They will miew for a long time, then stop, then die. Mothers outside have been known to die because they keep feeding their kittens when they've had little to no food themselves. So much is being drained from them, and they are also starving.

Some feral kitties can be quite ferocious when you first try to handle them. You can't catch them unless you use box or slam traps or a net, but some of these kitties are so feral that you have to cage them right away once you catch them. You cannot, yet, handle them. They may never let you handle them but in time, with right care and patience, they may. If you can rescue their kittens from the outdoors, while they are young, they can be tamed by good medical treatment, consistent feeding, and gentle handling. But with the older feral cats, if you were to rescue them, you would be taking a chance on some of them if you brought them indoors because a small percentage of them may not come around, as much as you would wish. Some come around, though, and some only do, in part. Most feral cats can be brought around to some degree of indoor adapting, and possibly all feral cats can, but, often, there is not enough time or resources to rescue the more feisty and temperamental feral cats. If a stray cat had ever been kept inside, there might not be much of a restoration cost in terms of time, and strays can easily end out having a good temperament.

So much rests on altering stray and feral cats, and on giving them regular food and water. Any outdoor kitty will change, after that. Stray and feral cats found around any area can multiply relatively quickly if they can get to food and not starve, and if no one intervenes and at least gets the males neutered, it will all be downhill for those kitties. Unneutered stray and feral males end out with battle scars, and many of them. If they are neutered, they won't get so many wounds from being outdoors. They may still get some, though, because other males do not know they are neutered and at first sighting, may take them on.

Frankly, some countries do not do enough to trap and neuter and spay loose outdoor kitties in their country. Countries that know they have an excess of stray and feral cats should invest in hundreds of small animal traps, pay a number of people to trap them, bring them in to get altered, and then return some of them to the exact area where they were found but set up centers around their country where some of them can be adopted. Then they should pay employees or outside people to transport groups of them to these adoption centers. In the USA and certain countries, people pay the pound or shelter now, for them to take the animal—be it a cat, a dog, or some other animal. They didn't used to have to pay. Government funds and/or donations and money from Wills kept them going.

It used to be free to bring in all animals. This changed around the fall of 2003 (when these animal outlets started to charge people). At first, the bring-in charge was low but it doubled, then tripled, per animal and even per litter. In some places, now, you have to make an appointment to leave an animal at a pound or shelter. All this 'change' is why fewer animals are being turned in and more are dying outside. Some felt there was greed that was inexcusable, but who can judge? Greed can be charging more for everything, even when you don't need to, or giving yourself a higher salary, too often, when you really don't need to. Etc. Who can know who that shoe is going to fit? It will fit some people, though. I've written a full book on greed—*Creeping Greed*. I think greed is rampant, but not every individual is greedy, just some are. Greed relates to not giving and not sharing.

It can also be hard to get through to a person on the telephone, anymore. Some places only take messages, claiming someone will call you back and you never know when or who will, and sometimes you miss their call. They may call you back after a day or two. Shelters and pounds are less accessible and by now, everyone knows this. This isn't what was initially intended but it is how take-ins have ended out.

It got even worse when the coronavirus came in. Everything became more difficult. Some of these animal-related places closed, or went by appointment only, and it was hard to get an appointment. If you took a stray cat in, or any cat, they turned people back at the gate or the door…or the gate or door was locked. A very few pounds and/or shelters would take emergency cases. They all got more authoritative. No one wanted to get the virus.

In any event, back to the subject of helping stray and feral cats. Once this procedure become systematic—i.e. Retrieve, Alter, Return or Adopt out—the stray and feral cat problem would become minimal, but it would take government money so non-useful government programs would have to take a

231

backseat to the government RARA Program. (You have to name it something but any name would do.) The Australian feral cats in the Outback, for example, would eventually die out if they were all altered, but they shouldn't be put back in the Outback, no matter what.

Again, the key to the success of a RARA program (or a similarly-named program) would be in the actual hiring of people, for pay, to go and trap these cats around different countries. It might take some time, and some people in the country would have to report where the stray and feral kitties were so the paid employees or outside people could come trap them, but over a period of time, the stray and feral situation would be genuinely well under control and outdoor kitties would not have to continually have to suffer and be so terribly and so continuously deprived. These kitties could be rescued. After being altered and receiving food and water 24/7, they would mellow out considerably. Homes could be found for many of them. Stray and feral cats could be altered so they don't produce more outdoor cats. And so it would keep on going.

Much good would come about because of such government-supported programs. Those kitties that are not able to be places (because not all kitties can be) could live out their lives in a large group shelter that was organized with separate rest areas for the kitties, and plenty of activity stimulation. A group shelter is set up so all the cats can mingle in an open area. In one house or building, there might be three or four rooms that a group of kitties can hang out in. If two kitties do not get along, for sure, one of them can go in with another group. These group shelters are needed all around the world—to be installed by governments, if need be, and clearly, they are needed to be helped by governments in a number of countries, so it is 'whosoever will'.

For now, though, the responsibility falls on citizens (and it hasn't been working, too well, for years). Unfortunately, some people look outside and see a male and because the kitty is a male, they subliminally think the kitty is all right being outside, just because it is a male. Males are not all that much larger or more muscular than the females are. A domesticated, bred-down kitty is a domesticated, bred-down kitty and they are all pretty small and so they are really helpless, outside, particularly in view of the many perils. They all need our protection and hands-on help, and possible eventual government intervention (the sooner, the better, and immediately would be good).

<u>What is sad is that any stray or feral kitty is actually considered a domestic kitty because the stray or feral kitty is part of a group of animals that has been domesticated, and had these kitties lived indoors from the time they were kittens, as they should have been doing, they would be manifesting the same behaviors as indoor-only kitties manifest.</u> These unfortunates missed out, in other words and they shouldn't have. <u>All</u> kitties are Domesticats, which is the whole point. A stray or feral kitty is just 'yet to be tamed'. It has the potential to be tamed. It takes time and patience to do this, though, and not a lot of people will take this on. Some do not know how to. (Anyone can learn how to from my *I Care for My Cats* book.)

A group of people should be employed by the governments to do this, too, but volunteerism will always be needed. Once the stray and feral rescue program really got going in various countries around the world, past a certain point, the problem would <u>continually</u> be diminishing until the problem kept on being reduced to 90/80/70/60/50/40/30/20/10/0% of kitties being forced to live outside and to be born outside. The more there are that get altered, the fewer there will be that need altering and since fewer litters will be born at every bend and turn, the problem will eventually cease to be, but there would have to be a maintain-the-kitty-population program in place, too, because some people are still going to lose or dump kitties.

<u>At birth, all kitties have the potential to start off and to remain tame and docile.</u> All kitties should live to be fifteen-years old or older. This doesn't happen if they are always outside. They live, on average, for only five to six years, which is close to 1/3rd of the number of years they should be living. Rescuing kitties by way of a RARA or similar government program should become a national goal all over the world and in every country for the sake of all kitties everywhere. It is time to give focus to increased and more intensified kitty rescue…and dog rescue, too, for that matter. It's really past time but probably, more awareness will be needed, first, which is why I wrote *I Care for My Cats* and this book. We have not been doing everything right, concerning the care of our cats (and dogs). We've only been doing things partly right, some of the time.

What is a deception is the impression that stays with people when they see, on TV or elsewhere, how ferocious some outdoor kitties have been when they've been picked up or handled by a human for the first time. Kitties will fight when they're first being caught because they think they are going to be hurt, killed, and possibly even eaten. It's instinctive for them to put up a fuss or fight and that ferociousness does not, at all, describe the total personality and temperament of the struggling, fearful kitty—not even close. Kitties being captured don't know to think otherwise, not at their crisis moment of capture. People think, 'wow, that cat was wild' and they subliminally conclude that if that kitty was, then other kitties will constantly and continually be like that, too. This is short-sighted and way off-the-mark thinking. It is mere rote thinking. People jump to wrong conclusions.

Really, kitties are wonderful and loving domesticated animals and because even feisty animals can settle down and be or become trusting and receptive to human handling, some people really do need to adjust their thinking. In truth, after the kitty realizes you are not going to harm it, and after you feed and care for the kitty and bring love and attention its way, the kitty will not be ferocious or even feisty when you put your hands on the kitty. Many animals are receptive to care and kindness when it comes right down to it. There are a number of procedures to follow, to help feisty kitties to ease into calmness and being tame and docile. It is all step-by-step. It won't happen right away and anyone involved will have to have patience, stay steady, and have some faith.

Kitties can change, over time. Sometimes, they change pretty fast. Eventually, with time and patience, the kitty will lose its fears in most cases, unless the kitty is absolutely too far gone, but even that assessment can sometimes be premature and wrong and the kitty, really, wasn't too far gone. Many times, even the ones that seem too far gone can still be cared for and loved, though from more of a distance. It depends on what is meant by 'too far gone', too. Different people might assess such a kitty differently. The 'too far gone' ones might just need more time and patience.

Stray and feral cats, in some cases, can be brought into homes. The first step toward taming such kitties is spaying or neutering and caring for all of their medical needs. (Some vets and vet clinic personnel really go through a lot when they have to handle certain stray and feral kitties. They always have long, thick gloves around for handling certain ones.) The second step is to keep them separated from other kitties in the home so they can develop bonds with the humans in the home first, if that is possible (and, usually, it is, after they've been spayed and neutered, medically treated, and given food and water, routinely). The altering realization has to enter the stray or feral cats' minds—that full realization will really mellow such kitties out. They'll lose the desire to need to mate. This realization kicks in faster for some kitties. All this time, they should be in a relatively small room with nowhere to hide—a room the caretaker will frequently enter. The third step is to attempt to introduce them to one or more other kitties that are already in the home, but some kitties that are transitioning from stray or feral to an in-home situation may not be able to be trusted around other kitties. You'll have to watch them very closely as you are doing this. If and when you introduce them to each other, always be close by. Make sure food and water are out, perhaps in two places.

From start to finish, it is a gamble, but I earnestly believe that stray and feral kitties can be all rescued and rehabilitated and that it is worth looking into and trying and that by putting these kitties under observation for a while before deciding on whether or not they can permanently live indoors, that this adequate-time observation is a wise first course of action. You won't be able to decide this in a day, however. <u>You have to give stray and feral kitties a fair chance and a fair amount of time for observation.</u> Some stray and feral cats will surprise you, though. <u>Some stray and feral cats are already pretty tame. And, some stray and feral cats will be more able to be tamed than is ordinarily believed.</u> Often, the negative image of stray and feral cats is exaggerated—especially with regards to the feral cats. In fact, <u>only a small percentage of outdoor cats are really all that feral.</u> It just seems like they are or could be and so people assume that most of them are. <u>Most stray and feral cats can be</u>

<u>rehabilitated or rehabilitated enough—enough to warrant keeping them alive.</u> This is an extremely important point and one that should not be forgotten.

Keep your guard up, though, when you first bring a stray or feral kitty into a civilized setting. A few of them are quite feisty and this is mainly because of intense fear, not hatred. The kitty does not hate you. This fear may seem unjustified to you, but it certainly doesn't to the kitty. You do not know what the kitty has experienced outdoors and its life may have been very difficult and the kitty may have been exposed to some very scary and dangerous situations.

If a stray or feral cat is taken in and the kitty doesn't know how to use a litter box, the kitty must be put in to a small room for a while, with food and water and a decent place to sleep and rest, and there should be at least one litter box. Put a small fecal clump in the litter box so the kitty will know to use it. Get a clump that was from another kitty in the home. The stray or feral kitty will smell the clump and realize that the boxed area is a good place to do its business. It will begin to use the litter box on a regular basis, in that small room. The kitty must realize it is captive, and is a guest but remember, you have to have the kitty altered and medically cared for first or at around the same time you bring the kitty in. Eventually (but later on), move the kitty and the litter box out of the small room (like a bathroom) and in to a bigger room (like a bedroom). Eventually, you will want to transition the kitty to the main part of the home. The kitty will seek it out any litter boxes (one or two of them if there are two litter boxes), because the kitty will now be familiar with its useful purpose. It is not apt to spray because any altering will have kicked in.

Kitties are intelligent. They can learn new habits and tendencies. Everyone must realize this and not think they cannot be rehabilitated. Don't get a mental block and think that they can't or won't change. They can and will. You may have to keep the stray or feral kitty in the small room for a while, though, so it will become even more deconditioned and deprogrammed. (This step-by-step approach almost always works as long as kitties are altered first. They, absolutely, have to be spayed or neutered first or they will not settle in. They must heal well from the surgery before you allow them to be around any other kitties. If they stay in a small room, like a bathroom, they will heal more safely from a surgery because they can't move around very much.) Again, you must regularly enter the room they are in. Talk soothingly to them, let them smell your hand. Bring them their food. Give them a treat or two, on occasion.

I've rehabilitated so many outdoor kitties, using this bathroom approach. A person rehabilitating kitties will have regular contact with any in the bathroom because the bathroom is used so often (reference the toilet, teeth brushing, and baths/showers). You can even take a shower when the kitty is in the bathroom—just crack the window so the steam will dissipate because you can't, yet, open the bathroom door.

Stray and feral cats may not always bury their feces—not at first. Usually, they do try, though. Many times in the wild, there is nothing to bury their feces with, or it is too difficult for them to do this. So, at first they may use litter in a home but they may not bury their feces under the litter. If you give them time, they eventually will, because it is instinctive for them to want to bury their feces. They know they smell, so to get rid of the smell, they know to bury them. This was is what happened with the ones that I took in.

At first with some of the kitties, no feces were buried, then just one or two were, but they were at least getting the idea. Eventually, all the feces were all buried but it was patience on my part to regularly go in and de-clump and to give them the benefit of the doubt and to work with the situation. As soon as they realized that the litter could be dug in, and that they could do their business in this dig-and-cover manner, they decided that this was something they wanted to do. It was a little smelly on occasion, but it was worth the wait for the trend to change. Eventually, complete covering occurred. I kept the litter de-clumped more frequently than usual, but that was no problem and I didn't mind doing that. Their behavior was changing, too, and that was good. They were becoming more receptive to a human coming in, and being around. Some of them, I could touch and pat soon after. Some, I had to wait a while.

This type of situation has been the case with stray kittens I've taken in, too. Most stray and feral cats will come around but it takes patience, time, determination, and a little grit. Altering the older kitties really mellows them out—big time—but the realizing that they are altered may take longer than you think. This somewhat depends on the age of the kitty (and possibly on how much they mated). <u>Isolating transition stray and feral cats or wild-ish kitties for a while helps them to gradually forget their past ways.</u> Kitties become what they see. <u>A new life can change them</u>. Once they know they are captive and cannot go outside, they adjust to being inside the home. If they don't see dangers around them anymore, they will settle down and be more relaxed. Of course, this principle relates to people, too. It's just a good principle to keep in mind, except that you cannot capture people. Some criminals are contained in jail or prison, though.

On the subject of litter boxes and litter, I use an old pair of kitchen tongs for de-clumping the litter box or boxes that are inside. (I don't mind putting bagged and wrapped-up clumps in the indoor trash for a short period of time because they're usually free of parasites, etc. i.e., my indoor-only kitties are healthy or they become healthy.) It's a good idea to wait until the clumps have thoroughly dried but that doesn't really matter. It's not that hard to pick up pieces of kitty excrement with a pair of tongs. (I plunk the tongs in an old, unused vase, when done.) It shouldn't bother you if you have to remove outdoor clumps, either. You should go around from time to time and remove those, too. No one should ever come to despise cats just because of occasional excrement on their lot or property. Stray and feral cats need our help, not our scorn and wrath. People pick up their dog's excrements. It is just as easy to pick up cat excrements (with a scooper or old pair of tongs).

There are many humane things we can do for helpless outdoor kitties. We clean up after our babies that wear diapers. Why shouldn't we go out and occasionally de-clump what is outside and why complain about doing that and why dislike cats because they have to do their business? It's easy to pick up clothes from the floor, isn't it? Well, it's easy to go around with tongs and put clumps in a bag and then staple the bag shut or wrap it in a sheet of newspaper and toss it.

Again, stray cats can be different than feral cats. Strays once had a home and were previously around humans, at least for a time. Temperament can enter in. Likely, outdoor kitties all have different experiences outside. At birth, a general nature pre-dominates and it relates to genetic make-up. But, behavior is learned, from the mom cat and from externals in the environment. The point is, you never really know what to expect when you encounter any outdoor kitty. Most are skittish, but some will come around and accept humans faster than others will. A few come around fairly quickly. Some are sleuths. They check everything out and then some. They know they must try to stay safe. They've learned (often the hard way) that they must proceed with caution. The ones that allow you to at least touch them when they are at the feeding site (and don't run away when you do) are possibly strays. The ones that seem to fear you and won't come near you are possibly feral, but not necessarily. They could be strays. It really doesn't matter if they are stray or feral cats. You have to start off at square one with all of them when you go about feeding and rescuing them.

The adage 'time heals' relates to taming stray and feral kitties and helping them, and also to the in-home gradual adaptability of both stray and feral kitties. Every one of these kitties need healing and security, quite frankly. They need to be settled down and to be under a responsible person's care and management. But, of course it would have been better if these kitties had been cared for inside of a home all along the way and from the very beginning. These outdoor kitties should never have been outside, but their existence is a reality and we have to recognize the related problems <u>now</u>, because they are problems. <u>It's never too late to try to change things or to turn things around. There's always a beginning point.</u> Again, my RARA proposal, I hope, will be taken seriously. Just think of all the good such a government-helped program would do. I'd rather see government money of the different nations go to a RARA or similar program than to what is probably pork-barrel waste. There is always plenty of that. Cats (and dogs) are living creatures.

If you put a stray or feral kitty in with your already settled-in kitty that is indoor-only, the entering kitty may mellow out, a little here and a little there, and just let go of old ways. The established kitty could pick up some undesirable behavior from observing the entering kitty, but this isn't likely because the established kitty will be set in its ways. Almost always, the entering kitty takes on the behaviors of the established kitty (or kitties) because they sense that they are the newcomer and the guest. You can't let fear govern your decision to put the two (or more) together. So much will depend on the ages and the general temperaments of the kitties that are at-issue. If the entering stray and feral is coming in to a multi-kitty home and the established kitties are tame, docile, and well-behaved, the entering kitty will almost always gradually conform to the ways of the established kitties, which is another reason why I believe that even feral cats can be tamed. You have to always proceed with caution, though, and go through the process at your own risk.

This gradual conformity approach particularly applies to kittens, but it can apply to many of the older stray and feral kitties, too. There are exceptions, but there is power in numbers. All of the well-behaved kitties will definitely impact any entering kitty. This is what I've experienced and seen but again, it is good to have a responsible adult around to intervene if there are any problems and skirmishes. My home was large enough for opposing kitties to find safe secluded spots. Most of the time I had smooth transitions. A couple of them fought but I would put a broom between them and they'd stop. Gradually, they stopped fighting. My rescues were all successful. I found homes for most of these taken-in kitties. A few I took to a no-kill shelter, after they'd been settled down and socialized in as much as was possible. They were fine.

If a kitty that is not trusting or friendly comes in to your home, give it time and work with the kitty. Try to have a little faith. Some kitties will completely change just within a few days. Some kitties take longer. Hang in there. Decide to love the kitty no matter what. Decide to make a commitment. If you only half-way do this, the kitty will sense that. Kitties respond to genuine love and caring. In that respect, they're like humans. <u>Eventually, the kitty will bond with the people in the home (assuming they are all generally calm), and those bonds will essentially replace the kitty's yen or desire to go outside.</u> But, the people in the home will still always have to be careful around doors so the once-outdoor kitty won't ever be able to scoot outside.

All indoor kitties, whether they've always been indoors or whether they've been outdoors, at all, need to have a spot or two around the home where they can be alone. They should also have a place where they can sit in the sun—like, next to a window. Kitties that have been used to being outside will miss the sun so it would be a kindness to arrange a spot in the sun for the kitty. If such a spot isn't available in your home, try to create one that will appeal to the kitty. Put a table by a window or build a shelf next to a window. There are special mounts you can attach next to a window that have comfortable kitty mattresses or have padding that the kitty can rest and sleep on so the kitty can enjoy the sun and enjoy looking out at nature's activities, particularly busy birds. You can fold over a small throw rug if you need to. Kitties love to watch busy birds. Kitties that have lived outside <u>love</u> to look out windows but that does not mean that they want to go back and live outside. After all, they are altered now, and their food and water is always in the home where they live.

A once-stray or feral kitty, after having its medical needs <u>fully</u> met, will settle into a new lifestyle and will enjoy such a place by a window. Altering,

243

de-worming, de-fleaing, de-miting, and grooming such kitties (a good initial bath is essential) really settles them down and helps them move towards docility, but it may take as much as a month or two before you will see clear-cut behavior changes and related consistent behaviors. Some kitties that are brought in may not take to baths. A bath may take two people to see it through. Some grooming shops have ways they use to contain kitties when they are bathing them. They use spray wash and rinse when a kitty is being contained. You want to get rid of fleas if it is flea season. You want to get rid of mites and bacteria on the skin or in the fur. Special shampoos have to be used.

Again, the effects of spaying and neutering can take a while to completely kick in. Unfortunately, too many outdoor kitties are never brought inside and there are so many that need to be brought inside and also brought to full health. More people need to decide to do this so kitties can be protected and rescued from a bad life (and have a longer life). Every neighborhood should be doing this all around the world. Different people should just jump in. There is such a thing as Neighborhood Watch. There should be such a thing as Neighborhood Cat Rescue.

Every one of the living-outside outdoor kitties had the initial potential to be very handsome or beautiful and maximally healthy and to live a long life, but quality and length of life is so significantly reduced for the outdoor kitty. Most outdoor kitties just don't have that healthy look, and, usually, they are stressed out. Often, their fur is matted and rough, their coats aren't shiny, and they are dirty; and, sometimes, their fur is full of burrs or thistles (and parasites). Kitties cannot remove mats by themselves, nor can they remove burrs or thistles all that well. Sometimes, outdoor kitties have scars on them, too, usually from fighting or from trying to get away from an angry cat (but obviously not getting away, fast enough). But, it really doesn't matter what the outdoor kitties look like now. It is how they can begin to look and still look that is important. Their outward appearance will greatly improve after they're all fixed up. If they have residual scars or any other issue, they will look better than they did and they will still be handsome or beautiful creatures.

One town in America recently voted that there be a ten-cat limit for kitties living outdoors, per owner. (They should have voted that these cats should only be inside but society hasn't come to that, yet.) A woman put her cats outside and she had more than ten, and these kitties were becoming a neighborhood nuisance. Hence, the noted town ordinance came around. The whole reportage distressed me because why weren't these kitties inside (or in other homes). <u>The more needed ordinance and law, which should really be all over America and all across the world, is that all kitties should be kept indoors.</u>

Perhaps, even, a limit of three or four kitties per household should be established, or at least openly recommended.

If someone has ten kitties and can't keep them all inside, then that person should find homes for them, whereby the new caretaker or caretakers would promise to keep them inside. <u>A person really isn't a full-fledged caretaker if the person puts a kitty outside.</u> On one level, the person is being irresponsible. Putting ten kitties outside is ten times more irresponsible, even though the woman's heart seemed to be in the right place, i.e., her feeding so many kitties was a kindness, but, the coin has two sides. Some of those outdoor kitties probably aren't eating real well, though, if there are any clashes or fights over food. Some of the kitties could roam away, and get lost. Likely, some already have.

Some would say ten cats is too high a number to have. Likely the woman isn't paying for vet care, either. (Out of sight, out of mind, in other words.) But, I shouldn't judge because I know there are people out there who do their best to care for all kitties in their charge (even outdoor ones), including medically. Some have even ended out starting a private shelter. Hopefully, the woman with the ten cats is at least paying to have them altered. If she is even just having the males altered, she is doing something right because she is keeping the kitty population down. Also voted in was that all the kitties had to wear ID tags on a collar. It was becoming a health issue in the neighborhood because the neighbor's yards were being used as litter box areas. Plus, there were cat noises so the kitties were disturbing the peace. (This leads me to suspect that some of them were not altered.)

Without being able to help themselves, this collection of kitties was becoming public nuisances. They needed to be indoors and maximally cared for, not minimally cared for like most kitties are if they are outside. This is not to say that putting food and water out for outdoor kitties is not important. It is very important. It will always cost money, for the food, but what is worth spending money on? Keeping kitties alive has to be at the top of the list, one would hope. Many people already want to Save Our Domesticats and more have been jumping on board and doing whatever is constructive that lines up with that goal.

If a person has indoor cats that are well cared for and they don't want them to mix with the outdoor cats, and if the cats outside that the person feeds aren't and never have been theirs and are stray or feral cats that need to be fed, that is one thing because some people do not want their indoor kitties to mix with the outdoor ones, inside their home. The person feeding the stray or feral cats would only be feeding them out of kindness and not because he and/or she once owned them, only to have put them outside. In such a case, the individual(s) should be commended, and even more so if he and/or she had been making an effort to find homes for some of the cats and to get them fixed up, medically. Some outdoor cats are easily and immediately catchable and homes can be found for them fairly easily. In other words, some kitties will let whoever feeds them pick them up. Some outdoor cats are sociable.

Sociability is the ability to socialize. I've found that in neighborhoods with houses that are encircled by other houses that cats are less apt to be feral. Very few of the kitties have a real wildness about them and are extremely difficult to catch. Some might run away, however. Kitties more on the outskirts and in country areas tend to be more skittish, feisty, and feral. Always, though, there are exceptions.

I do not like the word, feral, because people using the word think that all outdoor cats are feral. Not so. The word implies that the kitties are wild and hostile and dangerous and this is totally misleading. They should call feral cats, born-outside cats, and that would be more accurate. The word, feral, should stop being used. The word should be better qualified when it is defined. Feral ordinarily refers to cats that have never had any human handling because they were born outside. The majority of outdoor cats in home neighborhoods and communities aren't really feral. They've been put outside or were dumped at some point in time and after they had been around humans, to some degree.

247

Feral cats or the born-outside kitties have never had human contact. They've never been inside a home. You could start calling these kitties, bosk kitties, instead of feral kitties and so it would stand for born-outside kitties. That would bring forward more exactness when referring to a specific type of kitty that is outside. Bosc would work also, to refer to born outside cats. Or, just call them born outsiders or born-outside cats or kitties but don't refer to them as feral cats or kitties anymore if they were born outside because you will be mis-labeling a number of the other outdoor kitties that get mixed up with them. There are the born outsides, and there are the outdoor kitties and again, we should be careful about mis-labeling kitties.

Another new term on the scene (besides bosk or bosc) is Indie Kitty or Indies. These are cats that have had little to no human handling. This would refer to many of the outdoor kitties but it also refers to some of the indoor kitties if, for some reason or other they have not had human interaction or handling. This can happen if there are too many cats in a home or if a caretaker is too busy or is distant from the kitty. In other words, Indie Kitties are kitties that tend to keep a distance from human. Some may have even had a bad experience with one or more humans.

Whatever the reason or reasons, this more independent kitty (Indie Kitty) is skittish or shy or overly aloof. Such kitties need to become trusting and it will take thoughtful effort to help them become more trusting of a caretaker and those living in a home. They'll need focused love, whether they were outdoor kitties, brought inside, or kitties that were indoors but were not given adequate human handling and attention. Like with the born-outsides, these Indie Kitties can be kittens, of any age, or they can be cats that are no longer kittens. Yet, many people will call an outdoor Indie Kitty a feral. Even some of the born-outsides that won't let you catch them, in truth, could end out becoming sociable around humans, given time, patience, and appropriate medical care. They can actually become little friends, to a caretaker. They will become dependent on the caretaker.

Definitions are important, and so are descriptions. Again, to some people, feral implies that the kitties are 'too far gone'. In truth, even feral cats can be rescued, and they can settle down, considerably. People need to stop viewing kitties in short-sighted ways. This doesn't help needy kitties one bit. Everyone should want to intervene and bring outdoor kitties inside as soon as possible, too. It can be an adjustment for kitties to come inside to permanently live but most of them will adjust. <u>The word, feral, labels too many of the outdoor kitties and this labeling can sometimes discourage people from making an effort to bring them in.</u> This labeling has caused this to happen in the past, many times, and so the labelling has hurt kitties, not helped them.

Feral cats have the potential to be transitioned by way of a step-by-step process. It is all in the process, relative to transitioning any and all outdoor kitties. They can gradually learn new ways and adapt to a better life. They absolutely must be fixed up medically, though. First, they must be checked over and medical problems or disorders have to be tended to. Again, being altered will change their demeanor. When they are given foot and water on a continued basis, they will mellow out. When they get patted and stroked, they will come to realize that they are not in harm's way and will become more trusting.

Some of these transitioned kitties may still have some reservations around people some of the time but they will improve enough to where they will become responsive enough. Then again, there could be a total about-face turn to where they will be very relaxed, trusting, and responsive all the time. Either way, it is a kindness to get homeless kitties into a home where people are sensitive towards the ways and needs of kitties. Probably, too, some actual places that help these transition kitties could be established, here and there. There would have to be enough rooms, at these places.

There are degrees of understanding concerning kitties. Awareness about kitties grows and is not an overnight happening. It is good to make a portion of your readings be about kitties. Having pets should not be background. It should be foreground so you want to learn as much as you can about them.

11

Conclusion, and a Final Appeal

There have been too many purebred cats bred and born and on the one hand, it was fine that they were, but on the other hand, there have been too many of them. Because people wanted purebred cats, there was, inadvertently, less effort put in to rescuing the outdoor cats, as the strays and the ferals. It is a reality that fewer purebred cats should be being born and the key word is 'fewer'. Were this to be the case, there would be more effort, all across the board, to rescue all of the unfortunates—the outdoor ones that are forced to live in the <u>perilous</u> outdoors. A high percentage of the outdoor kitties could be rescued, fixed up, salvaged, and placed into home. People would want <u>them</u>, instead of wanting a purebred cat. Why has it taken so long for all the countries of the world to get more focused and organized and really go to bat for the cause of getting outdoor kitties indoors?

It's definitely better for kitties to be living indoors with a loving caretaker because their happiness and their survival depends on it. <u>Kitties need the comfort and the safety that can only be found inside of the four walls of a consistently, loving home.</u> Kitties deserve to be in homes where they are wanted and where the temperature is always a moderate range. Kitties deserve to be pampurred, but they cannot be pampurred if they are outside. Pampurring is out of the question for outdoor kitties.

Kitties put outside will usually leave an area, for some reason or other. So many people I've talked with tell me, "well, my kitty never leaves the porch (or patio) or the yard." Who are they trying to fool? Themselves, likely. But not me because I know the chance is always there for a kitty to leave, and to wander and roam. Many kitties leave, come back, leave, and come back. And so it goes. Some have said "well, I can make the fence higher," and I'm thinking, "OK, but when?" I inform people that there are <u>many</u> reasons why kitties should be kept safe, from the outdoors. Putting up a high fence won't solve the problem. Building a fence higher doesn't always work anyway, plus, building a higher fence costs money. (Few would even bother to do that, anyway.) The woman was off-the-mark with her thinking. She'd lost her kitty. Her kitty had jumped the fence, and just never returned. She obviously didn't want to bear the guilt that came from her losing her cat. The woman should go to square one and get on the right path of thought, which is that she should not let any kitty ever be outside. Only then can she heal, regarding the whole issue. Choices are not always correct. She had made the decision to put her cat outside. No one had made that decision for her. Logic always has to factor in. You play the odds at a racetrack. You shouldn't play them, reference your kitty.

One woman I spoke to indicated she would take the kitty outside with her when she read on her outside deck. She had no fenced yard. I gave her my opinion, which was that if you have a kitty outside with you at any time that a loose dog can walk by, and go after the kitty. The kitty can either be hurt, right there, or run away because of fright (and not return). Another kitty can cause this to happen, as well. In other words, even if you are outside with a kitty, something unexpected can happen. Besides, a caretaker would need to go inside from time to time, and so the temptation would be to leave the kitty outside and that is when the kitty could wander off or be frightened off by something, and run away. I, for one, could not concentrate on reading, or doing anything, were any of my kitties outside with me; I would worry too much about this and that. I'd be too anxious and it wouldn't be worth it. Kitties could be kept on a halter and leash, when a caretaker goes outside with them. That way, the kitty would be safe and contained. A caretaker might worry about running into a dangerous dog, but they should try their best to not go anywhere where a dog is apt to be.

I like the idea of caretakers building an outdoor area for their kitty or kitties. They would use wood and some kind of screen (that could not be damaged by any clawing). These sun/shade areas could be an extension of the home (and even have the crisscrossing patterned lattice as a part of the shade areas). There could be places up high that the kitty/kitties could jump up to so kitties can look down. They feel safe up higher. These safe places should also be put in to the home. Kitties prefer these upper places for resting and sleeping so they have to be large enough perches. (Perches are not only for birds.) A caretaker could pay to have a sunroom added, and design it to be conducive for a kitty. In other words, the kitty could be outside but be safer than the roaming outdoor kitties are. Sunrooms are always nice, no matter what.

Once a kitty leaves an area for a while, it can forget its old environment and its owner(s). It can also forget how to get back home. This happens all the time. Some people mistakenly think that kitties have phenomenal memories, but their memories aren't that good. Their memories are limited. It may seem like their memories are better than they are, but that is because they act on instinct and they act according to their own temperament. If your kitty, put outside, is going to become a different kitty and forget all about you and indoor ways, what's the point of even having the kitty? People whose kitties have wandered off for a time had to get totally re-acquainted with their kitty after the kitty finally returned (but not all of them do return). The kitty was just not the same. Some of these people eventually chose to never let their kitty go outside again. Often, the kitty had lost weight because it had not been able to find food or to find it very often. Often, the kitty came back with parasites, too.

One kitty I heard about came back skin and bones. The owner happened to see the kitty in a totally different area and he went over to him and they were somehow still able to connect (after several months had gone by), whereupon, the owner picked his kitty up and took him home and fed the kitty well and got him the appropriate veterinary care. It was a happy, nick-of-time rescuing and encounter. The kitty got to live and was restored to health (in as much as was possible). Hopefully, there'd been no organ deterioration, or any health issue that could crop up later.

There are people who think that indoor kitties are bored kitties. This is not true. They have everything they need and there are people around to keep them from being bored. If there are one or more other kitties in the home, they can't get too bored because they're always watching one another, communicating, and socializing. If kitties seem to sleep a lot, it's not because they're bored. They just naturally sleep a lot. Often, their sleeping isn't deep sleep. Kitties are instinctively always 'on guard', just in case something happens that could be catastrophic so they are not bored. They stay aware of what is going on in their environment, even when it is a safe one.

To keep kitties from being bored, though, if that is your concern, make sure there are windows that kitties can sit or lay next to while they are watching the birds, passing-by cars, pedestrians, dogs, and anything else that happens to be outside. Also, have kitty furniture around that they can climb up on, and put some toys out for the kitties. Use an interactive toy with them, on occasion, or buy play tunnels or similar items for them. Kitties are mature cats when they are one year of age and they rest more, after one year of age. They play with toys less. Playing with any toy at all tapers off from one to two years of age. They never seem to tire of an interactive toy, though. Mainly, kitties do not need to be busy and entertained the same way we do. Their natures are very different from ours. They don't need to keep up with the News, to read a book, or to take a class. They don't need to be going about cleaning the house, fixing dinner, or washing clothes. Kitties are complacent and are happy with a restful type of life. As they get older, they like to observe. They will stay curious. They especially love to be next to their caretaker, either resting or sleeping.

If you perceive your kitty is a little bored, then do what you can to correct the problem. Mainly, don't let the thought that indoor kitties are bored kitties deter you from bringing an outdoor kitty inside and keeping the kitty inside permanently because you might think that outdoor kitties are not safe kitties. I've gone into enough detail to illustrate that they are not safe outside and to cover why they aren't safe outside. Once outdoor kitties are made to be tame, or more tame, and they become socialized, they can be very enjoyable and safe to be around (with very few exceptions, if any exceptions).

<u>My appeal is that all kitties, everywhere, be kept indoors, no matter what their temperament.</u> Some countries have allowed the problem of stray and feral cats to become a huge and chronic problem. It's time to do much more for all kitties. All kitties should be in a home and around loving, caring, and concerned people.

For anyone who thinks it's all-right to leave kitties outside, remember that kitties are supposed to live to be a little over fifteen human years of age. A few have lived to be thirty. But outdoor kitties, especially in certain areas, die way too early. The only solution to that problem is to bring outdoor kitties inside to permanently live indoors and to do this 'as of yesterday' and to not allow kitties to be or go outside in the first place. Such simple action is within the range of possibility but it is going to take organized work and some determination to get the message out and get this done. It will take <u>focus</u>. There have to be proclaimers. Then there has to be doers.

Even the air that some kitties have to constantly breathe in when they are outside is polluted. You may not even know what kind of chemicals and toxins are in the air, where you are living. They can be bad. You can't see them or even smell them, in many cases. They are out in this 24/7; we don't have to be but they do. This, too, is a peril. It all depends on where they live. Being outside day and night, in bad air, is not good. It's like living in a small room with a chain smoker, in some cases. Some kitties can only find water that's polluted, too. If you care about animals at all, you want them to breathe in decent air and to drink clean and safe water. You will want them to have good health.

Occasionally, kitties have to be around radiation, of some kind. With radiation leakage, you never know where it's going to be. It can happen, and it causes damage to outdoor animals. Sometimes, there's government or military testing that directly or indirectly damages or kills outdoor animals. Such things are now better monitored, in some countries. A lot of things slip through the cracks, though. People who love animals have to become aware of all perils, big and small, so they can mobilize and also, so they can better mobilize to get all the outdoor kitties rounded up, cared for medically, and put in loving homes with dependable and faithful caretakers.

Remember, too, that if you put your kitty (or kitties) outside, you run the risk of angering your neighbors. If your kitty urinates around their home, or uses their garden as a litter area, neighbor won't be happy. If your kitty makes all kinds of noises that disturb their peace and sleep, then you'll also get complaints. There are other reasons why a neighbor can complain, but those two noted ones are the main reasons. If you are doing your best to bring outdoor kitties in and are feeding the strays, usually neighbors will be tolerant. When you think about it, these issues aren't all that problematic. Gardens can be cleaned out, a little noise is only temporary and there is, really, very little noise. It is always of short duration, too. But, if you become defensive and unco-operative, then the neighbors probably will, too. Try to placate and get along with your neighbors, and care about them, too, like you do the cats. Purpose to do this.

I know it isn't always easy to love thy neighbor in this present world, but strive to, at least, like your neighbor. Live by the Golden Rule, when and as you can. Concentrate on doing that. Try not to dislike your neighbor. Best to love thy neighbor as thyself, though. In other words, treat your neighbors well. Turn the other cheek if they are not as nice to you as you are to them or as you wish them to be. Say to yourself, "I know there's good there".

Clearly, I've covered the perils that exist outside, though I've surely missed many. <u>So now you understand, more inclusively, the majority of reasons why it is not safe outside for our domesticated kitties, whether they are urban or rural kitties.</u> I call all outdoor kitties, whether they have a home, are stray cats, or are feral cats, <u>misfortunates</u> because it is their misfortune to have to be outside. Most people think there are only four main perils-communicable diseases, being hit by cars, being killed by dogs, and wandering away from home and getting lost, but now you realize that those four just barely scratch the surface. There are many more perils out there that will kill, maim, and cause illness, pain, and suffering, and kitties are at a distinct disadvantage whenever they are born, put, dumped, and left outside. Always, stop and reflect on their many plights. There are more perils out there than is generally realized. I was not able to cover much medical in this book, but I cover it more inclusively in my compendium, *I Care for My Cats (and Other Animals)*. There are hundreds and perhaps even thousands of perils. Encourage others to keep kitties inside, too. Plant those kinds of seeds all over the place. Some of those seeds will sprout. Don't worry about opposition. Get the word around because kitties cannot, really, take care of themselves. They just aren't safe outside. They aren't now, and they won't be in the future. Time is of the essence.

12

Seven Cat Poems, with Introductions

I am including seven poems in this book that relate to plights of kitties, or to kitties in general. Most are directly outdoor-peril related poems. More of my kitty (and animal) poems are in my long cat book compendium. I write Introductions for all my poems. Each poem here includes their Introduction and the poems are in alphabetical order. The first one is about a black cat. The second one centers on a purrty interesting play on words. The third one relates to one subject I've covered rather extensively in this book—feeding outdoor kitties. The fourth one is about animal cruelty. The fifth one ties in with the title of this book. The sixth one relates to a released, possibly abandoned pet, and the seventh one relates to helping outdoor (stray and feral) kitties. Because I am including the poem's original Introductions, there will be some repetition, relative to what has already been noted in this book. Also, the poems were all written at different times, and over the years. These poems are in my poems and short works books, of which there are eight (and there are a few subsequent poems, too). (All kinds of poems are in the eight books.)

Blackie—the Introduction

There are lots of Blackie's out there, only they aren't just black, they're several different colors, and mixes of colors. Cats need our help. They've been suffering too long. There hasn't been enough awareness about all their plights. Not enough people have acquired the consciousness that our cats need help and need help now. Some people don't care about cats, at all. There are many reasons for the lack of awareness and consciousness. Hopefully, those reasons will gradually be stripped away, as education continues to enter the scene. Blackie deserved to be safe, protected, loved, and given nutritious food whenever he was hungry. He deserved to have everything that a well-cared-for indoor cat has. Why should it be otherwise?

In my book, *I Care for My Cats*, I cover the plight of cats, in depth. I cover many other subjects about cats, too (many, many, as the book ended out being mammoth in size, once the manuscript was finished). My consciousness about cats continually increased as I was writing the book. I know from whence I've come, in other words. The book is perhaps the longest book that's ever been written about cats. I was selective about what went in to the book. The book covers much material about cats—just about every subject imaginable is covered. It is a comprehensive guide about cats, and about their care. It's about animal rights, and other animals are noted, especially if they have been being neglected, mistreated, or abused. I tie it all in. This poem, along with my other cat poems, is in the *I Care for My Cats* book. There is a chapter that covers poetry about cats, but my poems are elsewhere in the larger book (wherever they fit in), besides just being in the poem chapter. Here is one of those poems—

Blackie—the Poem

Black cat, I can see your battle scars.
Still you are a handsome creature.
I don't care if you're plain looking.
That you're a cat is your best feature.

You somehow endure cold and heat.
I don't know how you can stand it.
How you've escaped dying so far
Has baffled me more than a bit.

You have much dust inside your fur.
You have to go look for your food.
You are a nice cat, and I know
That your disposition is good.

I see you are somewhat skittish,
But you are relaxed around me.
I see that you are on your guard
About all that you do and see.

You've learned to be cautious, at times;
Outside, there will be some fright.
I hope to rescue you, in time
And I understand your sad plight.

I'll wait 'til fleas are dead outside;

I know they could be on you.

I don't want them inside my home.

My indoor cats are quite a few.

I'll feed you with the other strays.

I know that you can be saved.

When summer's gone, and in autumn,

You'll come in, and will be bathed.

I'll, for sure, bathe you really well,

And flea shampoo I will use

Just in case there are still fleas--

Your skin, they can sure abuse.

I'll take time out to clean your ears.

Miticide, I'll put inside.

If there are mites inside of them,

They'll die, since they cannot hide.

I'll check your stools in case there's worms.

Doing that is no big deal.

I'll get you pills that kill the worms.

What's medical, I'll try to heal.

I plan to take you to the vet's.

You'll get shots and be altered.

Soon after you won't want to spray.

Your life will be more ordered.

It will take time and be some work,

But who is there to do this?

I want to make your life better

So the outdoors you will not miss.

You'll get dry food both day and night;

I'll give you food that is wet.

I'll also give you special milk.

You'll make a really fine pet.

Outside, you'll never go again.

There's too many perils out there.

There are some comforts in my home.

Nothing's going to be hard to bear.

In time, you'll settle in just fine.

Everything will be routine.

You will, also, be more relaxed.

I know you'll become serene.

It will be good to add you in

And to have you always around.

I'm more than sure that in the end

I'll be happy that, you, I found.

Do You Want A Cat?—the Introduction

This is an unusual free-verse poem because of the purr emphasis and use, found in thirty-six lines and a total of thirty purr words. Four of the words don't align with "purr' perfectly and their sound isn't exactly urr, but the sound is close and so they seem to work out OK as a purr word, anyway. The gist of the poem is that you'll make a cat very happy if you'll give it a good home. So many cats need good homes, and, actually, there are many people out there who could provide one or more cats with a good home. Two kitties in a home are best because they will bond and keep each other company when no one is around. They'll never feel lonely and two are not any more difficult to take care of, in the main, than one is. Also, as a caretaker, you'll get twice as much love back. Will you be one of these people to get one or more kitties? Cats are wonderful creatures. My rather long book, titled *I Care for My Cats (and Other Animals)—From the Cats in the Wild to the Domesticated Cats—A Practical and Comprehensive Reference for the Care and Protection of Kittens and Cats* is so extremely fact-filled. It has sixty chapters and is loaded with useful material. So . . . if you ever do get a cat, or two, or three, et al., you might consider getting ahold of the book.

Cats have been my life and they've taught me more than I can indicate. Likely, my poems wouldn't be what they are had it not been for my many experiences with cats. I hope that after you've read the poem you will answer the question, do you want a cat? with a "yes".

Do You Want a Cat?—the Poem

Cats are purrfect, hardly from purrdition.

True, they can be purrsnikity, at times,

but for every behavior there is a purrpose behind it.

Am I making myself purrfectly clear?

Purrhaps there isn't enough understanding

about why cats do what they do,

but cats really aren't that purrplexing.

It should be everyone's purrsuit

to come to understand the behavior of cats—

to understand their purrsonalities,

their tempurraments, and their ways.

Just remember, their behavior isn't always purrmanent.

Cats are definitely worth the money,

when they are purrchased.

So grab your purrse or wallet,

and go out and find a cat.

Many cats despurrately need a home.

Will one of those homes be yours?

Also, try to find a cat that purrs.

Purrchance you'll get one of those cats,

and also one that is purrky.

All cats are purrty, so keep to that purrspective.

I hope I've purrsuaded you to find and enjoy a cat.

Cats can be purrpetual companions

if you'll just give them a chance.

The purrequisite for all caretakers

is to be loving and caring

and purrceptive about the ways of cats.

There are lovely purrbreds around,

and mixed breeds are often purrferred.

Some people aren't that purrticular, though,

and they just want a nice cat

and should purrsist and purrsevere.

Others will have a purrsonal preference

until they find their special cat . . .

and even purrmit themselves to find two.

Feeding Outdoor Cats—the Introduction

I purposely didn't want to rhyme this poem because I wanted to pack more in, into more lines; therefore, it was done in blank verse. I probably should have written a poem on this subject before now because the subject matters so much to me and the subject is very important. I've written other poems about cats, too.

Cats forced to live outside are subjected to many perils, which is why I wrote a whole book about outdoor perils. One of the perils is that of starvation. Cats get non-nutritious food, bad food, or no food, when they are outside. Sometimes, they eat food that has parasites in it. People erroneously think cats can survive on small animals, including birds, but they cannot. They can't catch them all that well, they can't get to the meat, and there's not much meat on the animals they are able to catch. Besides, the meat can spoil really fast out in the open air and insects start to crawl all over it, too.

Domesticated cats need prepared cat food that's been processed. All over the world there are domesticated cats. They need this kind of food every day. Outdoor kitties don't get enough of this specially-formulated food so people have to put it out for them and this can't be skimped on and has to be consistently put out for them. Enough has to be put out for all cats forced to be outside and that is why more people need to be doing this good deed. Outdoor kitties are spread out, all over the world. True, it costs money to feed outdoor cats, but rewards will be in Heaven because people are supposed to care about 'all creatures, great and small'. Helping 'all creatures great and small' is in line with God's Will. It should be reward enough, however, just knowing you are doing something very helpful, which is, keeping outdoor kitties from starving and also from getting sick. You can't take your money with you.

Some outdoor kitties aren't actually strays, but there are so many strays out there that you may, mostly, be feeding strays if you put food outside. It all depends on where you live. There are also feral cats. A cat is a cat is a cat. Generally, an outdoor kitty that is owned by someone is fed at the owner's home and gets all or most their food there. A few kitties that have owners will also wander off, though, especially if they are ever hungry and their owner has not yet put food out for them or there isn't enough food being put out for them. You can never assume an outdoor kitty is owned by someone and this is key. Even if the kitty is wearing a collar, they could still be a stray. They could have been abandoned or wandered away.

Most outdoor kitties don't have collars and even if they do, there's usually no identifying tag or engraved plate on the collar. Cats do not have to wear an attached license tag around their neck, like dogs have to legally do, so unless an owner attaches a phone number on a collar the cat is wearing, no one will be able to trace an owner. There's no identifier. (There could be a name of the kitty but that is of little to no help.) Sadly, a collared kitty can end out being a stray. The kitty could have wandered off and become permanently lost some time ago or even recently, or, their previous owner could have moved away or simply abandoned them, thinking they'll be fine outside. Sometimes, too, a caretaker dies. Any of these situations have occurred, many times over. Kitties that have inserted identifier discs implanted are not scanned at regular homes, only at vet clinics so unfortunately, identifier discs are not of that much help if kitties are wandering around loose outside. Most stray and certainly feral kitties do not have identifier tags.

I have to assume that every kitty that comes to my home, for food, is not owned by anyone. I, of course, don't own them, and can't because I have several indoor cats I take care of. I've taken in many of these outdoor kitties, tough, and their kittens. I've had some of them altered. I've found homes for many of them—almost all of the ones that I've taken in and certainly all the kittens. A few I've taken to animal shelters and just hoped for the best for them. What else can you do, at times? Again, you can never assume that an outdoor kitty is not a stray, especially since most of them are, unless they are feral, or are owned by someone in the vicinity. Quite a few of them are actual feral cats. Again, just knowing you are feeding stray (and feral) cats should be your principal reward and reward enough. Cats are innocents, and in so many ways, they are actually helpless creatures because we have domesticated kitties so that each and every one of them are no longer 'wild' and able to live very long, outside. Feral kitties, in particular, rarely live very long outside or in the wild. This is so pitiable. All domesticated kitties need us to help them. They have no one else. My belief is that no kitty should ever be outside. All kitties can and should be indoor kitties.

This poem is a non-rhyming poem so it is blank verse. You can generally get more specific content into a poem with blank or free verse than you can with verse that rhymes but not in all cases because there can be exceptions to that. I tend to rhyme poems but I have a variety of types of poems in my overall grouping of poems.

Feeding Outdoor Cats—the Poem

The kitties living around my home
Have learned they have to wait a while.
They know food will be forthcoming
In a good-sized, deep plastic dish.

They know the food will taste just fine
And that it will constantly come.
They know there'll also be water
In a sturdy round container.

Food for them always gets put out
At least two or three times a day,
And that is with the dry cat food–
Leftovers go out, separately.

The food cannot be stale or spoiled.

It has to be safe for the cats.

Dry cat food is what's nutritious.

It has everything that they need.

I don't always see cats feeding.

A hidden camera would be nice.

Then I would see them when they ate

And know how many came and went.

I've fed them around thirty years.

It's been a hobby, on the side.

The cat food keeps adding in cost,

But it is what I love to do.

I always feed them, and times two;

They are fed on two different sides.

The food I put out gets eaten,

Then I put more out, later on.

I freshen the water every day

And will clean any container.

Sometimes they're cleaned out less often.

There are times when they look okay.

In the summer ants will come around

And they go after the cat food.

I put water in a pie pan
And set the food dish in that.

Ants will then drown in pan water.
I don't like it that ants drown,
But the cats have to get to food
And won't eat if ants are there.

Kitties show up in the morning.
They show up around sunset.
They also come 'round through the night
And will wait their turn if they must.

Sometimes I will hear two cats fight.
The fights don't last very long.
One cat will drive off a rival,
Then eat in security.

But then the other cat comes back
And eats from the dish that's there.
After a while all get their fill
But return when hunger calls.

I try not to miss a feeding.
I know the food will be eaten.
Oddly, something will remind me.
I think that God's in on this.

I won't stop feeding all the cats.

They deserve to eat, each day.

They get dumped, left, and this is wrong,

And kittens get born outside.

You can't know if others feed them.

You have to assume they don't.

You might be the only person

Who's putting food out for them.

If you put food out for kitties,

Just put out a little, at first.

Eventually they'll know you did.

They'll soon find it and then eat.

Who else do they have to feed them?

No one, is the answer to that.

Kitties have starved and are starving.

Seek them out and feed them now.

Lucky's Message—the Introduction

Lucky is a real cat. He was minding his own business one day and got horrifically victimized. Someone wanted him dead, and they shot an arrow straight through his head and neck area. Lucky somehow made it over to the house where he lived at and was then rushed to the vet clinic for emergency care. A policeman stopped the car the owner was in because it was speeding, and when he saw what had happened, he gave them a police escort to the vets.

Miraculously, Lucky made it through the surgery, but he ended out having some lingering problems. Lucky's message is 'please keep me inside all the time because I want to stay safe'. (Or, at least, that is my message, for Lucky.)

Whoever shot Lucky has his thinking scrambled. He should have wanted to help Lucky. It doesn't take that long or cost that much to rescue a cat that's forced to live outside. In this case, though, Lucky had a home. Unfortunately, many outdoor kitties don't. No one knows how far Lucky had to walk. Lucky could have been far from home and shot at some distance away from home, or, someone in the neighborhood could have shot the arrow into him. Either way, it was cruel and senseless to do what was done. Even walking a short distance before he got to his familiar porch must have been excruciating and frightening. Again, the message is that cats should all have homes and stay inside where they can be maximally safe from all outdoor perils, of which there are hundreds. The shooting of bullets, rifle shot, bee-bees, and arrows are but some of these many perils.

Lucky's Message—the Poem

I was given the name of Lucky,

But I was an unlucky cat.

Somebody tried to bump me off.

I am unhappy about that.

I do not want to go outside

And I now want to stay indoors.

Another arrow, I don't want.

Arrows will leave you with some sores.

The arrow someone aimed at me

Was shot from a really close range.

Why did that horrid guy hurt me?

I think he had to be deranged.

I used to be a happy cat,

As I just went about my day.

Will you please now keep me inside?

I hope that you will not say 'nay'.

Everybody was quite surprised

That I got through the surgery.

I suffered, and, it was so bad,

And the ordeal was so scary.

I have to be very still now,

But at least I'm able to eat.

I'll never be quite the same, though.

I think that I should have a treat.

I've felt the pain now, for a while,

Since that traumatic, awful time.

It was hard for me to walk home

After that germ had done his crime.

I really am not a bad cat.

There is no cat I know that is.

I wish that the shooter would just

Evaporate like sparkling fizz.

I am sure that he would not like
Being shot with a swift long arrow.
I could have so easily died.
I've never even been his foe.

He could have chosen to like me
If he had thought more about it.
I don't want to harm anyone.
Do I intend harm? Not one bit.

No cat is ever bad, at all.
But there's some people who can be.
All kitties should be protected,
It should not only include me.

People who chose to be so mean
Cannot be thinking very straight.
I am lucky to be alive.
Dying had almost been my fate.

Outdoor Perils—the Introduction

This short poem drives a point in and makes a clear statement. There are hundreds (maybe thousands) of outdoor perils that outdoor kitties (and dogs) can encounter. We domesticated cats, and because we did, they are now too small and helpless to survive outside. One CATegory (or chapter) in my book, *I Care for My Cats*, makes note of what these perils are (CATegory 13). The chapter was expanded to be its own book, titled *The Outdoor Perils of Cats* (i.e. this book).

Kitties belong inside so they can be kept safe by their caretaker or caretakers. Keeping kitties inside is a pet issue of mine–they should never be outside, and 'never' is the key word. Another key word is 'negligence', and it should be obvious what I mean by that. No matter what the reason or the excuse, no cat should be outside, ever. All kitties should always be inside. It is not that difficult or expensive to see that kitty litter is always available to indoor kitties. There are only plusses to keeping kitties inside.

Outdoor Perils—the Poem

Trusting little kitty that is roaming all about,
Be warned that outside, something bad can get you.
Be careful of the dangers that can be anywhere
And know that outdoor perils are more than a few.

It's easy to think that kitties are safe outside.
It's wrong to put them out and minimize their care.
Outdoor kitties are unsafe and miserable,
Because of all the perils, they really do not fare.

Bring all cats inside, now, and do not hesitate.
Outside, kitties suffer from heat, cold, lack, and stress.
Make an earnest effort to keep kitties inside.
You'll protect them and all cum, vet bills will be less.

The Sad Cat—the Introduction

I love all animals, and I despise seeing animals stuck in small cages. You see them in markets, in transit trucks for selling, and in a number of places, really. You especially see this kind of thing in foreign countries. Cats and dogs end out being in small cages at pounds and shelters, too. At animal shelters where unwanted animals are euthanized, many of the older animals don't stand a chance. People are inclined to prefer kittens over grown cats. It's as simple as that. There are, of course, exceptions to this, but not many. Some older cats are adopted or placed, but they tend to be the younger older cats. Many kittens are adopted and purchased, especially around late spring and during the summer and the early fall. For one reason or another, certain of these kittens end out at an animal shelter, when they get bigger. As more time goes by, some end out going there twice, over a period of time. Some may go more than twice. *The Sad Cat* is about all these poor cats that end out at a pound or shelter and were unwanted. People should fight hard to keep their kitties. Worst-case scenario, they could try to find a new caretaker for them, on their own, if they feel they must part with their kitty.

People should 'look before they leap' and think it through when they get a pet because when a pet is brought into a home, it is a commitment, and a pet owner should plan to keep the pet until the pet dies. So that a cat will live as long as possible, the cat should be kept indoors all the time because there are so many outdoor perils for cats. I cover this very subject (and many others) in my book, *I Care for My Cats*. Any poems about cats that are in my poems and short works books will also be found in my cat book. There are several cat and other animal poems and short works in those books.

Kitties do not have to be housebroken because they always take to using litter. Dogs should all be housebroken, early on, so they can be inside as much as possible. These days, more dogs are kept inside or kept inside more often than ever before, and this includes even the bigger dogs. They're let outside to do their business, then they are quickly let back in. It is sad to know that animals are constantly being euthanized, around the world. In some countries, some animals are shot or their throats are slit, if they are unwanted. Some are drowned. Euthanizing is humane. Still, there should be very little euthanizing. There should be fewer births. That's the key. Some of those animal breeders out there should change careers (or hobbies). Euthanizing should only be for legitimate medical reasons, and not because an animal is unwanted. (Also, see the short work about dogs in *I Care for My Cats*; it is titled *The Wronged Dog* because he is also treated very badly. *I Care for My Cats (and Other Animals)* is also about animal rights, so other animals are noted. I am somehow able to weave everything in. *The Wronged Dog* is also in my second poems and short works book.

I hope more cats (and dogs) will be kept inside and also permanently kept, until the pet dies a natural death. Way too many cats (and dogs) are allowed to mate, and more laws should be passed to prevent this from happening. I have a number of pet peeves relative to the subject of cats, dogs, and other animals. (All these are in my long cat compendium, which covers other animals as well as cats.) Because the world is an imperfect one, it naturally follows that the care and protection of animals has been and is imperfect. More people need to jump on the bandwagon of animal concern. (In my third poem book–*Next Poems and Short Works*–there is a short story titled, *A Future for Animals*. It is also at the end of *I Care for My Cats*. There are also four short stories about cats, in that book. They are in CATegory 57 of *I Care for My Cats*, and the four stories are my new type of short story (i.e. the Sans=Dialogue Story).

The advantage of writing free verse is that you are able to write a poem like this one. It is one of my few really short poems. People have said that it has impact; it covers a serious topic.

The Sad Cat—the Poem

I was a kitten once.

Everyone seemed to want me,

and they liked to be around me.

They watched me as I went about,

and they gave me toys.

They laughed and smiled at me,

and they patted me, too.

They took care of me, routinely,

and talked about me with their friends.

Then I became a cat.

People weren't so doting or embracing.

They kept ignoring me.

I ended out at a local shelter.

I was in a really small cage

and they wouldn't let me out.

I tried to sleep when I could

but I was a bundle of nerves.

It was so strange and scary there,

and I just wanted to get away.

It was real hard to move around

so I rested, in the wire cage.

Sadly, no one came to get me

and people just kept walking by.

They kept ignoring me, too,

and it all made me very sad.

A few people looked at me quickly

but they just kept on going.

I could tell they didn't want me,

And didn't want to be with me.

But all the kittens got attention,

and some time, and some smiles.

I so wanted to be loved and held

like was happening with the kittens.

I just wanted to be happy again

and to be back at my home.

I wanted to be loved and patted

and to be safe, and secure.

But I presently wasn't

And would I ever be?

I just couldn't be sure . . . .

Tuffy Cat—the Introduction

I wanted to write *Tuffy Cat* because this one particular kitten meant a great deal to me. She was special and extraordinary. But, as with other kitties that

I had previously taken in, I had to give her over to a loving person and family because I already had other kitties to take care of and these kitties needed me to not spread myself out too thin. (I had probably been giving Tuffy Cat too much attention, for one thing). I had to keep to a quota because I kept on bringing in stray kitties to fix them up and then place them into homes. There were quite a few strays and ferals around where I lived. Strays and ferals were an ongoing problem that, sadly, most residents near where I lived did not take much interest in. All in all, it was best I parted with sweet little Tuffy Cat, but I felt sick at heart when I did, and I missed Tuffy Cat immediately and I always will. There have been so many cats (kittens and older ones) that I had to reluctantly give over to people who were essentially strangers. Secretly, I wanted to keep them all and take care of them myself but that could never be because there were always new cats to bring in and I only had so much room and so much time.

The poem somewhat reveals the sadness foster care people feel, when they have to let go of a kitty. I went through this, many times. I worry about some of them, today. You do the best you can for them. You hope it was enough. You hope the home ended out being a good one for them. Foster care people have to give up control, which isn't always easy to do. Anyone who takes in kitties to find them a home is well aware of the anguish that can be experienced when placing kitties into homes. Some prospective homes are a bit borderline, to be frank; a judgment call is required. You always worry about placed kitties, though. It is emotionally difficult to place kitties. Some homes are clearly great. Some homes may seem OK, but are they? You always hope you did the right thing but you never really know and this can eat at you for the rest of your life. Some people might misrepresent something. I like the idea of home visits.

Tuffy Cat—the Poem

Tuffy Cat, Tuffy Cat, you're considerably cute,

And when you get older, you'll be a real beaut.

I so love to watch you throughout all the day–

That's whenever you eat and sleep, or run or play.

One day, you happened to come along my pathway

But I knew that your visit would be a short stay.

You grew on me quickly and you entered my heart

'Till, truth told, I didn't really want us to part.

I brought you indoors and everything was just fine

And for, at least, a while you were happily mine,

But I have to trust others who will carry the torch

After I take in strays that come up on my porch.

I will quickly take them to a veterinarian,

And give them good food that has helpful nutrition.

I will bring them inside from the cold and the heat,

To find them an owner who they will, in time, meet.

So I got you all fixed up, as best as I could,

And enjoyed being with you, like anyone would.

I had to place an ad so an owner I'd find

(Though the memory of you would stay in my mind.)

Then along came someone wanting to love you, too.

Her cat had just died and she really wanted you.

With reluctance I, then, was forced to let you go.

And then, for quite some time, I was feeling real low,

But my other sweet kitties were always around,

So, by them and with them, I some solace found.

I thought about you often as time went by.

When I think about you, I am left with a sigh.

Tuffy Cat, Tuffy Cat, I hope you're all right–

That you're safe and you're happy all day and all night.

Index

blood relatives 194

blood sample 164

bloodstream 125

bloodsucking 148

blood test 74, 170

blowfly 5, 172

board 112, 218, 246, 251

boards 103, 180

boas 130

Boas 127

boats 34, 36, 40

bodies 6, 14, 19, 81, 97, 143, 151, 204

body 10, 11, 17, 18, 51, 58, 70, 71, 72, 74,
86, 96, 98, 102, 106, 112, 119, 134,
135, 144, 151, 166, 172, 181, 208, 214

body heat 10, 17

body temperature 18

body weight 208

bond 192, 221, 243, 264

bonded 196

bonds 3, 236, 243

bone 10, 131, 145, 216

bone damage 131

bones 4, 55, 202, 213, 216, 254

bone splinters 216

bony 6

book ix

books 7, 13, 86, 137, 220, 259, 277

boots 14, 34

border 193

bored 83, 128, 254, 255

bored kitties 254, 255

born 3, 14, 17, 79, 88, 93, 99, 104, 105,
107, 182, 184, 186, 202, 217, 219, 220,
224, 227, 228, 233, 247, 248, 251,
258, 272

born-outside cats 247, 248

born outsides 248

bosc 248

bosk kitties 248

botflies 173

botfly 5, 173

bottle 56

bottled water 36

bow and arrow 88

bowel movement 74

bowl 94, 95, 99, 205, 226

bows 86

brace 181

brain 111, 161, 162, 163, 171

branch 141

branches 116, 117, 141, 148

brands 178

Brazil 137, 138, 139

breathe 18, 87, 156, 177, 182, 256

breathing 18, 125, 169, 175

bred 3, 11, 75, 107, 109, 115, 137, 189,
233, 251

bred down 11, 107, 109, 115, 189

breed 10, 102, 133, 135, 138

292

cheek 257

chemical 175

chemical-free 175

chemicals 155, 168, 170, 176, 256

Chengdu 27

chest 214

chew 55, 168, 182, 224

chicken 216

chicks 18

chiggers 4

Chihuahuas 95

child 168, 181

children 5, 13, 49, 67, 68, 72, 97, 105, 134, 143, 157, 160, 161, 167, 168, 220, 223

chill 9

China 23, 25, 27, 28, 138

China Sea 25

choke 55

Cholla 97, 123

Cholla cactus 123

choosing 185

cigarette 48

cigarette butts 48

Cimicidae family 147

circumstances 76, 133, 166

cities 22, 27, 42, 79, 89, 135, 139, 148, 168, 215

citizens 79, 80, 219, 233

clashes 226, 245

claw 4, 57, 61, 159, 176, 206

clawing 62, 253

claws 67, 70, 116, 125, 152, 203

claw scratch 57

claw wounds 4

clay 196

clay litter 196

clean 7, 28, 34, 58, 64, 65, 66, 70, 106, 119, 151, 162, 165, 167, 173, 188, 197, 240, 256, 262, 270

cleaning 161, 168, 255

cleaning solvents 161

clean water 197

clear plastic 180

climate 9, 18, 122, 125, 136

climate-controlled 18

climates 139, 147

climb 92, 100, 111, 114, 115, 116, 117, 121, 141, 147, 201, 255

climbers 114

climbing 168, 201

clinic 56, 85, 92, 98, 99, 103, 125, 126, 132, 133, 160, 166, 178, 192, 216, 235, 272

clinic personnel 235

clinics 24, 28, 103, 131

clip 17, 124

clipping 125

closet 37

clothes 240, 255

clothing 142

dirt 7, 64, 69, 94, 95, 146, 174, 177, 178

dirt particles 69

dirty 6, 69, 70, 93, 152, 173, 177, 186, 197, 207, 216, 244

disaster 21, 22, 27, 28, 31, 33, 35, 37, 38, 40, 44, 46, 48, 50, 53

disasters 21, 24, 25, 28, 29, 32, 34, 40, 41, 43, 45, 46, 47, 49

discharge 97

discoloration 144

disease 4, 27, 31, 32, 55, 74, 148, 149, 150, 202

diseases 6, 63, 148, 149, 151, 190, 258

dish 68, 83, 99, 147, 178, 197, 204, 205, 212, 213, 214, 215, 222, 269, 271

dishes 163, 176

disinfectant 58

disorders 249

disorientation 43, 214, 254

disoriented 2, 8, 18, 31, 48, 64

disposition 261

distracting 72, 102, 121

distressed 245

disturb 257

docile 75, 221, 234, 235, 242

docility 75, 244

doctors 24

does xi, 8, 10, 12, 13, 16, 18, 19, 31, 46, 47, 51, 55, 60, 61, 68, 71, 80, 82, 83, 85, 93, 108, 117, 121, 122, 126, 131, 139,

153, 157, 160, 162, 165, 166, 170, 192, 196, 201, 206, 208, 224, 234, 237, 243

dog 12, 13, 64, 80, 81, 90, 91, 93, 94, 96, 99, 101, 117, 121, 135, 160, 162, 164, 168, 169, 174, 178, 186, 197, 213, 230, 234, 240, 252

dog attack 64, 93

dog attacks 93

dogs 5, 13, 19, 23, 31, 35, 38, 50, 69, 73, 80, 81, 87, 89, 90, 91, 92, 93, 94, 95, 96, 98, 99, 100, 107, 112, 114, 117, 123, 128, 129, 133, 136, 138, 139, 149, 150, 157, 160, 161, 163, 165, 167, 178, 179, 193, 197, 200, 203, 212, 213, 234, 241, 255, 258, 268, 275, 277, 278

domestic 5, 10, 11, 22, 24, 26, 29, 32, 37, 38, 42, 46, 49, 60, 61, 68, 87, 105, 111, 112, 115, 116, 117, 129, 132, 136, 138, 164, 193, 201, 203, 227, 233

domestic animals 5, 22, 24, 32, 38, 46, 49, 117

domesticated 11, 75, 76, 87, 88, 90, 110, 111, 115, 116, 127, 151, 163, 164, 197, 200, 203, 217, 228, 233, 235, 258, 267, 268, 275

domesticated animals 88, 111, 151, 163, 197, 235

domesticated kitties 11, 75, 87, 228, 258, 269

domesticated kitty 116, 127

299

knowledge 87, 211

L

label 170

labeling 248, 249

lactating 186

lactation 229

ladders 117

lame 93, 169

lance 58

landfall 42

land leeches 148

land mines 193

Landscaping a Small Lot 137

landscaping rocks 18

La Niña 10, 150

lap 165, 166, 167, 215

laps 161

lap up 165, 166, 167

large dogs 13, 90

large mart 167

larvae 5, 172, 173, 216

larvae cysts 5

Latin 38

lattice 253

law 37, 68, 87, 103, 106, 110, 127, 131, 167, 245

lawn 7, 168, 176

laws 57, 81, 105, 107, 112, 136, 165, 278

lead 4

leap 114, 277

learn 65, 75, 76, 87, 107, 126, 154, 157, 175, 192, 206, 220, 225, 227, 233, 238, 249, 250

learned 100, 115, 153, 177, 190, 211, 240, 261, 269

learned behavior 115

leash 95, 197

leaves 6, 17, 116, 166, 173, 174, 175, 176, 180, 252, 253

leavings 208, 209

ledge 157, 181

leeches 148

leftover 214

leftover human food 214

leftovers 55, 213, 214

leg 91, 93, 120

legal 128, 131

legislation 166

legs 70, 92, 127, 145, 181

lesions 74, 173

Leukemia 6

levies 32, 34

Leyte Island 39

libraries 211

library 13

lice 172

license 268

license tag 268

lick 69, 106, 120, 165, 166, 167, 170, 177

licking 7, 58, 160

lids 216

lie 113

life 1, 3, 31, 44, 47, 56, 76, 77, 83, 84, 91,
    110, 111, 137, 138, 140, 159, 168, 170,
    189, 193, 210, 219, 221, 227, 237, 239,
    244, 249, 255, 263, 264, 282

life span 76, 227

life spans 227

light 9, 18, 41, 120, 130, 135, 173, 183,
    184, 193

light-colored 173

lightning 6, 8, 48, 69

lightweight 83

limb 121, 135

limbs 10, 22, 93, 181

limp 119

limping 93, 120, 159

lion 90, 99

lions 89, 99

liquid 57, 161, 162, 163, 178

list 1, 4, 7, 20, 32, 74, 160, 246

litter 56, 64, 89, 93, 104, 145, 174, 176,
    177, 178, 183, 186, 188, 196, 200, 217,
    220, 221, 222, 231, 237, 238, 239, 240,
    246, 257, 276, 278

litter box 56, 174, 188, 221, 222, 237,
    240, 246

litters 103, 104, 105, 184, 227, 233

livelihood 32, 49

liver 166

livestock 32

Living and Travelling in the South-West 137

living creatures 30, 49, 145, 241

lizards 204

locality 92, 206

local pound 94, 96, 104, 187, 208,
    209, 210

London 154

London Zoo 154

lonely 3, 92, 194, 264

long-fur 14, 16, 44, 123

long-furred 44, 123

long sentence 1, 4

loose dog 31, 95, 96, 252

loose dogs 31, 95, 96

Los Angeles 49

loss 5, 27, 43, 73, 115, 170, 208

lost 2, 8, 22, 26, 27, 32, 33, 36, 43, 44, 50,
    64, 79, 89, 99, 131, 135, 159, 192, 224,
    246, 252, 254, 258, 268

loud noise 33

loud noises 33

Louisiana 32, 36, 41, 51

Louisiana State University 36

love 6, 76, 87, 94, 112, 129, 152, 164, 169,
    186, 192, 195, 207, 235, 243, 248, 255,
    257, 264, 270, 277, 282

loving 87, 110, 111, 164, 189, 190, 200,
    235, 251, 256, 257, 281

New Jersey 41

New Mexico 48

New Orleans 32, 34, 35, 36

News 21, 48, 51, 111, 116, 138, 192, 255

newspaper 240

newspapers 33

New York 41

night 12, 13, 14, 15, 16, 17, 30, 72, 80, 83, 89, 90, 92, 100, 128, 135, 147, 156, 165, 205, 206, 212, 213, 256, 263, 271, 283

night temperatures 12

Nile 148

nine lives 1

noise 2, 152, 160, 168, 257

noises 33, 68, 206, 246, 257

no-kill 60, 210, 242

no-kill shelters 210

non-toxic 166, 175, 176

North Carolina 130

Norwegian 11

Norwegian Forest Cat 11

nose 18, 144

notes 276

nuisance 16, 121, 134, 245

nursing 17, 185, 222

nurtured 44

nutrients 206, 219

nutrition 6, 44, 226, 282

nutritional 213

nutritious 225, 260, 266, 270

O

observation 108, 236

occult 111

ocean 9, 26, 39, 40, 49, 51, 52, 154

ocean currents 52

odor 217

offense 106, 199

offensive 178

office 163

officials 37, 131, 146

oil 54

ointment 18

older 14, 15, 47, 100, 102, 104, 105, 115, 142, 143, 152, 161, 187, 201, 212, 229, 234, 239, 242, 255, 277, 281, 282

older cat 102, 115, 277

older cats 102, 115, 277

older kittens 15, 143

older kitties 14, 100, 152, 212, 239

older kitty 102, 212

opening 182, 183, 185, 187

open wound 59

open wounds 59

optional xi

ordeal 17, 35, 36, 43, 84, 97, 173, 274

ordinance 245

organ 37, 106, 131, 161, 254

organ deterioration 254

321

sick kitty 199

Sidewinders 129

sing 222

size 14, 58, 100, 114, 127, 135, 166, 168, 217, 219, 223, 227, 260

skills 115, 203

skin 4, 9, 10, 18, 57, 58, 59, 61, 73, 94, 97, 120, 121, 122, 123, 124, 125, 126, 140, 142, 143, 144, 147, 172, 173, 244, 254, 262

skinny 74

skin salve 73

skirmishes 242

skittish 56, 76, 156, 191, 195, 210, 212, 220, 224, 241, 247, 248, 261

skunk 5, 189

skunks 203

slam 108, 132, 209, 229

slamming 82

slashes 4

sleep 10, 16, 51, 68, 82, 83, 114, 116, 158, 172, 188, 237, 243, 254, 257, 279, 282

sleeping 79, 86, 90, 92, 98, 158, 159, 172, 253, 254, 255

Sleeping Sickness 151

sleeps 158

slide 26

slither 127

slivers 6, 120

slug 170, 175

slug bait 175

slug poison 170

slugs 4, 204

small animals 11, 90, 145, 156, 178, 188, 190, 204, 266

small cage 169, 277, 279

small cages 277

small dogs 90, 95, 136

small prey 197

small room 221, 222, 236, 237, 238, 256

small wildlife 107

smell 2, 8, 117, 152, 161, 162, 179, 237, 238, 256

smells 2, 162, 209

smoke 21, 43, 47, 48, 142

smoke inhalation 47

smoker 256

snail 175

snails 4, 204

snake 126, 127, 128, 129, 130, 131, 132, 133

snake bite 131, 132, 133

snake bites 131, 132

snake owners 128

snake poles 132

snakes 5, 100, 118, 127, 128, 129, 130, 131, 132, 133, 134, 143, 193, 197, 204

snake types 130, 131

sneak 114, 155

sniffer 178

snow 6, 10, 12, 13, 15, 30, 130

snow and ice 6, 10, 12, 13, 15, 30, 130

snowing 12, 16

snows 10

soap 70, 97

sociable 247, 249

social 56, 224

socialize 247

socialized 222, 224, 242, 255

socializing 254

society 128, 165, 245

soft 62, 69

soggy 8, 214

solid 67, 111

solid food 67

solo 105, 141, 193, 194

solo cat 105

solo cats 105

solo kitties 193

solution 75, 214, 256

solvents 161

sore 72, 120

sores 273

soul 163

souls 109

sounds 179

source 67, 217, 223

South America 52, 101, 133, 135, 136, 137, 139, 142, 146

Southern California 49

South Korea 141

South-West 89, 123, 137, 186, 202

spay 57, 230

spayed 7, 14, 103, 188, 228, 236, 238

spaying 235, 244

S.P.C.A. 36

spears 73

species 88, 110, 127, 128, 148, 173

speed 78, 79, 83, 170

Sphinx 12

spider 143, 144, 186

spiders 5, 100, 143, 144, 184, 186, 193

spikelets 121

spill 162, 164, 165, 166

spillage 162

spills 161, 162, 163, 167

spine 181

splinter 122

splinters 6, 63, 119, 120, 126, 216

spoil 55, 267

spoiled 4, 55, 214, 270

spoiled food 214

spoils 54, 109

spores 73

spot 71, 82, 131, 135, 136, 151, 166, 186, 217, 243

spots 71, 79, 97, 152, 158, 242

spotted 128, 134, 150

spray 142, 218, 237, 244, 263

spraying 150, 171, 217

strength 9, 28, 135

stress 3, 8, 17, 68, 102, 194, 198, 209, 220

strike 67, 129, 131, 135

stronger 31, 90, 116, 176, 223

strychnine 169

study 174

stung 5, 74, 125, 126, 140, 143, 146,
147, 151

subliminally 233, 234

submerge 135

success 124, 150, 232

suckle 104, 229

suckling 104, 187, 222, 229

suckling time 104, 229

sudden 5, 43, 69, 86, 144, 158, 161, 215

sudden death 144, 161

sudden movements 69

suffer 7, 11, 12, 22, 24, 33, 38, 64, 99, 102,
109, 115, 119, 123, 126, 146, 152, 172,
199, 214, 220, 225, 232

suffering 12, 24, 28, 54, 84, 143, 164, 169,
198, 200, 258, 260

suicide 32, 121, 161

Sumatra 26

summer 14, 19, 32, 46, 48, 152, 262,
270, 277

sun 6, 12, 14, 18, 19, 30, 59, 182, 197, 208,
214, 243, 253

sunami 25

sunbath 56

sunburn 6, 12

sunburned 18, 19

sun exposure 18, 59

sun rest 197

sunroom 253

sunshine 57

supplement 31

supplies 40, 41, 81

supply 40, 185, 215, 228

suppress 91

surgeries 83

surgery 83, 84, 238, 273, 274

survival 22, 36, 251

survive 10, 24, 38, 65, 75, 83, 154, 195,
203, 207, 266, 275

swabs 70

swallow 55

sweater 11

sweep 5, 125, 143

swelling 97

swim 35, 50, 102, 135, 157

swimming 6, 136, 157

swimming pool 6, 136, 157

swimming pools 6, 136, 157

swollen 72

symptom 119

symptoms 170, 178

syringe 56

system 44, 74, 149, 167, 171

systems 10

winds 9, 16, 21, 22, 25, 34, 39, 40, 42, 43, 45, 123, 133

wind storms 6

wind swirls 6, 25, 29, 33, 41, 42, 46, 51

wine 58, 152

winter 6, 10, 12, 14, 17, 19

wire cage 280

wire mesh 102

wires 183

wiring 182

Wisconsin 110

wolf 89

wolves 5, 89, 90, 99, 100

women 68, 189

wood 59, 62, 119, 122, 129, 174, 253

wooded areas 118

wool 11

words 28, 37, 40, 68, 89, 90, 101, 107, 108, 115, 132, 145, 153, 184, 190, 207, 208, 221, 233, 246, 247, 248, 253, 257, 259, 260, 264

work 28, 36, 71, 97, 106, 117, 121, 177, 179, 207, 208, 209, 215, 220, 221, 222, 239, 243, 248, 252, 256, 263, 278

workers 44, 50, 71, 138, 211

working xi, 96, 177, 184, 210, 233

worldwide 151

worm 171, 172

worms 4, 74, 144, 148, 172, 262

wound 56, 57, 58, 60, 97, 102, 109, 119

wounded 120, 159, 201

wounds 4, 57, 59, 60, 230

writing 7, 188, 260, 279

Wronged Dog 278

Wyoming 47, 48

X

x-ray 84, 102, 181

x-rays 84, 181

Y

Yamanashi 29

yard 37, 98, 112, 129, 139, 171, 177, 197, 252

yards 163, 176, 190, 246

yell 61, 62

yellow and red 130

yellow jacket 5, 125, 140

yellow jackets 5, 140

Yolanda 39, 41

young children 168

young people 6, 88, 128, 223

yowing 62

Z

zones 23, 26